Modern
Equity Investing
Strategies

Modern
Equity Investing
Strategies

Anatoly B. Schmidt

New York University Tandon School of Engineering, USA

World Scientific

NEW JERSEY · LONDON · SINGAPORE · BEIJING · SHANGHAI · HONG KONG · TAIPEI · CHENNAI · TOKYO

Published by

World Scientific Publishing Co. Pte. Ltd.
5 Toh Tuck Link, Singapore 596224
USA office: 27 Warren Street, Suite 401-402, Hackensack, NJ 07601
UK office: 57 Shelton Street, Covent Garden, London WC2H 9HE

Library of Congress Cataloging-in-Publication Data
Names: Schmidt, Anatoly B, author.
Title: Modern equity investing strategies / Anatoly B. Schmidt,
    New York University Tandon School of Engineering, USA.
Description: [Singapore] ; [New Jersey] : [World Scientific], [2022] |
    Includes bibliographical references and index.
Identifiers: LCCN 2021022918 (print) | LCCN 2021022919 (ebook) |
    ISBN 9789811239496 (hardcover) | ISBN 9789811239502 (ebook) |
    ISBN 9789811239519 (ebook other)
Subjects: LCSH: Fixed-income securities. | Stock exchanges.
Classification: LCC HG4650 .S37 2022 (print) | LCC HG4650 (ebook) | DDC 332.64--dc22
LC record available at https://lccn.loc.gov/2021022918
LC ebook record available at https://lccn.loc.gov/2021022919

British Library Cataloguing-in-Publication Data
A catalogue record for this book is available from the British Library.

For any available supplementary material, please visit
https://www.worldscientific.com/worldscibooks/10.1142/12347#t=suppl

Desk Editors: Nimal Koliyat/Lai Ann

Typeset by Stallion Press
Email: enquiries@stallionpress.com

"The author has been successfully teaching the material in this book to NYU Master's students for the last 8 years. As equity analytics continues to evolve, this field-tested almanac is an indispensable guide to the past, present, and future."

Peter Carr, Ph.D.
Professor, Chair of the Finance and Risk Engineering Department
NYU Tandon School of Engineering, USA

"In the secular shift taking place in equity investing from judgment-based to quantitative and systematic, Dr. Schmidt's book is a needed addition to the body of knowledge, which will hopefully be used as a reference or textbook by the next generations of quants seeking to build a career in the space."

Emmanuel D. Hatzakis, Ph.D., CFA, FRM
Professor, Director of the Masters Programs in Finance & Financial Engineering, School of Business at Stevens Institute of Technology, USA

"Alec Schmidt's new book provides a tour d'horizon of all aspects of the theory and practice of financial markets that one would wish to cover in a profound undergraduate lecture. Its 15 chapters cover material that is seldom found in one volume, ranging from market microstructure, portfolio theory and volatility modelling to a broad coverage of trading strategies and their statistical validation. The book is very well-balanced and profound, and it does not neglect important parts of the literature that have fallen out of fashion in some quarters (like the inventory models in market microstructure that are often sacrificed in textbooks in favor of asymmetric information models). Chapters on agent-based models and opinion mining represent cutting-edge developments in empirical finance. Overall, an excellent addition to the textbook literature that I will warmly recommend to the students of our Quantitative Finance program."

Thomas Lux, Ph.D.
Professor, Chair of Monetary Economics and International Finance
University of Kiel, Germany

"This book is a comprehensive, well-structured and up-to-date guide to quant equity investment and trading practices, which should be of great interest to students of finance and to mathematically inclined market practitioners. The author's unusual background enables him to combine deep first-hand knowledge of financial market dynamics with the mathematical rigor of a physicist and the accessible narrative style of a seasoned educator. This work will prove informative to new students of equity investment and to those already familiar with it, who wish to refresh or improve their knowledge. I thoroughly recommend it."

Frank McGroarty, Ph.D.
Professor of Computational Finance and Investment Analytics
Director of Centre for Digital Finance
University of Southampton, UK

In memory of my parents, Ida and Boris Schmidt.
To my children, Mark and Sabina.

About the Author

 **Anatoly (Alec) Schmidt** is Adjunct Professor at Financial Engineering Departments of the NYU Tandon School and Stevens Institute of Technology. He was also Visiting Professor at Nanyang Technological University and Moscow Financial Academy. Alec holds a Ph.D. in Physics and has worked in the financial industry for more than 20 years, most recently as Lead Research Scientist at a market data analytics company, Kensho Technologies. Alec has published two books, *Quantitative Finance for Physicists: An Introduction* (Elsevier, 2004) and *Financial Markets and Trading: Introduction to Market Microstructure and Trading Strategies* (Wiley, 2011), and multiple papers in peer-reviewed journals on agent-based modeling of financial markets, portfolio management, and trading strategies.

Preface

This book is a result of my evolving interests in quantitative finance. Like many physicists, I landed in this field in the 1990s when the financial industry started actively hiring quants. This career change was painful at times but ultimately gratifying. I described it along with other travails of an émigré from the former USSR elsewhere (Schmidt, 2013).

I started working in an institutional FX brokerage where I did analysis of trader behavior, market impact of trading, and high-frequency trading strategies. I was also curious about the major directions in quantitative finance and how physicists could contribute to it, in particular, using the agent-based modeling. Then I wrote a book about this subject (Schmidt, 2004).

A few years later, I used my brokerage experience (including a stint at an algorithmic trading agency) to write a book on financial market microstructure and algorithmic trading (Schmidt, 2011).

Since 2013, I have worked at a financial market data analytics company where I was involved in various projects related to equity investing: from analysis of market impact of alternative data to deriving optimal portfolios.

My teaching experience at the financial engineering programs of the NYU Tandon School and Stevens Institute of Technology has lead me to believe in the need for a single source that covers all topics I mentioned above: from the modern equity market structures to deriving optimal portfolios to implementing and back-testing active trading strategies to optimal trade execution.

This book will satisfy the demand among the college majors in Finance and Financial Engineering and mathematically versed practitioners for an overview of both the classical approaches in equity investing and modern trading strategies scattered in the periodic literature. While the book describes quantitative concepts and models in a rigorous fashion, it will not overburden the reader with math beyond the college undergraduate calculus and statistics curriculums.

Acknowledgments

My students' curiosity was an important stimulus for writing this book. Conversations with the faculty members of the Finance and Risk Engineering Department at the NYU Tandon School and the Financial Engineering Master's Program at the Stevens Institute of Technology helped me choose the book's contents. Discussions with the participants of the international conferences *Computing in Economics and Finance* and *Forecasting Financial Markets* that I attended for many years advanced my research interests. I am also grateful to the editors of the World Scientific for attentive chaperoning of the publishing process.

Contents

About the Author   ix

Preface   xi

Acknowledgments   xiii

Notations and Abbreviations   xxiii

Introduction   xxvii

Part I: Modern Equity Markets   1

**Chapter 1. Equity Markets: Traders, Orders,
    and Structures**   3

  1.1 Introduction 3
  1.2 Traders 3
  1.3 Orders and Limit Order Book 6
  1.4 Market Liquidity 9
  1.5 Equity Market Structures 12
     1.5.1 Continuous order-driven markets 13
     1.5.2 Oral auctions 15
     1.5.3 Call auctions 15
     1.5.4 Quote-driven markets and hybrid markets . . 16
  1.6 The US Equity Markets 17
     1.6.1 NYSE 17
     1.6.2 NASDAQ 18
     1.6.3 Alternative trading systems 19
  1.7 High-Frequency Trading 20
  Notes 24

Chapter 2. Models of Dealer Markets   25

2.1   Introduction 25
2.2   Risk-Neutral Inventory Models 25
    2.2.1   Garman's model 26
    2.2.2   The Amihud–Mendelson model 29
2.3   Risk Aversion 29
2.4   Inventory Models with Risk Aversion 32
2.5   Information-Based Models 34
    2.5.1   Kyle's model 35
    2.5.2   The Glosten–Milgrom model 38
Notes 42

Chapter 3. Models of the Limit-Order Markets   43

3.1   The Taker's Dilemma 43
    3.1.1   Introductory comments 43
    3.1.2   The CMSW model 44
    3.1.3   The Parlour model 45
    3.1.4   The Foucault model 46
    3.1.5   New developments 48
3.2   Market Microstructure Models 51
    3.2.1   Introductory comments 51
    3.2.2   Roll's model 51
    3.2.3   The Glosten–Harris model 54
    3.2.4   Structural models 55
    3.2.5   Modeling of trading impact 57
3.3   Empirical Findings 61
    3.3.1   Intraday patterns 61
    3.3.2   Order flows and market impact 62
Notes 63

Part II: Market Dynamics   65

Chapter 4. Dynamics of Returns   67

4.1   Introduction 67
4.2   Prices and Returns 67
4.3   The Efficient Market Hypothesis 69
4.4   Random Walk and Predictability of Returns 71
4.5   Empirical Findings 73

4.6 Corrections in the US Equity Markets 76
    4.6.1 The model 76
    4.6.2 Corrections in major US equity indexes . . . 78
    4.6.3 Corrections for the US equity sector ETFs . . 79
4.7 Fractals in Finance 84
Notes 86

Chapter 5. Price Volatility   **87**

5.1 Introduction 87
5.2 Basic Notions 87
5.3 Conditional Heteroscedasticity 89
5.4 Integrated Volatility 93
5.5 Market Risk Measurement 95
Notes 99

Chapter 6. Agent-Based Modeling of
Financial Markets   **101**

6.1 Introduction 101
6.2 Adaptive Equilibrium Models 103
6.3 Non-Equilibrium Price Models 107
6.4 The Observable Variables Model 109
    6.4.1 Modeling price–demand relationship 111
    6.4.2 Why technical trading may be successful . . . 112
    6.4.3 Modeling the birth of a two-sided market . . 114
Notes 117

Part III: Portfolio Management   **119**

Chapter 7. Mean–Variance Portfolio Theory   **121**

7.1 Introduction 121
7.2 Portfolio Selection 121
    7.2.1 Portfolio with one risky asset and one risk-
        free asset 122
    7.2.2 Portfolio with two risky assets 123
    7.2.3 Portfolio with two risky assets and one risk-
        free asset 125
7.3 The Markowitz Model 127
7.4 Portfolio Diversification 130

7.4.1 Introductory comments 130
7.4.2 Partial correlations-based mean variance . . . 130
7.4.3 Diversity booster 139
7.5 Optimal ESG Portfolios 143
Notes 148

Chapter 8. Portfolio Optimization   **149**

8.1 Introduction 149
8.2 Shrinkage in Portfolio Theory 149
8.3 The Black–Litterman Model 151
8.4 Robust Portfolio Optimization 153
Notes 155

Chapter 9. Risk-Based Asset Allocation   **157**

9.1 Introduction 157
9.2 Equal Weight Portfolio 157
9.3 Minimum Variance Portfolio 159
9.4 Maximum Diversification Portfolio 161
9.5 Risk Parity Portfolio 161
Notes 163

Chapter 10. Factor Models   **165**

10.1 Introduction 165
10.2 Capital Asset Pricing Model 165
10.3 The Arbitrage Pricing Theory 168
10.4 Multi-Factor Models 171
     10.4.1 Implementation issues 171
     10.4.2 The Fama–French models 173
     10.4.3 Smart betas 175
Notes 176

Part IV: Active Trading Strategies   **177**

Chapter 11. Technical Analysis-Based Strategies   **179**

11.1 Introduction 179
11.2 Trend Strategies 182
     11.2.1 Filter rules 182
     11.2.2 Moving-average rules 183
     11.2.3 Channel breakouts 185

11.3 Momentum Strategies 187
    11.3.1 Time series momentum 187
    11.3.2 Moving average convergence/divergence . . . 191
11.4 Oscillators 193
    11.4.1 Relative strength index 193
    11.4.2 Stochastic oscillators 193
11.5 Complex Geometric Patterns 194
Notes 196

Chapter 12. Arbitrage Strategies   **197**

12.1 Introduction 197
12.2 Hedging Strategies 199
12.3 Pair Trading 201
    12.3.1 Cointegration and causality 201
    12.3.2 Pair selection 203
12.4 Beta Hedging 206
12.5 Momentum Arbitrage 208
12.6 Arbitrage Risks 209
Notes 215

Chapter 13. News and Sentiment-Based Strategies 217

13.1 Introduction 217
13.2 Textual News Sentiment 218
13.3 Impact of Financial and Macroeconomic News . . . 219
    13.3.1 Impact of corporate earnings on stock prices 220
    13.3.2 Market impact of macroeconomic news . . . 224
    13.3.3 Market sentiment indexes 231
13.4 Opinion Mining 233
    13.4.1 Blogging platforms 233
    13.4.2 Google searches 234
Notes 236

Chapter 14. Back-Testing of Trading Strategies   **237**

14.1 Introduction 237
14.2 Performance Measures 239
14.3 Resampling Techniques 243
    14.3.1 Bootstrap 243
    14.3.2 Markov chain Monte Carlo 245
    14.3.3 Random entry protocol 247

14.4 Comparing Trading Strategies 248
        14.4.1 Bootstrap reality check 248
        14.4.2 New developments 250
    Notes 251

Chapter 15. Execution Strategies   253

    15.1 Introduction 253
    15.2 Benchmark-Driven Algorithms 255
        15.2.1 Time-weighted average price 255
        15.2.2 Volume-weighted average price 255
        15.2.3 Percent of volume 256
        15.2.4 Participation weighted price 257
    15.3 Cost-Driven Algorithms 257
        15.3.1 Risk-neutral framework 257
        15.3.2 Risk-averse framework 259
    15.4 The Taker's Dilemma in Optimal Execution 264
        15.4.1 Introductory comments 264
        15.4.2 The random walk model 266
        15.4.3 Modeling execution of pegged orders 267
    Notes 269

Appendix A: Probability Distributions   271

    A.1 Basic Notions 271
    A.2 Commonly Used Distributions 275
        A.2.1 The uniform distribution 275
        A.2.2 The binomial distribution 275
        A.2.3 The Poisson distribution 276
        A.2.4 The normal distribution 276
        A.2.5 The lognormal distribution 277
        A.2.6 The Cauchy distribution 278
        A.2.7 The gamma distribution 278
        A.2.8 The geometric distribution 278
    A.3 Stable Distributions and Scale Invariance 279

Appendix B: Elements of Time Series Analysis **281**

B.1 The ARMA Model 281
  B.1.1 The autoregressive model 281
  B.1.2 The moving average model 284
  B.1.3 The ARMA model 284
B.2 Trends and Seasonality 288
B.3 Multivariate Time Series 289

References 293

Index 317

Notations and Abbreviations

All variables are in italics. Scalar values are denoted with the regular font (e.g., X), while vectors and matrices are denoted with bold letters (e.g., $\boldsymbol{X}$). For example, $\boldsymbol{\sigma}$ is covariance matrix and σ^2 is variance. The matrix transposes are denoted with primes (e.g., $\boldsymbol{X}'$) and the matrix determinants are denoted with $|\boldsymbol{X}|$. The following notations are used interchangeably: $X(t_k) \equiv X_k$, $X(t_{k-1}) \equiv X(k-1)$. $E[X]$ denotes the expectation of the variable X.

The following abbreviations are used across all book chapters:

ACF	autocorrelation function
ADR	American depositary receipts
AIC	Akaike information criterion
APT	arbitrage pricing theory
AR	autoregressive process
ARCH	autoregressive conditional heteroscedasticity
ARMA model	autoregressive moving average model
ATS	alternative trading system
BB	best bid price
BO	best offer price
B&H strategy	buy-and-hold strategy
BLM	Black–Litterman model
BRC	bootstrap reality check
BV	book value
CAPM	capital asset pricing model
CARA	constant absolute risk aversion

CBOE	Chicago Board Options Exchange
CCAPM	consumption capital asset pricing model
CFTC	Commodity Futures Trading Commission
CIR	cumulative impulse response
CSM	cross-sectional momentum
CRRA	constant relative risk aversion
DB	diversity booster
DMVP	diversified mean–variance portfolio
DMVPT	diversified MVPT
ECN	electronic communication network
EGARCH	exponential generalized autoregressive conditional heteroscedasticity
EMA	exponential moving average
EMH	efficient market hypothesis
ERBP	equal risk balance portfolio
ERCP	equal risk contributions portfolio
ESG	environmental, social, and (corporate) governance
ETL	expected tail loss
EWBP	equal-weight benchmark portfolio
EWMA	exponentially weighed moving average
EWP	equal-weight portfolio
FIFO rule	first-in-first-out rule
FINRA	Financial Industry Regulatory Authority
FPT	first passage time
FX	foreign exchange
GARCH model	generalized autoregressive conditionally heteroscedastic model
HaSP	head-and-shoulder pattern
HFT	high frequency trading
ICAPM	intertemporal capital asset pricing model
IGARCH	integrated generalized autoregressive conditional heteroscedasticity
IID	independent and identically distributed
IPO	initial public offering
IS	implementation shortfall
LOB	limit order book

MA	moving average
MACD	moving average convergence/divergence
MBS	mortgage-backed securities
MCMC	Markov chain Monte Carlo
MDD	maximum drawdown
MDP	maximum diversification portfolio
MinVP	minimum variance portfolio
ML	machine learning
MLE	maximum likelihood estimate
MSE	means square error
MV	market value
MVP	mean–variance portfolio
MVPT	mean–variance portfolio theory
NASDAQ	National Association of Securities Dealers Automated Quotations
NBBO	national bid and offer
NYSE	New York Stock Exchange
OLS	ordinary least squares
OTC market	over-the-counter market
PaMVP	partial correlations-based MVP
PDF	probability density function
PeMVP	Pearson's correlations-based MVP
POV	percentage of volume
PWP	participation-weighted price
RA	risk aversion
ROE	return on equity
RPP	risk parity portfolio
RSI	relative strength index
SEC	Securities and Exchanges Commission
SMA	simple moving average
SUE	standardized unexpected earnings
TABSs	technical analysis-based strategies
TSM	time series momentum
TWAP	time-weighted average price
VaR	value at risk
VAR	vector autoregression model
VIX	volatility index
VWAP	volume-weighted average price

Introduction

Investing in finance implies acquiring assets for receiving future profits. In a nutshell, there are two types of assets: real assets and securities. Real assets include commodities, real estate, machines, and intellectual properties, such as patents and art. Securities are financial assets that represent ownership of real assets and their cash flows. They include stocks, bonds, currencies, and various derivative contracts, such as options and futures, to name a few. Thus, investing is a very wide field. This book is devoted to equity investing, and more specifically, to the equities that represent ownership of publicly traded corporations. The term *stock investing* is also often used since the units of equity are called stocks (or shares).

One should answer three major questions for successful investing: What, When, and How (to buy and/or sell), There is no single answer to any of these questions. The problem is that investing, and finance in general, is not based on some fundamental laws in the sense that is used in natural sciences. Rather, the theories in finance are mere models derived using some assumptions on market dynamics (e.g., the *random walk hypothesis*) and human behavior (e.g., the notion of *rational investors*). And often, these models fail (Derman, 2011). Therefore, the stock portfolios need permanent management for adapting to ever-changing market conditions. Many practitioners agree that portfolio management is as much art as science (Grinold & Kahn, 2000; Jacobs & Levy, 2016).

The third question (How) is not a typical portfolio management topic. However, trading is the means for forming and rebalancing stock portfolios, and optimal execution is very important for minimizing capital losses caused by the trading process (Johnson, 2010; Kissell, 2020).

Most textbooks on investments and portfolio management focus on two classical theories (see, e.g., Bodie & Merton, 1998; Luenberger, 1998; Elton *et al.*, 2009). The first one is the mean–variance portfolio theory (MVPT) pioneered by Markowitz (1952). MVPT formulates the problem of estimating portfolio asset weights as an optimization problem. Namely, MVPT determines portfolio asset weights that minimize portfolio risk measured by the variance of portfolio return. While MVPT has a beautiful mathematical framework, various conceptual and implementation problems complicate its usage in practice. These problems and their possible remedies are described in this book.

Another classical approach in portfolio management is the *capital asset pricing model* (CAPM) according to which security returns are proportional to the market return. The *arbitrage pricing theory* (APT) offered by Ross (1976) expands the CAPM into a linear multi-factor model. This approach has received further development in the Fama and French (1993, 2015) factor models and in their multiple variations that are sometimes called *smart betas* (see, e.g., Ang, 2014).

Besides the classical theories, I also describe several heuristic strategies widely used in modern equity investing. They include risk-based asset allocation, technical analysis-based trading strategies, arbitrage strategies, and alternative data-based investing.

Finally, to answer the third question (How), I offer an overview of the modern equity market organization and optimal execution strategies.

The book is organized into four parts. Part I (Modern Equity Markets; Chapters 1–3) is devoted to the modern equity markets. I start by introducing the major types of traders, trading orders, and market structures (Chapter 1). Then I present various models of dealer markets (Chapter 2) and limit-order markets (Chapter 3).

Part II (Market Dynamics; Chapters 4–6) addresses the basic models of price dynamics. I discuss the efficient market hypothesis and predictability of stock returns in Chapter 4. Various price volatility models are described in Chapter 5. Finally, I introduce the concepts of agent-based modeling of financial markets in Chapter 6.

Part III (Portfolio Management; Chapters 7–10) describes various approaches in portfolio management. I start with MVPT and its modifications including partial correlations-based MVPT, diversity booster, and optimal ESG portfolios (Chapter 7). Then I proceed with portfolio optimization methods (Chapter 8) and risk-based asset allocation (Chapter 9). The CAPM, APT, and various factor models are described in Chapter 10.

Part IV (Active Trading Strategies; Chapters 11–15) is devoted to various opportunistic trading strategies, their back-testing, and optimal trade execution. Specifically, I offer an overview of the technical analysis-based strategies in Chapter 11. Arbitrage strategies and alternative data-based strategies are the subjects of Chapters 12 and 13, respectively. In Chapter 14, I describe resampling techniques used for rigorous back-testing of trading strategies. Optimal execution strategies are introduced in Chapter 15.

Lastly, for self-contained presentation of the material, I include in the appendix a description of probability distributions and elements of time series analysis that are used in this book.

Part I
Modern Equity Markets

Chapter 1

Equity Markets: Traders, Orders, and Structures

1.1 Introduction

This chapter offers a big picture of modern equity markets: who the traders are, what types of orders they can submit for initiating trading, how these orders are processed, and how markets are organized.

1.2 Traders

Let me start with the people who trade. Traders can be partitioned into two groups: *proprietary traders* and *brokers* (or agency traders). The former trade for their own money (or their employer's capital). Depending on the context, I will use the terms "proprietary traders" and "investors" interchangeably. Harris (2002) provides a detailed taxonomy of various proprietary trader types. Here, I offer a somewhat simplified classification. Namely, I discern *profit-motivated traders* and *utilitarian traders*. Profit-motivated traders trade only when they expect to gain from trading.

Utilitarian traders trade if they need some additional benefits besides (and sometimes even instead of) profits. Investors who trade for managing their cash flows are a typical example of utilitarian traders. For example, when investors sell part of their portfolio to get cash for buying a house or investors invest into their pension plans on a periodic schedule regardless of the market conditions, their trades may be not optimal in the eyes of purely profit-motivated traders.

Hedgers are another type of utilitarian traders. The goal of hedging is to reduce the risk of owning a risky asset. A typical example is buying put options for hedging equities. Put options allow investors to sell stocks at a fixed price.[1] The immediate expenses of buying options may be perceived as a loss. Yet these expenses can protect the investor from much higher losses in the case of falling stock price. In the economic literature, utilitarian traders are often called *liquidity traders* to emphasize that they consume the liquidity that is provided by *market makers* (or *dealers*). I describe the concept of market liquidity in Section 1.4.

Profit-motivated traders can be partitioned into *informed traders*, *technical traders*, *arbitrageurs*, and dealers. Informed traders make their trading decisions using information on the asset fundamental (or fair) value. It is based on the company's profits, cash flows, product quality, competitors, etc. Informed traders buy security only if they believe that it is underpriced in respect to its fundamental value and sell when security seems overpriced. Since buying (selling) pressure causes prices to increase (decrease), the trades of informed investors move security price toward its fair value. Note that the fundamental value is not static. New information, e.g., discovery of a new technology, introducing a new product by the company or its competitor, CEO's resignation, and serious accident, can abruptly change the stock valuation.

Informed traders are called also *value investors* or fundamental investors (Graham & Dodd, 2008). Also, informed investors with *risk aversion* are called *rational investors* (see Sections 2.3 and 4.3 for details). Sometimes, *insiders* (mostly the company's chief executives and board members) are called truly informed investors since they may have information about their company that is unavailable to the public. It should be noted, though, that trading based on insider information is illegal.

Technical traders believe that all information that is necessary for trading decisions is incorporated into historical price dynamics. Namely, technical traders use multiple price patterns described in the literature for forecasting future price direction (see Chapter 11).

Estimates of the fundamental value of a security may vary across different markets. Also, security prices may significantly fluctuate around its fair value. Traders who explore these opportunities are called *arbitrageurs* (see Chapter 12).

As I indicated above, dealers supply liquidity to other traders. It is said that they make market in securities that they trade. Traders who trade with market makers are sometimes called *takers*. In some markets, traders who are registered as dealers (also called *dedicated market makers*) receive some privileges, such as exclusive handling of some securities and lower market access fees. In return, dealers are required to always provide securities in which they make the market for buying and selling during trading hours. Dealers make profits from the difference between the sell price and the buy price that they establish. This implies that there are takers in the market who are willing to buy a security at a price higher than the price at which they can immediately sell this security. It seems like easy money, providing that the asset price does not change and there are equal flows of buy orders and sell orders. However, due to price volatility, there is always a risk that dealers have to replenish their inventory by buying security at a price higher than the price they sold this security at in the near past. This may be caused by a sudden spike in demand caused by either informed or liquidity traders. Similarly, dealer's loss may occur when the takers exert selling pressure. I describe the dealer market models in Chapter 2.

Brokers do not trade for their own money; they execute orders for their clients. To emphasize the institutional character of a broker, the term *brokerage* is also used. Brokerage revenues are based on commissions for trading and other services for their clients. Typical brokerage services include matching their clients' buy and sell orders, connecting to the markets, *clearing* and *settlement*, providing market data and research, and offering credit. Settlement implies delivery of traded assets to the trading counterparts (buyers and sellers). Clearing denotes all brokerage actions that ensure settlement according to the market rules. These include reporting, credit management, and tax handling. Brokerage clients should deposit money for trading into their accounts. They may also open *margin accounts* that offer cash loans from the broker for buying additional shares (so-called *trading on margin*) or borrowing shares for *short selling*.

Short sellers assume that stock price will fall in a near future. They sell the borrowed shares at a current price and later buy the same number of shares back at a lower price and return the shares to the broker (so-called *buying to cover*).

Trading on margin can increase losses if asset price moves in an adverse direction. If these losses exceed some threshold, the broker may issue a *margin call*, which requires the trader either to liquidate part of his asset position or to add more capital to his account.

The institutions that trade for investing and asset management of their own or their clients' capital (pension funds, mutual funds, money managers, etc.) are called the *buy-side*. The *sell-side* institutions provide trading services to the buy-side. Some large sell-side firms have brokerage services and are called *broker-dealers*.

1.3   Orders and Limit Order Book

When traders decide to make a trade, they submit *orders* to their brokers. Orders specify trading instrument, its quantity (size), market side (buy or sell), and possibly other conditions including price that must be met for conducting a trade. When an order meets its counterpart in the market, a transaction occurs and it is said that both orders are *matched* (or *filled*). Traders submit orders upon some market conditions. If the market conditions change before the order is matched, the trader can cancel and possibly resubmit an order with other properties. Then, the *latency* problem may become important since traders do not receive confirmations of their trades instantly. If a trader attempts to cancel the order while it is being transacted, the cancellation fails.

There are two major order types: *market orders* and *limit orders*. Price is not specified for market orders and these orders are filled at the best price available at the order arrival time. Namely, a buy (sell) market order is filled at the current best *ask* (*bid*) price. Limit buy and sell orders are *quoted* in the market with their bid and ask (or *offer*) prices, respectively. Prices of limit orders are sometimes called *reservation prices*. The highest bid and the lowest ask present in the market are called *best bid* and *best ask* (or just bid and ask), respectively. The difference between the best ask and the best bid is called the *bid/ask spread* (see more in Section 1.4). During trading hours, one can observe so-called *bid/ask bounce* of transaction prices that is caused by trades randomly initiated by buyers and sellers. As a result, sequential transaction prices fluctuate between the best ask and best bid prices. It is said that any price within (outside) the

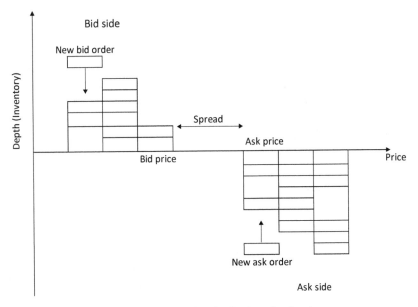

Fig. 1.1. Example of a limit order book.

spread is *inside* (*outside*) *the market.* The half-sum of the best bid and the best ask is called *mid-point price* (or just *mid-price*). Limit orders specify the worst price (highest ask or lowest bid) at which traders agree to trade. If a better price is available for matching the limit order at the time of its arrival to the market, the transaction is done at the better price. Limit orders are not guaranteed to be filled. For example, a limit buy order is placed below the best bid, but price does not fall that low. Limit orders that are not immediately filled are stored in the *limit order book* (LOB) until they are matched or cancelled (see an example of the LOB in Fig. 1.1). It is important to remember that the aggregated order size at any price in the LOB is finite. Hence, a large market order may wipe out the entire LOB inventory at the best price and get filled not at a single (best) price, but within some price range. As a result, the best available price worsens — at least temporarily. It is said that large orders have *market impact* (which is price impact; see Section 3.2). Note that some markets permit only limit orders.

Generally, limit orders are automatically cancelled at the end of trading day. To prevent such a cancellation, an option known as *good-till-cancelled* may be available. Usually, such an option has a limited duration (e.g., 1 month).

For a trader, the choice between a limit order and market order (when the latter order is permitted) may be non-trivial. For example, a trader assuming a *long position* can submit a market buy order and fill an order at current best offer price. In other words, the trader becomes a taker.

Another option is to submit a limit order at a current best bid (or even at a lower) price, that is, become a maker. It is said that takers pay the spread, which is the cost of immediacy. Indeed, there is a risk that the price will move in an adverse direction and the maker order will not be filled within the acceptable time horizon. I call this choice the *taker's dilemma* and discuss it in Sections 3.1 and 15.4.

If a limit order is submitted across the bid/ask spread, it is called *marketable limit order*. For example, a limit buy order is submitted at a best ask (or even higher) price. Why would anyone submit such an order? This may happen if a trader wants to quickly make at least a partial fill, but not beyond the chosen price.

Some markets permit *hidden limit orders*. These orders have a lower priority in respect to visible limit orders at the same price, but higher priority than the limit orders with a worse price. Sometimes, orders can be partially hidden. In the latter case, when the visible order part is filled, it is replenished with the hidden amount and the order position in the LOB is preserved. An example of the LOB where an order B has a hidden amount of 500 shares before and after filling a market order with 400 shares is given in Table 1.1.

Cancel-and-replace limit orders allow traders to change the order size without losing the order position in the LOB.

Table 1.1. Example of LOB with hidden amount.

LOB before		Market order	LOB after	
Order	Size	Size	Order	Size
A	100	400	B	200(300)
B	200(500)		C	100
C	200			

In some markets, limit orders can be *pegged*. There are three ways to define pegged order. The first two of them involve pegging to the best price on the same or opposite side of the market, respectively. Also, orders can be pegged to the bid/ask mid-price. The price of an unfilled pegged order moves along with its peg.

Equity markets have an option to submit *market-on-open* and *market-on-close* orders. These orders are submitted in advance for executing at the next market opening and closing, respectively.

Stop orders can be treated as limit orders since they, too, specify filling price. However, price has a different role in stop orders: it constrains possible loss rather than yields the realized profit. Indeed, after buying security at some price, a trader may want to sell it using a limit order at a higher price for locking in the profit. On the contrary, a sell stop order is submitted at a price that is lower than the current security price, which restricts a loss in the case of a possible adverse price movement. Hence, stop order may be considered as a form of hedging with options. The difference is that hedging has the immediate cost of buying options, while stop orders can be cancelled any time and have transaction fees only if they are filled.

Some other instructions may be provided with trading orders. *Fill-or-kill orders* are filled at their arrival in the market. Any portion of such an order that cannot be immediately filled is cancelled. Even a stricter constraint is used in the *all-or-none orders*: these orders can be filled only completely, or not at all.

1.4 Market Liquidity

Market liquidity is a notion that is widely used in finance. Yet it has no strict definition and in fact may have different meanings. Generally, the term *liquid asset* implies that it can be quickly and cheaply sold for cash (i.e., money). Hence, cash itself is an ideally liquid asset. On the contrary, real estate and antiques are not very liquid.

In the context of financial markets, liquidity characterizes the ability to trade an instrument without notable change of its price. A popular saying defines liquidity as the market's *breadth, depth, and resiliency*. First, this implies that the buying price and the selling price of a liquid instrument are very close, that is, the bid/ask spread is small. The size of the bid/ask spread is an important object in the market microstructure theory. Here are the common definitions and components of the spread (de Jong & Rindi, 2009):

The *quoted spread* between ask A_t and bid B_t that is averaged over T periods equals

$$S^Q = \frac{1}{T} \sum_{t=1}^{T} (A_t - B_t). \tag{1.1}$$

In terms of the asset fundamental price, P_t^*, the averaged spread is

$$S = \frac{1}{T} \sum_{t=1}^{T} 2q_t(P_t - P_t^*). \tag{1.2}$$

In (1.2), q_t is 1 for buy orders and -1 for sell orders. Since the value of P_t^* is not observable, the *effective spread* in terms of mid-price $M_t = 0.5(A_t + B_t)$ is usually used:

$$S^E = \frac{1}{T} \sum_{t=1}^{T} 2q_t(P_t - M_t). \tag{1.3}$$

Sometimes, the *realized spread* is applied in post-trade analysis:

$$S^R = \frac{1}{T} \sum_{t=1}^{T} 2q_t(P_t - M_{t+1}). \tag{1.4}$$

Note that that mid-price M in (1.3) and (1.4) is calculated at times t and $t+1$, respectively.

I have already indicated that the bid/ask spread from the taker's point of view is the price for immediacy of trading. Now, let us examine the main components of the bid/ask spread, which are determined by dealers (market makers). First, the spread incorporates the dealers' operational costs, such as the trading system development and maintenance, and clearing and settlement. Indeed, if dealers are not compensated for their expenses, there is no rationale for them to stay in this business. Dealer inventory costs, too, contribute into the bid/ask spread. Since dealers must satisfy order flows on both sides of the market, they maintain inventories of risky (and sometimes undesirable) instruments. Glosten & Harris (1988) combine the operational and inventory costs into a single *transitory* component since their effect on the security's price dynamics is unrelated to security's fair value. The details of the inventory market microstructure models will be discussed in Chapter 2.

Another component of the bid/ask spread reflects the dealer's risk of trading with counterparts who have superior information about the true security value. Informed traders trade on one side of the market and may profit from trading with dealers. Hence, dealers must recover their losses by widening the spread. Generally, these losses are passed to uninformed traders. This component of the bid/ask spread is called the *adverse-selection* component (see the details in Chapter 2).

The depth of a limit-order market implies that there are multiple orders in the LOB, possibly from various market makers. Therefore, order cancellations and transactions in a liquid market do not affect notably the LOB inventory available for trading.

Finally, market resiliency means that if some LOB inventory loss does occur, it is quickly replenished by market makers. In other words, market impact of trading has a temporary character (see Section 3.2).

Various liquidity measures are discussed in the literature. Sometimes, inverse liquidity (illiquidity) measure, based on the price impact caused by trading volume, is used (Amihud, 2002):

$$\text{ILLIQ} = \frac{1}{N} \sum_{k=1}^{N} |r_k| / V_k. \tag{1.5}$$

In (1.5), r_k and V_k are return and trading volume, respectively, for time interval k. This formula is rooted in the Kyle's (1985) model, which will be discussed in Section 2.5.

Gomber *et al.* (2015) offer another liquidity measure based on a relative market impact of simultaneous *round trip trade* (i.e., simultaneous buying and selling a given number of securities).

Schmidt (2016) used the percentage of time with a two-sided market for analysis of contributions of high-frequency traders to liquidity of the institutional FX market.

1.5   Equity Market Structures

Equity markets differ in their organization and trading rules. Some markets that are highly organized and regulated by the government agencies are called *exchanges* (or *bourses* in non-English-speaking countries). In the United States, trading of stocks, bonds, and several other securities is regulated by the *Securities and Exchanges Commission* (SEC). Trading of commodities (including spot, futures, and options) is regulated by another government agency, the *Commodity Futures Trading Commission* (CFTC).

Historically, exchanges were founded by their members (dealers and brokers) for trading among themselves. In our days, most exchanges have become incorporated. Still, generally, only the members can trade at exchanges. Two major exchanges in the USA are the New York Stock Exchange (NYSE) and NASDAQ (see the details in Section 1.6). An alternative to exchanges is the *over-the-counter* (OTC) *markets* where dealers and brokers can trade directly. Businesses must go through *initial public offering* (IPO) at some exchange in order to start trading their securities. Then, it is said that the security is listed on this exchange. After IPO, the issuer sells this security to investors in a *primary market*. Subsequent trading of securities among investors other than the issuer is conducted in the *secondary market* (or *aftermarket*). Trading of exchange-listed securities in the OTC markets is referred to as trading on the *third market*.

Market structure is determined by the specifics of *execution systems* and *trading sessions* (Harris, 2002; de Jong & Rindi, 2009). There are two major execution systems: *order-driven markets* and *quote-driven markets*. In terms of trading sessions, order-driven markets can be partitioned into *continuous markets* and *call markets*. Some order-driven markets are *auctions* in which trading rules ensure that trading occurs at the highest price a buyer is willing to pay and at the lowest price a seller is willing to sell at. The process of defining such a price is called *price discovery* (or *market clearing*). An example of auction price discovery is described below.

Another form of order-driven markets is *crossing networks* (called also *dark pools*). Price discovery is not implemented in crossing networks. Instead, prices used in matching of buy and sell orders are derived from prices in other (primary) markets. Accordingly, the term *derivative pricing* is used.[2] Orders submitted to crossing networks are prioritized by their arrival time. The main advantage of crossing networks is that trading in these markets is confidential. As a result, it does not have direct impact on price in the primary markets. Therefore, crossing networks are attractive to those traders who trade very large orders (*blocks*) and want to hide their intentions. The disadvantage of trading in the dark is that it may encounter significant *order imbalance*. It is calculated as a difference between aggregate demand and aggregate supply and is also called *excess demand*. As a result, the portion of filled orders (*fill ratio*) in dark pools may be rather small. More details about dark pools are given in Section 1.6.

1.5.1 *Continuous order-driven markets*

In continuous order-driven markets, traders can submit their orders at any time while the markets are open. Trading hours vary in different markets. For example, the exchanges NYSE and NASDAQ are open on Monday through Friday; they start trading at 9:30 A.M. EST and close at 4:00 P.M. EST. On the contrary, the OTC markets have extended trading hours (so-called *pre-market hours* and *after-market hours* that last up to 4 h outside the exchange trading hours).

In order-driven markets, traders can trade among themselves without intermediary dealers. In other words, every trader can become a maker by placing a limit order. Those limit orders that are not immediately matched upon arrival are entered into the LOB according to the price–time priorities. Price priority has the primary precedence, which means that an order with a better (or, it is said, more aggressive) price is placed before orders with worse prices.

Time priority means that a new order is placed behind the orders that have the same price and entered the market earlier. Matching of a new taker order with maker orders stored in the LOB occurs upon the *First In, First Out* (FIFO) principle, that is, older maker orders are filled first. It is said that the first order with the best price is on *top of the order book*. Hence, the higher (lower) the bid (ask) order price is, the closer this order is to the top of the LOB. A new limit bid (ask) order that is higher (lower) than the current top of the book forms a new top.

In some markets, the size precedence rule is used and the largest order on top of LOB is filled first. In other markets, priority is given

Table 1.2.   Example of LOB.

Order	Price	Size
Ask2	10.35	200
Ask1	10.30	200
Bid1	10.25	100
Bid2	10.23	200

to the smallest order. Some markets use *pro rata* allocation. If aggregated bid size exceeds aggregated offer size, then all bid orders are partially filled proportionally to their size.

Consider a few examples of matching in an order-driven market (see Table 1.2).

Let the LOB have the following bid orders:[3] B1 — 100@10.25 (best bid), B2 — 200@10.23; and the following ask orders: A1 — 200@10.30 (best ask), A2 — 200@10.35. A market buy order of a size less than or equal to 200 will be filled at the price $P = 10.30$. If the size of the market buy order equals 200, it completely matches A1 and the bid/ask spread increases from $s = 10.30 - 10.25 = 0.05$ to $s = 10.35 - 10.25 = 0.1$.

Market buy order of size 300 will be matched as 200@10.30 + 100@10.35. What if you want to buy 500 units, which is higher than the entire offer inventory? Then, you can submit a limit order that will be stored in the LOB until a new seller decides to match it. For example, you may want to submit a bid of 500@10.35. This would result in the immediate matching of 400 units, and the remaining 100 units become the new best bid. Such an order would not be optimal, though. One may submit two orders: a market order of 400 shares and a limit order 100@10.26. The latter one is still on top of the LOB and it saves some money due to its filling at a lower price. On the contrary, a bid 100@10.35 is more attractive to the sellers and will likely be filled faster.

If a bid is submitted inside the market, that is, $10.25 < P < 10.30$, it is placed before B1 and becomes the new best bid. The bid/ask spread then decreases from $s = 0.05$ to $s = 10.30 - P$. If a bid is submitted with a price in the range $10.23 < P \leq 10.25$, it is placed in the LOB between the bids B1 and B2. Finally, a bid with a price $P \leq 10.23$ is placed behind the bid B2.

1.5.2 Oral auctions

In *oral auctions* (or *open-outcry auctions*), traders (brokers and dealers) gather in the same place (floor market). Traders are required to communicate (using shouting and hand signals) their trading intentions and the results of trading to all market participants. This ensures transparency of the trading process.

Order precedence rules and price discovery in oral auctions are similar to those in continuous order-driven markets. However, there may be some additional secondary precedence rules. In particular, *public order precedence* gives priority to the public traders in respect to the floor traders.

Open-outcry auctions used to be the main trading venue in the past. In our days, most of the floor markets have deployed electronic trading systems that are used along with open outcry or have replaced them completely.

1.5.3 Call auctions

In call auctions, trading occurs at predetermined times. Call auctions can be conducted several times a day (so-called *fixings*) or at the openings and closings of continuous sessions. Orders submitted for given call are batched and executed simultaneously at the same price. Prior to auction, all submitted orders are placed according to the price–time precedence rules. Aggregated demand and supply are calculated assuming that traders willing to buy (sell) at a price P will also buy (sell) at a price lower (higher) than P. The auction price is defined in such a way that yields a maximum aggregate size of matched orders. Consider an example of price discovery in a call market with the orders listed in Table 1.3.

The maximum trading volume here corresponds to the price of 9.80 (see Table 1.4). The aggregate supply at this price (with a size of 800) is matched completely. However, part of the aggregate demand $(900 - 800 = 100)$ is not filled within the current call. Thus, the order that was the last to join the list of buyers involved in this fixing is filled only partially.

If the rule of maximum aggregate size of matched orders does not yield a unique price, the auction price is chosen to satisfy the rule of minimum order imbalance. If even the latter rule does not

Table 1.3.   Example of the pre-auction order book.

Buyers			Sellers	
Order	Size	Order price	Order	Size
		9.95	S1	700
B1	100	9.90	S2	300
B2	200	9.85	S3	400
		9.85	S4	200
		9.85	S5	100
B3	600	9.80	S6	300
B4	500	9.75	S7	500
B5	600	9.70		

Table 1.4.   Price discovery in the order book listed in Table 1.3.[a]

Price	Aggregate demand	Aggregate supply	Aggregate trading size	Order imbalance
9.95 and higher	0	2,500	0	2,500
9.90	100	1,800	100	1,700
9.85	300	1,500	300	1,200
9.80	**900**	**800**	**800**	**100**
9.75	1,400	500	500	900
9.70 and lower	2000	0	0	2,000

[a]Maximum trading values in bold.

define single price, the auction price is chosen to be the closest to the previous fixing price.

The advantage of call auctions is that the entire interest in given security is concentrated at the same time and is visible to all traders. On the contrary, continuous markets offer much more flexibility for choosing trading decisions.

1.5.4   *Quote-driven markets and hybrid markets*

In the quote-driven markets, only dealers submit maker orders. All other traders can submit only taker (market) orders. Price discovery in these markets means that market makers must choose such bid and ask prices that will at least cover their expenses (let alone generate profits) and balance buy and sell order flows. The theoretical models of dealers' strategies are discussed in Chapter 2. Some markets combine quote-driven and order-driven systems in their structures. The NYSE and NASDAQ are examples of such *hybrid markets*.

1.6   The US Equity Markets

As I indicated above, the main US primary markets are the NYSE and NASDAQ. There are also several US regional exchanges that were created primarily to list local companies that could not afford to become listed in the national exchanges. Current regional exchanges include the Boston, Chicago, Pacific, and Philadelphia exchanges.[4] Some *alternative trading systems* (ATSs) have been recently transformed into exchanges. They include BATS, Direct Edge, and IEX. More details about ATSs are given below.

1.6.1   *NYSE*

The NYSE has been the major US equity market. A brief history of the NYSE trading system, including recent changes, is offered by de Jong & Rindi (2009) and Hendershott & Moulton (2011). In 2007, the NYSE was merged with the pan-European electronic market Euronext. Hence, the name of the new corporation is the NYSE Euronext. The latter was acquired by the Intercontinental Exchange (ICE) in 2013. However, both NYSE and Euronext retain their brand names.

The NYSE was founded as an open-outcry auction back in the end of the 18th century and has evolved since then into a complex hybrid market combining an open outcry with a quote-driven (dealer) market, and an electronic LOB. For every stock traded on the floor, there is a designated dealer (*specialist*) who maintains the LOB and makes the market using his own account when there is lack of liquidity from other traders. Another specialists' duty is conducting the opening and closing auctions.[5] Importantly, the specialists are not allowed to trade ahead of their customers at the same price on the same side of the market. In fact, trading by brokers and dealers for their own account using the knowledge of their customers' pending orders (so-called *front running*) is illegal.

In 2007, the NYSE introduced the Hybrid Market architecture based on the merger of the NYSE with the *electronic communication network* (ECN) Archipelago (see more about ECNs below). The new system significantly expanded automatic execution and limited the role of the specialists. Traders now can directly submit their orders to the electronic LOB bypassing brokers and specialists unless their order size exceeds one million shares. An important reason for launching the Hybrid Market was the new SEC rule (so-called SEC Regulation NMS Order Protection Rule). This rule requires all equity markets to honor better-priced quotes available in other *fast markets* before filling orders at the market's own prices. Sub-second-order execution is required for the status of fast market, which is implemented in the Hybrid Market.

Market orders and marketable limit orders in the Hybrid Market are by default executed automatically. There are, however, stock-specific price ranges (so-called *liquidity replenishment points*) that determine the limits for price jumps and volatility. If these limits are reached, trading is converted from automatic to the auction execution.

Hendershott & Moulton (2011) have shown that introducing the Hybrid Market has reduced an average execution time from 10 seconds to less than one second. This, however, increased the bid/ask spread (i.e., cost of immediacy) by about 10%.

1.6.2 *NASDAQ*

NASDAQ was founded by National Association of Securities Dealers (NASD) in 1971. In 2007, NASD was consolidated with the member regulation, enforcement, and arbitration functions of the NYSE into the Financial Industry Regulatory Authority (FINRA). Currently, FINRA is the largest independent regulator for all securities firms doing business in the United States.

NASDAQ is a purely electronic market: it does not have a physical floor, and its dealers and brokers are connected via an electronic network. The specific feature of NASDAQ is that several competing dealers can make market for the same company (rather than one specialist in the NYSE). In the past, the NASDAQ computer system was used only for quoting prices and trading was conducted over the phone. It became clear during the market crash of 1987 how inefficient telephone-based trading is. As a result, an electronic order matching system was implemented. At present, the dealers' orders in the NASDAQ are consolidated into the integrated entry and execution system with LOB.

1.6.3 *Alternative trading systems*

ATSs are designed for direct matching of buyers and sellers. They are regulated by the SEC, but are not registered as exchanges. Thus, ATSs cannot list new securities. ATSs serve as alternative sources of liquidity and compete with exchanges for customers using lower execution latency and fees. Advanced technology that facilitates *high-frequency trading* (HFT) is what allows ATSs to compete with exchanges. There are two main types of ATSs: (1) ECNs and (2) crossing networks (dark pools that were introduced above).

ECNs allow their customers to submit their orders via electronic networks. Those orders that are not immediately matched form LOB according to the rules typical for the order-driven markets. The ECN LOB is visible to all ECN customers (orders usually are anonymous, though). Hence, price discovery is a distinctive feature of ECNs. One immediate advantage that ECNs offer to their customers is the possibility to trade before and after regular trading hours when the main exchanges are closed. Usually, only limit orders are permitted at these times.

In recent years, the line between exchanges and ECNs has become blurred due to mergers and acquisitions. For example, as was indicated above, the ECN Archipelago was merged with the NYSE in 2006. Also, one of the first ECNs, Instinet, was bought by NASDAQ in 2006. The BATS Exchange was founded as ECN in 2005, but it became an exchange in early 2009. Another ECN, Direct Edge, became an exchange in 2010.

As I mentioned above, there is no price discovery in crossing networks. Instead, orders are matched upon prices quoted in the primary markets. Historically, the first dark pools being independent agencies (such as the ITG acquired by Virtu Financial in 2019, and Liquidnet) offered anonymous block trading. Average trade sizes in these venues could reach tens of thousands of shares. In more recent times, several large brokers-dealers, such as UBS, Credit Suisse, and Goldman Saks, implemented crossing networks for internalization of their customers' orders. In these dark pools, brokers can trade for their own account against their customers, too. At present, this type of crossing networks is responsible for the major share of the dark pool trading. Typical order size in these dark pools is in the range of two to five hundreds of shares.

1.7   High-Frequency Trading

HFT is characterized by very short time periods of holding assets or, in other words, by extremely high *portfolio turnover*.[6] While some HFT strategies imply holding a portfolio for hours, sub-minute and even sub-second intervals have become common. The basic HFT strategies include statistical arbitrage and event arbitrage (see Chapter 12), optimal execution of large orders sliced into smaller pieces (see Chapter 15), and market making. The latter strategy is stimulated in some markets by offering rebates for providing liquidity. These rebates, while being very small (fraction of a penny per share), may provide an additional incentive for market making, which is a risky business (see Chapter 2).

In any case, the idea behind HFT is "to be the first" — either in making price or in *scalping* price inefficiencies. Usually, the HFT strategies are completely automated (and sometimes are called "algos"). Needless to say, advanced computer systems are required for implementing the HFT strategies. Moreover, in order to minimize the data transfer latency, many HFT firms use *co-location*. Namely, they deploy computer servers in the immediate proximity to trading floors. Other HFT firms use microwave data transfer that is supposed to be a bit faster than transfer through copper wires (rainy weather may eliminate advantages of microwave transmission, though). Obviously, building or leasing microwave transmission towers is a serious investment that can be justified only by superior trading profits.

By some estimates, HFT in 2016 accounted for about 10–40% of equity trading in the United States (Aldridge & Krawciw, 2017). The proponents of HFT emphasize increased liquidity and stability among the benefits that HFT brings to financial markets (Aldridge, 2010). Hendershott *et al.* (2011) found that HFT narrows spreads, reduces adverse selection, and reduces trade-related price discovery for large-cap stocks.

However, HFT is not free from controversies. Indeed, the danger of "algos gone wild," (as Donefer, 2010, puts it) is real: automated trading of extremely large asset volumes at the speed of light may lead to unforeseeable consequences. It is true that automated market making constitutes a significant share of liquidity of modern equity markets. However, high-frequency traders are not regulated in the same way as "true" dealers are and can therefore leave the market any time if they find that the profit opportunities have evaporated or that their models cannot handle unforeseen market dynamics. This can potentially lead to significant disruption in markets rather than to its stabilization.

An instructive example of a major market disruption was the "flash crash" on May 6, 2010, when the Dow Jones index fell about 600 points within 5 min and then recovered within the next 10 min. A joint CFTC-SEC (2010) report identified a single large order (~$4 billion) to sell the Standard & Poor's 500[7] (S&P 500) *futures*[8] that provoked a chain of events leading to the crash. This order was placed by a large fundamental trader using an algorithm programmed to sell the entire order within 20 min without regard to price. Usually, trading of such a large order may take a few hours. Several HFT firms noticed unusually intense selling and attempted to profit from it. Hoping that the sell-off would end soon, they were buying the S&P 500 futures and hedging long positions by selling stocks that constitute the S&P 500 Index (see more about hedging in Chapter 12). However, after accumulating futures above some threshold, HFT firms started selling futures back. While many market participants withdrew due to high volatility, other HFT firms kept trading among themselves, creating a so-called "hot-potato effect." The selling algorithm that handled the original large order reacted at intense trading with an increasing selling rate. Ultimately, the selling pressure could not be absorbed by the buyers anymore, and the price of the S&P 500 futures fell dramatically. This had led to the sell-off in the stock market. Further damage was prevented only when automatic functionality in the futures market paused trading for several seconds. After trading resumed, increased buying interest recovered the equity markets. Kirilenko *et al.* (2017) provide further analysis of the flash crash. While this event was not triggered by HFT, it certainly highlighted the liquidity risk posed by possible withdrawal of

HFT firms from trading. Indeed, the "hot-potato effect" caused by a few competing HFT firms trying to outsmart each other implies that high trading volume is not necessarily an indicator of high liquidity. In order to mitigate similar crashes in the future, SEC introduced circuit breakers that halt trading of a stock for 5 min if the price moves 10% within a 5-min period.

Schmidt (2016) describes another example of withdrawal of the HFT firms in the global FX market during the intervention of the Bank of Japan in 2011.

Several other controversies accompanied the proliferation of HFT. In particular, it was revealed in 2009 that some brokers offered to the HFT firms a service that puts other market participants at a disadvantage and/or additional risk. This service is called direct sponsored (or "naked") market access. It allows customers to access the market without the latency of time required for compliance monitoring. Trading done through the sponsored access was not controlled by brokers and regulators and therefore involved increased market risk. The SEC prohibited brokers and dealers from providing sponsored access to their customers in 2010.

One more controversial practice implemented by some exchanges involves "flash orders." These orders can be perceived as a sophisticated form of "front running." Flash orders allow the HFT firms to view order flow information prior to when it becomes available to other market participants. The HFT firms may then post matching orders with prices better than those available at the moment. For example, an exchange that receives an order must route it to another (rival) exchange if the latter has a better price. According to the current regulation, this should be done within one second. Instead of immediate routing, the exchange creates a "flash" that is displayed just for a few dozen milliseconds. This flash can attract an HFT firm that fills the order at a price better than the one available in a rival exchange. While the SEC considered a ban on "flash orders" in 2009, it was not implemented. Nevertheless, most exchanges stopped offering flash orders to their customers.

Then, there are the HFT activities known as "quote stuffing," "spoofing," and "layering," in which large numbers of orders are placed and cancelled almost immediately. The HFT firms might engage in this practice to provoke other market participants to trade at a "new" price, which in fact is never available due to quick cancelations. For example, to buy stock at a lower price, an HFT firm places and quickly cancels sell orders below the ask price. This may create an impression of selling pressure and motivate the dealers to cancel current bids and resubmit them at a lower price. Then, the HFT firm buys at the lower price. Lewis (2014) offers a colorful description of various HFT practices used by the Wall Street traders.

One cause of future "flash crashes" might be some combination of "quote stuffing" with so-called "stub quotes." This practice was sometimes used by market makers who are obligated by exchanges to provide liquidity on both sides of the market. If market makers were not willing to trade at the moment, they might set unreasonably low bids and high offers. In 2010, the SEC banned stub quotes and mandated that market makers' quotes be within 8% of the *national best bid and offer* (NBBO). While quote stuffing was not banned outright by the SEC, FINRA and the exchanges consider submission of orders without intent of trading as market manipulation and may fine the traders who use it.

"Pooling" is another form of market manipulation in which two traders agree to trade between themselves at artificial prices (and compensate each other's losses) in order to create an impression of an impending change of market price.

Further sophistication of HFT fueled by the technological progress is inevitable. This creates a problem for buy-side firms unwilling or unable to participate in the expensive technology race. The Investors Exchange (IEX) answered the buy-side concerns by implementing a "speed bump." In a nutshell, it is 38-mile coil of optical fiber placed in front of the trading engine, which yields a 350-μs delay in processing trading orders. The SEC approved IEX as an official exchange in 2016. After that, the NYSE and NASDAQ implemented their own versions of the "speed bump."

Some electronic FX trading platforms offered new solutions for leveling the field between the HFT firms and other clients. One of them is introducing of a *minimum quote life* (MQL), which does not permit cancelling the orders stored in the LOB for some period of time (typically in the range from 50 to 250 ms). Another solution is randomization of the LOB, i.e., replacing the FIFO rule for order matching with a random choice of an order at best price.

These solutions were debated, but so far have not been implemented in the equity markets.

Notes

1. See, e.g., Hull (2006) for a definitive description of the options theory and its applications.
2. This term should not be confused with the pricing financial instruments called derivatives, e.g., options (Hull, 2006).
3. The notation 100@10.25 implies that the number of shares is 100 and the share price is $10.25.
4. There were several other regional exchanges in the past. However, the financial market landscape has been dramatically changed in recent years due to mergers and acquisitions. In particular, the Boston and Philadelphia regional exchanges were acquired by NASDAQ in 2007, and one of the former primary markets, the American Stock Exchange, was acquired by the NYSE Euronext in 2008.
5. The NYSE closing process is more complicated than the classical auction (Hasbrouck, 2007).
6. Portfolio turnover is the daily traded volume divided by the total number of shares outstanding for each stock (Emrich, 2009).
7. S&P 500 is a stock market index that measures the market-cap weighted stock performance of the 500 largest companies listed on the US stock exchanges.
8. Future contracts (futures) are financial instruments that allow investors to bet on the future value of an asset.

Chapter 2

Models of Dealer Markets

2.1 Introduction

As I indicated in Chapter 1, market makers in order-driven markets provide liquidity for takers and make money from the bid/ask spread. The challenge for the dealers' business model is that there is always a danger that the flows of buy orders and sell orders are not balanced. For example, if there is selling pressure, the price decreases. Then the dealer (who has an obligation to maintain inventory) may have to sell an asset at a price lower than the price at which he bought the asset some time ago. In the long run, the price may revert, but the problem is that the dealer with limited cash resources can become broke before restoring his inventory. There are two theoretical approaches for describing dealers' strategies that are collectively called *market microstructure models*: *inventory models* and *information-based models* (O'Hara, 1995; Hasbrouck, 2007; de Jong & Rindi, 2009). This chapter is devoted to these models. Also, I introduce here a concept of *risk aversion* that is widely used in economics and finance, particularly in the mean–variance portfolio theory (see Chapter 7).

2.2 Risk-Neutral Inventory Models

In this section, I discuss several models that address market maker's risk associated with maintaining inventory and how the size of the bid/ask spread can compensate for this risk.

2.2.1 *Garman's model*

The problem of the dealer's inventory imbalance was first addressed by Garman (1976). In his model, a monopolistic dealer assigns ask (p_a) and bid (p_b) prices, and fills all orders. Each order size is assumed to be one unit traded for one unit of cash. The dealer's goal is, as a minimum, to avoid bankruptcy (running out of cash) and failure (running out of inventory). The dealer also attempts to maximize his profits. Arrivals of buy orders and sell orders are assumed to follow independent continuous Poisson processes[1] with price-dependent rates $\lambda_a(p_a)$ and $\lambda_b(p_b)$, respectively. This process implies a high number of takers who submit multiple (albeit small) independent orders. Note that the buy (ask) rate depends on ask (bid) price.

Garman's model employs the concept of *Walrasian equilibrium*, in which lower prices drive demand and suppress supply while higher prices decrease demand and increase supply. As a result, price settles at a value that equates supply and demand.[2] Hence, it is expected that $\lambda_a(p_a)$ is a monotonically decreasing function while $\lambda_b(p_b)$ monotonically increases (see Fig. 2.1).

The probability of a buy (sell) order to arrive within the time interval $[t, t + dt]$ equals $\lambda_a dt$ ($\lambda_b dt$). First, Garman determines the

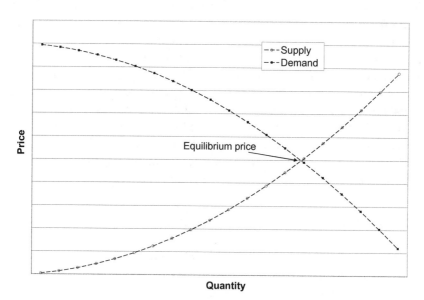

Fig. 2.1. Walrasian equilibrium.

units of cash, $I_c(t)$, and stocks, $I_s(t)$, that are held by the dealer at time t. If $N_a(t)$ and $N_b(t)$ are the total numbers of stocks sold and bought by the dealer since the beginning of trading $(t = 0)$, then the inventory dynamics are described as

$$I_c(t) = I_c(0) + p_a N_a(t) - p_b N_b(t), \tag{2.1}$$

$$I_s(t) = I_s(0) + N_b(t) - N_a(t). \tag{2.2}$$

Next, Garman calculates the probability $Q_k(t)$ that $I_c(t) = k$. Since each order size is one, there may be three events at time $t - dt$ that yield the cash position of k units: the dealer had $k - 1$ units of cash and sold one stock; the dealer had $k + 1$ units of cash and bought one stock; the dealer did not trade. Then $Q_k(t)$ satisfies the following relation:

$$Q_k(t) = \lambda_a p_a dt [1 - \lambda_b p_b dt] Q_{k-1}(t - dt) + \lambda_b p_b dt [1 - \lambda_a p_a dt]$$
$$\times Q_{k+1}(t - dt) + [1 - \lambda_a p_a dt][1 - \lambda_b p_b dt] Q_k(t - dt). \tag{2.3}$$

This allows one to calculate the derivative

$$\frac{\partial Q_k}{\partial t} \approx [Q_k(t) - Q_k(t - dt)]/dt = \lambda_a p_a Q_{k-1} + \lambda_b p_b Q_{k+1}$$
$$- (\lambda_a p_a + \lambda_b p_b) Q_k. \tag{2.4}$$

A similar equation can be derived for the probability $R_k(t)$ that $I_s(t) = k$.

In Garman's model, the dealer cannot borrow cash or stocks. Therefore, the trader must ensure that both $Q_0(t)$ and $R_0(t)$ are always less than unity. Indeed, the equalities $Q_0(t) = 1$ and $R_0(t) = 1$ imply that the trader definitely runs out of cash or stocks, respectively. This goal can be formulated in terms of the *gambler's ruin problem*.[3] Using this approach and the approximate solution of (2.4), Garman has shown that

$$\lim_{t \to \infty} Q_0(t) < 1 \quad \text{if} \quad \lambda_a p_a > \lambda_b p_b. \tag{2.5}$$

Similarly,

$$\lim_{t -> \infty} R_0(t) < 1 \quad \text{if} \quad \lambda_b > \lambda_a. \tag{2.6}$$

Hence, to avoid bankruptcy or failure, the dealer must maintain the bid/ask spread that satisfies the following conditions:

$$\lambda_a p_a > \lambda_b p_b, \qquad (2.7)$$

$$\lambda_b > \lambda_a. \qquad (2.8)$$

These conditions still do not guarantee full protection from bankruptcy or failure since the probabilities in (2.5) and (2.6) differ from zero. Also, this result points at the necessity for the dealer to set a bid/ask spread but it does not specify its size and positioning of mid-price. In order to obtain an analytical estimate for the bid/ask spread, Garman (1976) relaxes the condition (2.8) to

$$\lambda_b = \lambda_a. \qquad (2.9)$$

Then the bid and ask prices can be defined by choosing such a bid/ask spread that maximizes the shaded field in Fig. 2.2. The relation (2.9) still implies imminent failure at some point in time.[4] Hasbrouck (2007) indicates that "... with realistic parameter values, the expected ruin time is a matter of days." Hence, while Garman's model emphasizes importance of the bid/ask spread for dealer's strategy, it cannot serve as a practical advice for market making.

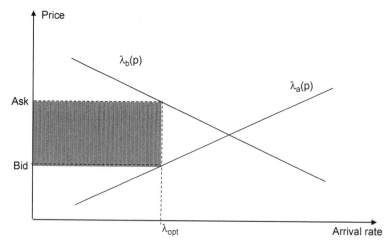

Fig. 2.2.   Bid/ask spread in Garman's model for the case (2.9).

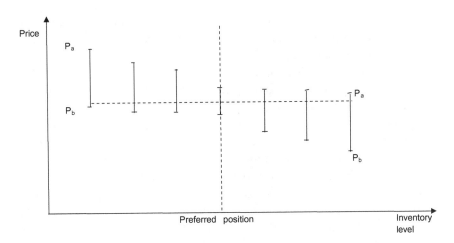

Fig. 2.3. Bid/ask spread in the Amihud–Mendelson model.

2.2.2 *The Amihud–Mendelson model*

One significant simplification of Garman's model is that the dealer establishes pricing in the beginning of trading and does not adjust it to ever ever-changing market conditions. This problem was addressed by Amihud & Mendelson (1980) by reformulating Garman's model so that the bid and ask prices depend on the dealer's stock inventory. Specifically, the dealer has an acceptable range and a "preferred" size of the inventory. The dealer maximizes trading profits by manipulating the bid/ask prices when inventory deviates from the preferred one. Amihud & Mendelson (1980) obtain their main results for linear demand and supply functions. Within their model, the optimal bid price and ask price decrease (increase) monotonically when inventory is growing (falling) beyond the preferred size. Also, the bid/ask spread widens as inventory increasingly deviates from the preferred size (see Fig. 2.3). The practical conclusion from the Amihud–Mendelson model is that the dealers should manipulate the bid/ask spread and mid-price for maintaining preferred inventory.

2.3 Risk Aversion

Humans are generally driven not only by their greed but also by their fears (Akerlof & Shiller, 2010). The concept of *risk aversion* is widely used in psychology, economics, and finance. In general, risk aversion is routinely observed in everyday life: many investors put significant part of their savings in risk-free assets, such as savings bank accounts and CDs, or in less risky money markets and bond markets rather than invest all their capital in potentially more rewarding yet ever volatile equity markets.

In the academic context, risk aversion denotes an individual's reluctance to choose a bargain with uncertain payoff over a bargain with certain but possibly lower payoff. The concept of risk aversion was empirically tested and theoretically advanced in studies of *behavioral finance*, the field that focuses on psychological and cognitive factors that affect people's financial decisions (Kahneman & Tversky, 2000; Statman, 2019). In the widely popularized experiments with volunteers, Kahneman & Tversky (2000) suggested making choices in two different situations. First, participants assumed to have $W_0 = \$1,000$ and were given a choice between (1a) gambling with probability $p = 50\%$ to gain $W_1 = \$1,000$ and probability $1-p = 50\%$ to gain nothing ($W_2 = 0$), or (1b) sure gain of $W_3 = \$500$. In the second experiment, participants assumed to have $W_0 = \$2,000$ and were given a choice between (2a) gambling with probability $p = 50\%$ of a loss $W_1 = -\$1,000$ and probability $1 - p = 50\%$ to lose nothing ($W_2 = 0$) and (2b) sure loss of $W_3 = -\$500$. All options in both experiments yield the same expected gain of $1,500. Indeed, the expected participant wealth W equals

(1a): $E(W) = W_0 + pW_1 + (1 - p)W_2 = \$1000 + 0.5^*\$1000 + 0.5^*0$
$$= \$1500,$$

(1b): $E(W) = W_0 + W_3 = \$1000 + \$500 = \$1500,$

(2a): $E(W) = W_0 + pW_1 + (1 - p)W_2 = \$2000 - 0.5^*\$1000$
$$-0.5^*0 = \$1500,$$

(2b): $E(W) = W_0 + W_3 = \$2000 - \$500 = \$1500.$

Hence, risk-neutral participants would split equally among these situations. Yet, the majority of participants had chosen option (b), i.e., certain payoff, in the first experiment. On the contrary, the majority of participants preferred option (a) in the second experiment, i.e., they were willing to gamble hoping to avoid their loss.

Such an outcome implies that the majority of participants were risk-averse.

In classical economics, *utility functions*, $U(W)$, of wealth W are used for quantifying risk aversion. The notion of utility function is rooted in the efficient market hypothesis, according to which investors are rational and act exclusively for maximizing their wealth (see Section 4.3).

Findings in behavioral finance indicate that the utility function generally is not linear upon wealth. One of the widely used utility functions is the *constant absolute risk aversion* (CARA):

$$U(W) = \exp(-aW). \qquad (2.10)$$

The parameter a is called the *coefficient of absolute risk aversion.* The important property of the CARA function is that its curvature is constant:

$$z_{\text{CARA}}(W) = -U''(W)/U'(W) = a. \qquad (2.11)$$

While it is very convenient to use CARA in theoretical analysis due to its exponential form,[5] absolute risk aversion may not always be an accurate assumption. Indeed, loss of \$1,000 may be perceived quite differently by a millionaire and a college student. Therefore, the *constant relative aversion function* (CRRA) is also used:

$$U(W) = W^{1-a}/(1-a) \quad \text{when} \quad a \neq 1$$
$$= \ln(W) \quad \text{when} \quad a = 1. \qquad (2.12)$$

In this case, the constant coefficient of relative risk aversion equals

$$z_{\text{CRRA}}(W) = -WU''(W)/U'(W) = a. \qquad (2.13)$$

All three popular utility functions (CARA, CRRA, and the logarithmic one) are concave, which implies diminishing marginal utility of wealth. Importantly, the utility functions are ordinal, i.e., their values are meaningless; only their differences are important. Hence, the utility functions can have an arbitrary additive constant.

Risk-neutral investors have a linear wealth utility function but some very ambitious investors act as risk seekers, which can be described with a convex utility function.

I shall return to the concept of risk aversion in describing the mean–variance portfolio theory in Chapter 7.

2.4 Inventory Models with Risk Aversion

Both the Garman and the Amihud–Mendelson models are derived for risk-neutral dealers who are concerned only with their profits. The latter model implies dealer's risk aversion only in that the dealer focuses on reducing deviations from preferred inventory.

Stoll (1978) was the first to explicitly introduce the concept of risk aversion in the inventory models. In the original Stoll's model, the dealer modifies his original portfolio to satisfy demand from liquidity traders in asset i and compensates his risk by introducing the bid/ask spread. Stoll considered a two-period model in which the dealer makes a transaction at time $t = 1$ and liquidates this position at $t = 2$. The price may change between (but not within) the trading periods. The main idea behind the Stoll's approach is that the dealer sets such prices that the expected CARA utility function of the entire trader's portfolio does not change after two transactions described above

$$E[U(W)] = E[U(W_\mathrm{T})]. \qquad (2.14)$$

In (2.14), W and W_T are the terminal wealth of the initial portfolio W_0 and the terminal wealth of the portfolio after both transactions, respectively,

$$W = W_0(1 + r), \qquad (2.15)$$

$$W_\mathrm{T} = W_0(1 + r) + (1 + r_i)Q_i - (1 + r_f)(Q_i - C_i). \qquad (2.16)$$

Here, r, r_i, and r_f are returns[6] for the entire portfolio, for the risky asset i, and for the risk-free asset, respectively; Q_i is the true value of the transaction in asset i; C_i is the present value of the asset i. Hence, Stoll assumes that the dealer knows the true value of the asset i. Note that $Q_i > 0$ when the dealer buys and $Q_i < 0$ when the dealer sells.

For obtaining an analytical solution, Stoll (1978) sets $r_f = 0$, expands both sides of (2.16) into the Taylor series around mean wealth $\overline{W}$, and drops the terms of order higher than two:

$$E[U(W)] \approx E[U(\overline{W})] + U''(W - \overline{W}) + 0.5U''(W - \overline{W})^2. \qquad (2.17)$$

The asset return is assumed to have the normal distribution

$$W = N(W_0, \sigma_p). \qquad (2.18)$$

Ultimately, the Stoll's model yields the relation

$$c_i(Q_i) = C_i/Q_i = z\sigma_{ip}Q_p/W_0 + 0.5z\sigma_i^2 Q_i/W_0. \qquad (2.19)$$

In (2.19), z is the coefficient of relative risk aversion (2.13), σ_{ip} is the covariance between the asset i and the initial portfolio, Q_p is the true value of the original portfolio, and σ_i^2 is variance of the asset i. If the true price of the asset i is P_i^*, then the prices of the immediacy to sell Q_i^b to (to buy Q_i^a from) the dealer P_i^b (P_i^a) satisfy the following relations:

$$(P_i^* - P_i^b)/P_i^* = c_i(Q_i^b), \qquad (2.20)$$

$$(P_i^* - P_i^a)/P_i^* = c_i(Q_i^a). \qquad (2.21)$$

Then the bid/ask spread is defined from the round-trip transaction for $|Q_i^a| = |Q_i^b| = |Q|$

$$(P_i^a - P_i^b)/P_i^* = c_i(Q_i^b) - c_i(Q_i^a) = z\sigma_i^2|Q|/W_0. \qquad (2.22)$$

Hence, the bid/ask spread depends linearly on the dealer's risk aversion, trading size, and asset volatility, but is independent of the initial inventory of the asset i. However, bid price and ask price are affected with the initial asset inventory: the higher the inventory is, the lower bid price and ask price are.

An obvious shortcoming of the Stoll's model is that it assumes complete liquidation of the asset position at $t = 2$. The Stoll's original work was expanded by Ho & Stoll (1981) into a multi-period framework. In the latter, the true trading asset value is fixed while both order flow and portfolio return are stochastic. Namely, order flow follows a Poisson process and return is a Brownian motion with drift.[7] The dealer's goal is to maximize utility of his wealth at time T. This problem can be solved using the methods of dynamic programming.[8] The intertemporal Ho–Stoll model shows that the optimal bid/ask spread depends on the dealer's time horizon. Namely, the closer to the end of trading, the smaller is the bid/ask spread. Indeed, as duration of exposure to risk of carrying inventory decreases, so does the bid/ask spread being the compensation for taking this risk.

In general, the bid/ask spread has two components. The first one is determined by the specifics of the supply and demand curves (assumed to be linear in the Ho–Stoll model), and the second one is an adjustment due to the risk the dealer accepts by keeping inventory.

This adjustment depends on the same factors as the bid/ask spread in the Stoll's one-period model (2.20): risk aversion, price variance, and the size of transaction. Also, similarly to the two-period model, the bid/ask spread is independent of the asset's inventory size.

Ho & Stoll (1983) offered another generalization of the original Stoll's (1978) model that describes the case with competing dealers. Namely, dealers in this work can trade among themselves and with liquidity traders. It was assumed that dealers have the same risk aversion but their endowments can vary. Liquidity traders trade with the dealer(s) who offer the best price. When several dealers offer the best price, the matching dealer is chosen randomly. The bid/ask spread in this model, too, depends on the product $z\sigma_i^2|Q|$ and decreases with the growing number of dealers since they all share the same risk.

2.5 Information-Based Models

The idea behind the information-based models is that price is a source of information that investors can (and should) use for their trading decisions (O'Hara, 1995; de Jong & Rindi, 2009). For example, if security price falls, investors may assume that price will further deteriorate and refrain from buying this security. Note that such a behavior contradicts the Walrasian paradigm of market equilibrium, according to which demand grows (falls) when price decreases (increases).

The information-based models are rooted in the *rational expectations theory*. Namely, investors and market makers assume rational behavior of their counterparts and behave rationally themselves in the sense that all their actions are based on the information available to them and they are focused on maximizing their wealth (or some utility function in the case of risk-averse agents). Asset price in information-based models reaches an equilibrium state that satisfies investors' expectations. Obviously, informed investors trade only on one side of the market at any given time. The problem of maintaining asset inventory that market makers face while trading with informed investors is called *adverse selection*.

In this chapter, I consider two classical information-based models that were introduced for describing different markets. The first one is Kyle's (1985) model for the batch auction markets. Another model was offered by Glosten & Milgrom (1985) for addressing the adverse selection problem in sequential trading.

2.5.1 *Kyle's model*

Kyle (1985) considers a one-period model with a single risk-neutral informed trader (insider) and several liquidity traders who trade a risky security with a risk-neutral market maker (dealer). The batched auction setup implies that the market clears at a single price. Hence, the bid/ask spread in this model is irrelevant. The insider knows that the security's value in the end of the period has the normal distribution

$$v = N(p_0, \sigma_0^2). \tag{2.23}$$

The insider submits an order of size $x(v)$ that optimizes her profits in the end of the period. Liquidity traders submit their orders randomly and their total demand y is described with the normal distribution

$$y = N(0, \sigma_y^2). \tag{2.24}$$

Note that buy orders and sell orders from liquidity traders have $+/-$ signs, respectively, and are balanced. Hence, mean value of y is zero.

Both random variables v and y are independently distributed. The dealer observes the aggregate demand, $z = x + y$, but is not aware what part of it comes from the informed trader. The dealer sets the clearing price $p(z)$ that is expected to optimize his profits. Naturally, $p(z)$ increases with growing aggregate demand. The insider's profit equals

$$\pi_I = x(v - p). \tag{2.25}$$

Kyle obtains the equilibrium price (i.e., the price that yields the optimal profits for both dealer and insider) analytically for the case when the clearing price depends linearly on demand:

$$p(z) = \lambda z + \mu. \tag{2.26}$$

In (2.26), λ characterizes inverse liquidity. Indeed, lower λ (higher liquidity) leads to lower impact of demand on price. Sometimes, inverse liquidity is called illiquidity (see Section 1.4). It follows from (2.25) and (2.26) that

$$E[\pi_I] = x(v - \lambda x - \mu).\tag{2.27}$$

As a result, the optimal insider's demand equals

$$x = (v - \mu)/2\lambda.\tag{2.28}$$

Equation (2.28) can be represented in the following form:

$$x = \alpha + \beta v, \quad \alpha = -\mu/2\lambda, \quad \beta = 1/2\lambda.\tag{2.29}$$

Then, all variables of interest can be expressed in terms of the model parameters (p_0, σ_0, and σ_y). Indeed, since v and z have normal distributions, it can be shown that $E[v|z]$ has the following form[9]:

$$E[v|z] = p_0 + \frac{\beta(z - \alpha - \beta p_0)\sigma_0^2}{\sigma_y^2 + \beta^2\sigma_0^2}.\tag{2.30}$$

In equilibrium, the right-hand sides of (2.26) and (2.30) must be equal for all z. Then the model parameters have the following form:

$$\alpha^* = p_0\sigma_y/\sigma_0, \beta^* = \sigma_y/\sigma_0,\tag{2.31}$$

$$\mu^* = p_0,\tag{2.32}$$

$$\lambda^* = \sigma_0/2\sigma_y.\tag{2.33}$$

The equality (2.32) $\mu^* = p_0 = E[v|z = 0]$ implies that the dealer sets price at its mean (true) value in case of zero demand. Note also that the inverse liquidity in equilibrium (2.33) is determined with variances of price and demand.

An interesting property of Kyle's model is that the price variance conditional on the aggregate demand equals

$$\text{Var}(v|z) = \sigma_0^2/2,\tag{2.34}$$

which is only one half of the unconditional price variance. The result (2.34) implies that the order flow provided by liquidity traders distorts the information available to informed traders. Indeed, even if insider knows that the traded security is overpriced and hence is not interested in buying it, a large idiosyncratic buy order from a liquidity trader will motivate the dealer to increase security price.

Now, let's consider profits and losses of all market participants. It follows from (2.27) that the expected insider's profit equals

$$E[\pi_I] = 0.5\sigma_y\sigma_0. \tag{2.35}$$

Note that only the expected insider's profit is positive. In fact, insiders may experience a loss according to (2.25), when the idiosyncratic rise of demand from liquidity traders leads to the condition $v - \lambda z - \mu < 0$. Trading cost of liquidity traders turns out to be equal to the insider's profit (de Jong & Rindi, 2009)

$$E[\pi_L] = E[y(p - v)] = \lambda\sigma_y^2 = 0.5\sigma_y\sigma_0. \tag{2.36}$$

Hence, the expected insider profits are funded with losses incurred by liquidity traders.

The total dealer's profits in Kyle's model are zero. The good news is that the dealer has no losses. There is a general rationale for expecting the dealer's zero profits (unless he is monopolistic). The so-called *Bertrand competition model* demonstrates that competing businesses that make identical products inevitably lower the product price until it reaches the product marginal cost. Why then does anyone bother to run batch auctions? Firstly, the auction owners receive transaction fees. And secondly, a constantly informed investor is just an unrealistic abstraction.

Kyle (1985) considers also a model with K auctions that are held at times $t_k = k\Delta t = k/K$; $k = 1, 2, \ldots, K$. Note that the discrete model approaches a continuous auction when $\Delta t = 1/K$ decreases. It is assumed that the order flow from liquidity traders follows the Brownian motion: $\Delta y_k = N(0, \sigma_y^2 \Delta t)$. The insider's demand is

$$\Delta x_k = \beta_k(v - p_k)\,\Delta t. \tag{2.37}$$

The dealer sets a price that depends linearly on total demand:

$$p_k = p_{k-1} + \lambda_k(\Delta x_k + \Delta y_k). \tag{2.38}$$

In the end of the auction k, the dealer's expected profits have the form

$$E(\pi_k | p_1, \ldots, p_{k-1}, v) = \alpha_{k-1}(v - p_{k-1})^2 + \delta_{k-1}. \tag{2.39}$$

In equilibrium, the coefficients in (2.37)–(2.39) satisfy the relations

$$\lambda_k = \beta_k \sigma_k^2 / \sigma_y^2, \tag{2.40}$$

$$\beta_k \Delta t = \frac{1 - 2\alpha_k \lambda_k}{2\lambda_k (1 - \alpha_k \lambda_k)}, \tag{2.41}$$

$$\alpha_{k-1} = 1/[4\lambda_k(1 - \alpha_k \lambda_k)], \tag{2.42}$$

$$\delta_{k-1} = \delta_k + \alpha_k \lambda_k^2 \sigma_y^2 \Delta t. \tag{2.43}$$

In contrast to the single-period model, price variance is now time-dependent:

$$\sigma_k^2 = (1 - \beta_k \lambda_k \Delta t)\sigma_{k-1}^2. \tag{2.44}$$

Since the system of Eqs. (2.40)–(2.44) is nonlinear, a numeric iterative procedure is needed for solving it.

In the multiple-period model, the insider splits her orders into small pieces with sizes varying with time. Such a strategy has become a standard protocol for filling large orders (see Chapter 15). In practice, this leads to positive autocorrelations in order flows, which implies some predictability of the insider's actions. However, this is not the case in Kyle's model, which allows the insider to hide her orders behind uncorrelated orders submitted by liquidity traders. Ultimately, however, security price reflects the entire insider's information, which limits her profits.

2.5.2   *The Glosten–Milgrom model*

In the sequential trading model derived by Glosten & Milgrom (1985), risk-neutral dealer sets bid price and ask price for trading one unit of security with informed traders (insiders) and uninformed (liquidity) traders, one trade at a time. The type of trader who trades at a given time is chosen randomly. Another assumption is that each trader can trade only one unit of security (or none). To obtain analytical results, Glosten & Milgrom (1985) consider a simple case when the security value V can have either high value $V = V_H$ (that reflects good news) with probability θ or low value $V = V_L$ (bad news) with probability $1 - \theta$. Insiders and liquidity traders trade with probabilities μ and $1 - \mu$, respectively. In this framework, insiders buy on

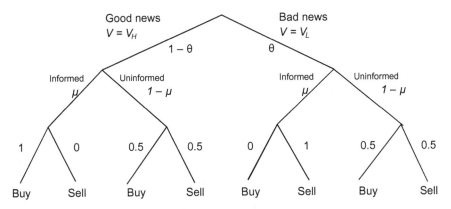

Fig. 2.4. Event diagram for the Glosten–Milgrom model.

good news and sell on bad news, while liquidity traders buy and sell with equal probability of 0.5. The event diagram for this model is shown in Fig. 2.4.

As in Kyle's model, the dealer in the Glosten–Milgrom model is not expected to make profits due to the Bertrand competition, and insider profits are equal to the liquidity trader's loss. The dealer sets prices that are *regret-free* in the sense that these prices are the dealer's expectations of the security's value based on the trading signals that he receives. Let's denote buy and sell events as B and S, respectively. Then, the dealer sets the following bid b and ask a:

$$a = E[V|B] = V_L Pr(V = V_L|B) + V_H Pr(V = V_H|B), \quad (2.45)$$

$$b = E[V|S] = V_L Pr(V = V_L|S) + V_H Pr(V = V_H|S). \quad (2.46)$$

The conditional probabilities in (2.45) and (2.46) can be calculated using the *Bayes'* rule[10]:

$$Pr(A|B) = \frac{Pr(B|A) Pr(A)}{Pr(B)}. \quad (2.47)$$

For example,

$$Pr(V = V_L|B) = Pr(V = V_L)\frac{Pr(B|V = V_L)}{Pr(B)}. \quad (2.48)$$

Note that

$$Pr(B) = Pr(V = V_L)Pr(B|V = V_L) + Pr(V = V_H)Pr(B|V = V_H)$$
$$= 0.5(1 + \mu(1 - 2\theta)). \tag{2.49}$$

Hence,

$$Pr(V = V_L|B) = \frac{\theta(\mu \times 0 + (1 - \mu) \times 0.5)}{0.5\,(1 + \mu(1 - 2\theta))} = \frac{\theta(1 - \mu)}{(1 + \mu(1 - 2\theta))}. \tag{2.50}$$

Similar calculations of all terms in (2.45)–(2.46) yield

$$a = \frac{\theta(1 - \mu)V_L + (1 - \theta)(1 + \mu)V_H}{1 + \mu(1 - 2\theta)}, \tag{2.51}$$

$$b = \frac{\theta(1 + \mu)V_L + (1 - \theta)(1 - \mu)V_H}{1 - \mu(1 - 2\theta)}. \tag{2.52}$$

Then, the bid/ask spread equals

$$s = a - b = \frac{4\theta(1 - \theta)\mu(V_H - V_L)}{1 - (1 - 2\theta)^2\mu^2}. \tag{2.53}$$

According to (2.53), the bid/ask spread increases with growing number of insiders (i.e., with higher μ), which demonstrates the effect of adverse selection. The bid/ask spread has a particularly simple form when good news and bad news arrive with equal probability $\theta = 0.5$:

$$s = \mu(V_H - V_L). \tag{2.54}$$

In this case, the bid/ask spread grows linearly with the number of informed traders.

The Kyle and Glosten–Milgrom models have been expanded in several ways. In particular, Easley & O'Hara (1987) considered an extension to the latter model in which traders may submit orders of small and large sizes. In general, informed traders are motivated to trade large amounts to benefit from their knowledge as much and as soon as possible. However, large orders reveal private information to the entire market and therefore cut insider's advantage. In one option, both informed and uninformed investors can trade small and large orders. In other words, all traders are *pooled* together.

This helps to hide some private information with small orders and improve price for large orders. Another option for informed investors is to *separate* themselves from liquidity traders so that informed traders trade only large orders. Note that adverse selection grows with order size. On the contrary, there is no adverse selection in trading small orders, and therefore, the dealer can establish zero bid/ask spread for small orders. Since informed traders maximize their profits, they will trade in the separate mode only if trading at a worse price is compensated with sufficiently large amounts. If this does not happen due to a particular choice of the model parameters, trading is conducted in the pooling mode.

In another model offered by Easley & O'Hara (1992), the bad/good news bifurcation in the root of the trading event diagram in Fig. 2.4 is complemented with the *no-news* case, in which only liquidity traders may want to trade. Also, liquidity traders have an option of *no trade* besides the buy/sell choice. The no-news case increases the probability of uninformed trading, thereby decreasing the bid/ask spread.

Subrahmanyam (1991) discusses the effects of multiple informed traders on liquidity. In this case, private information and, hence, profits are shared by several insiders. Then, while liquidity increases with the number of risk-neutral insiders, a growing number of risk-averse insiders can, in fact, decrease liquidity. Namely, liquidity decreases with a small but growing number of insiders as risk aversion causes them to trade more cautiously. However, after the number of insiders reaches some threshold, their sheer number yields increasing liquidity.

Back & Baruch (2004) considered two models that explore the relationships between the Kyle and Glosten–Milgrom frameworks. In the first model, orders from liquidity traders arrive as a Brownian motion and dealers see only total demand (as in Kyle's model). In another model, these orders arrive as a Poisson process, and the dealer sees them. The Back–Baruch model differs from the Glosten–Milgrom model in that the insider can optimize her times of trading. Back & Baruch (2004) have found that there is an equilibrium in which the insider employs a mixed strategy randomizing at each instant between trading and waiting. They have also shown that the distinction between this modified Glosten–Milgrom model and Kyle's model is unimportant when orders are small and arrive frequently.

Notes

1. Poisson process is described in Appendix A. This process is often used in simple models of order dynamics (see, e.g., Farmer *et al.*, 2005).
2. Note that the Walrasian paradigm is questioned in the information-based models (see Section 2.5).
3. For a description of the gambler's ruin problem, see, e.g., Ross (2007).
4. Hopefully, dealer's failure is a less dramatic event than bankruptcy.
5. Recall that both derivatives and integrals over exponential functions are exponential functions.
6. See Section 3.1 for the formal definition of return.
7. Brownian motion is introduced in Section 4.4.
8. Applications of dynamic programming to finance are reviewed by O'Hara (1995).
9. The following relations for two normally distributed random variables X and Y are used in derivation (2.28): $E(Y|X = x) = E(Y) + \mathrm{Cov}(Y, X)\mathrm{Var}((X)^{-1}(x - E(X)); \ \mathrm{Cov}(Y, X) = E(XY) - E(X)E(Y)$.
10. The process of incorporating new information into the variables of interest using Bayes' rule is called Bayesian learning. See more on Bayes' rule, e.g., O'Hara (1995) and Ross (2007).

Chapter 3

Models of the Limit-Order Markets

3.1 The Taker's Dilemma

3.1.1 *Introductory comments*

Chapter 2 was devoted to the microstructure models for the dealer markets. With proliferation of order-driven continuous trading platforms, theoretical research has focused on the markets where each trader being a liquidity taker can submit either a market order (or marketable limit order), or a non-marketable limit order. In the latter case, one can say that taker submits a maker order.[1] The critical question for a taker in an order-driven market is whether to submit a market order for immediacy of execution and for minimizing an opportunity cost or to submit a limit order, which saves the bid/ask spread (and possibly more if the order is placed outside the market) but has uncertainty of execution. An obvious compromise is placing a limit order inside the market, which narrows the bid/ask spread and increases probability of filling. The ambiguity of this choice, which I call *the taker's dilemma* (Schmidt, 2011), remains a challenge for both academics and practitioners.

In this chapter, several popular models of limit-order markets that address the taker's dilemma are described. I start with introducing one of the first contributions to analysis of this problem by Cohen *et al.* (1981). I call it the *CMSW model*. Then, I proceed with the models offered by Parlour (1998), Foucault (1999), and their more recent extensions (Parlour & Seppi, 2008; Rosu, 2009).

I shall continue discussing the taker's dilemma in respect to the optimal execution problem in Section 15.3.

3.1.2 *The CMSW model*

In the CMSW model, all traders attempt to maximize their wealth, which consists of cash and a risky asset. Traders trade only at a set of fixed points of time. Trading costs include a fee for submitting a limit order and another fee paid in case an order is filled. It is assumed that trading is symmetric on both sides of the market. Hence, only buy-side trading is considered. Ask price is defined exogenously as the random walk with price shocks summed up between the trading times according to the compound Poisson process:

$$\ln S_t(\Delta) = \ln S_t + \sum_{i=1}^{N(\Delta)} Z_i. \tag{3.1}$$

In (3.1), Δ is the time between trading points, price shocks Z_i are an independent and identically distributed variable with zero mean, and $N(\Delta)$ is a Poisson process with arrival rate ν.

At each time, the trader can choose not to trade or obtain a long position with either a market buy order or a limit bid order with a price below the current ask price. The CMSW model is formulated as a dynamic programming problem of maximizing trader's wealth.

It follows from the CMSW model that the probability to fill a limit order is always less than unity. It should be noted that this probability can be further estimated using the notion of the *first passage time* (FPT). Say the ask price at $t = 0$ is $S = S_a$ and the price of the bid order is $S_a - s$, i.e., the bid/ask spread equals s. We assume that the bid order is matched when $S(t) \Leftarrow S_a - s$. By definition, FPT for given shock s equals the time of the first instance when $S \Leftarrow S_a - s$. The probability distribution for FPT in the case of the Brownian motion without drift equals (Feller, 1968)[2]

$$f_{\text{FPT}}(s,t) = \frac{s}{\sqrt{2\pi\sigma^2}} t^{-3/2} \exp\left(-\frac{s^2}{2\sigma^2 t}\right). \tag{3.2}$$

It follows from (3.2) that $f_{\text{FPT}}(s, t)$ for given s has the following asymptote at long times:

$$f_{\text{FPT}}(s,t) \sim t^{-3/2}. \tag{3.3}$$

As a result, the expected value of FPT

$$E[\text{FPT}] = \lim_{t \to \infty} \int_0^t t f_{\text{FPT}} dt \tag{3.4}$$

is infinite. However, the probability for the first passage at fixed time t is finite. Since filling of a market order is certain, there is a jump in probability when the order type is changed. According to the CMSW model, if a bid price approaches the ask price (i.e., $s \to 0$), the jump in probability disappears when trading costs are neglected.

In the CMSW model, the bid/ask spread is determined with transaction costs. If the spread is wide, traders submit new limit orders that have lower spread but still have lower loss than market orders. When the spread narrows to the extent that fees for submitting limit orders negate their gain, traders may want to submit market orders. In the CMSW model, this effect is named *gravitational pull*. Order matching widens the spread as market orders wipe out the top of the LOB. Ultimately, the spread attains some equilibrium value. Growth of the market thickness in the CMSW model is determined with the increasing order arrival rate, and the bid/ask spread decreases as the market becomes thicker.

3.1.3 *The Parlour model*

In the model introduced by Parlour (1998), risk-neutral traders trade a risky asset with the fundamental value of v. Each trader perceives the asset value as $v\beta(t)$ where $\beta(t)$ is randomly distributed over the interval $(\underline{\beta}, \overline{\beta})$. Bid (B) and ask (A) prices are defined exogenously. Their values remain fixed and satisfy the condition $A < v < B$. Since order execution does not affect the values of A and B, this implies that market depth is infinite. Trading time is divided into $t = 0, 1, \ldots, T$ periods. Only one trader can trade at a given time. Hence, time t is also the trader's index. Traders buy or sell one asset unit with probability of 0.5. The active LOB accounts only for limit orders that were submitted by traders, that is, exogenous liquidity that maintains prices A and B is neglected. If the active LOB is empty, the exogenous liquidity provider matches market orders. Orders are matched using the FIFO rule (see Section 1.5). Namely, if the active bid LOB at time t has n_t^B orders and a trader submits a bid order, it is placed in the end of the order book, and $n_{t+1}^B = n_t^B + 1$. If a trader submits a sell order, it matches with the first bid order in the active LOB, and $n_{t+1}^B = n_t^B - 1$. Whether a trader t submits a market or limit order depends on his evaluation of the asset value. If a buyer's asset value estimate satisfies the condition $v\beta(t) > A$, he submits market order; otherwise, the buyer submits bid order at price B.

Similarly, a seller submits market order if $v\beta(t) <$ B; otherwise, he submits limit ask order at price A.

The optimal trading strategy cannot be defined in advance since the probability to fill a limit order depends on the actions of those traders who enter the market later. For example, a bid order that has the kth position in the active LOB is filled only if there will be at least k market sell orders submitted in future. However, the problem can be solved with the backward recursion. Namely, for trader T, submitting a limit order does not make sense since he is the last one in the sample. Say trader T happens to be a buyer. If $v\beta(T) >$ A, he submits a market buy order; otherwise, he does nothing. Similar logic applies to trader T being a seller. Now that we know whether trader T changed the active LOB, we can consider trader $T-1$. If he is a seller and $n_{T-1}^{S} = 0$, then he can submit a sell limit order, which will be executed if trader T submits a buy market order. However, this order cannot be executed within the remaining trading time if $n_{T-1}^{S} > 0$. This protocol can be continued from trader $T-1$ to trader $T-2$, and so on.

The Parlour model in equilibrium has some properties that coincide with empirical findings in equity markets (Biais *et al.*, 1995). In particular, market orders are more likely submitted after the market orders on the same side of the market. Indeed, one may expect that a buy order diminishes liquidity on the ask side, which motivates the seller to submit a limit ask order. Another interesting result is that a buyer (seller) is more likely to submit a market order in the case of a thick LOB on the bid (ask) side. On the contrary, a thick LOB on the ask (bid) side motivates a buyer (seller) to submit a limit order.

A variation of the Parlour model in which the direction of trade is determined by the value of $\beta(t)$ drawn from the uniform distribution[3] is offered by de Jong & Rindi (2009).

3.1.4 *The Foucault model*

Foucault (1999) addresses the so-called *winner's curse* problem. In the context of the limit-order market, this problem implies that the order on top of the LOB, i.e., the highest bid (lowest ask), is filled (picked-off, as Foucault puts it) by a sell (buy) market order first. Yet, this order may be mispriced, that is, the asset price may become lower (higher) after the transaction.

Foucault (1999) offers a model that describes a mix of market and limit orders in equilibrium. In this model, a single asset is traded at discrete moments of time $t = 0, 1, \ldots, T$, where T is random, that is, there is a probability of $1 - \rho$ that trading ends at any time. It is assumed that the asset value follows the random walk

$$v(t) = v(t - 1) + \varepsilon(t). \tag{3.5}$$

In (3.5), $\varepsilon(t)$ are IID innovations caused by public news. Innovations are assumed to have only values $\pm\sigma$ with the probability of 0.5. Note that σ is a measure of price volatility.[4] Then, the payoff of the asset at time T is

$$V(T) = \nu(0) + \sum_{t=1}^{T} \varepsilon(t). \tag{3.6}$$

At each time t, a new risk-neutral trader submits an order for one unit with a reservation price that has the trader's individual estimate $y(t)$

$$R(t) = v(t) + y(t). \tag{3.7}$$

It is assumed that $y(t)$ is independently and identically distributed, and can take values $y_h = L$ and $y_l = -L$ with the probability of 0.5. Furthermore, the values y_h and y_l are used to denote the trader type. In the end of trading, the utility function of a trader who traded the asset at price P is

$$U(y) = q(V(T) + y - P). \tag{3.8}$$

In (3.8), the values of $q = 1$ and $q = -1$ correspond to buyers and sellers, respectively. Traders choose between buy orders and sell orders, and may submit market orders or limit orders. If there is no difference in the outcome of submitting market order or limit order, it is assumed that traders submit a limit order. For certainty, limit orders live only one period and cannot be revised. If a limit order submitted at time t is not filled at time $t+1$, it is cancelled. If the LOB is empty, the arriving trader submits both ask and bid limit orders.

The state of the book is defined with bid $B(t)$ and ask $A(t)$ prices. If the bid side is empty, $B(t) = -\infty$; if the ask side is empty, $A(t) = \infty$.

In the simple case with $\sigma = 0$, the asset value v is constant and there is no winner's curse problem. The stationary bid/ask spread in this case equals

$$s^* = 2L(1 - 0.5\rho)/(1 + 0.5\rho). \tag{3.9}$$

In the generic case with non-zero volatility, Foucault (1999) shows that the bid/ask spread in equilibrium equals

$$S^* = \sigma + 2(2L - \sigma)/(2 + \rho) \quad \text{when} \quad \sigma < 4L/(4 + \rho), \tag{3.10}$$

$$S^* = 2\sigma + 8L/(4 + \rho) \quad \text{when} \quad \sigma \geq 4L/(4 + \rho). \tag{3.11}$$

Hence, the bid/ask spread increases with volatility. The first terms in the right-hand sides of (3.10) and (3.11) being proportional to σ account for the winner's curse. Namely, these trading costs relate to the case when a trader submits a bid (ask) order with a price higher (lower) than the asset future value. Hence, this order is filled (unfortunately for the trader) at sub-optimal price. As a result, the bid/ask spread (i.e., the cost of market orders) increases, which motivates traders to submit limit orders. This, in turn, decreases the probability of execution at higher volatility. The second terms in the right-hand sides of (3.10) and (3.11) reflect the execution costs. Obviously, increasing ρ, i.e., smaller probability of impending end of trading, leads to a smaller bid/ask spread and to a higher probability of execution.

3.1.5   *New developments*

The Parlour (1998) and Foucault (1999) models are attractive in that they are sufficiently simple to have tractable solutions but, nevertheless, offer rich and testable implications. Therefore, these models serve as the starting points for further analysis of the limit-order markets.

Foucault *et al.* (2005; Foucault, Kadan, and Kandel [FKK]) studied how the traders' patience affects order placement strategy, the bid/ask spread, and market resiliency. The latter is measured with the probability that the bid/ask spread after liquidity shock returns to its initial value before the next transaction. FKK made several assumptions to obtain a tractable equilibrium solution. In particular, there is an infinite liquidity source for buying (selling) an asset at price A (B); $A > B$. This liquidity source defines the outside spread, $K = A - B$. All prices here and further are given in units of ticks. Buyers and sellers arrive sequentially according to a Poisson process and trade one asset unit. Each trader can place one market order or limit order, which depends on the state of the LOB and trader's impatience level. The latter is a measure of trader's perceived opportunity cost[5] and can have two values: low δ_P and high δ_I; $\delta_I > \delta_P$. The proportion of patient traders, $0 < \theta < 1$, remains constant. Limit orders can be submitted j ticks away from the current best price ($j = 0$ for market orders) and cannot be changed or cancelled. Namely, order bid price and order ask price equal $b - j\Delta$ and $a + j\Delta$, respectively, where $b \geq B$ and $a \leq A$ are the best bid and the best ask, respectively; Δ is the tick size. Therefore, *inside spread* equals $s = a - b$. It is expected that limit orders must narrow the spread. The trader's utility function contains a penalty proportional to the execution waiting time and impatience level. Namely, the expected profits of trader i ($i = I, P$) with filled order j are equal:

$$\Pi(i, j) = V_b - a\Delta + j\Delta - \delta_i T(j) \quad \text{for buyers,} \quad (3.12)$$

$$\Pi(i, j) = b\Delta - V_s + j\Delta - \delta_i T(j) \quad \text{for sellers,} \quad (3.13)$$

where $V_b > A\Delta$ and $V_a < B\Delta$ are the buyers' and sellers' asset valuations, respectively. Hence, for a given spread s, traders place orders to maximize the value:

$$\max \pi(i, j) = j\Delta - \delta_i T(j). \quad (3.14)$$

In (3.14), $j \in (0, 1, 2, \ldots, s - 1)$. The strong constraints in the FKK model yield a tractable solution for the equilibrium placement of limit orders and expected execution times. It shows, in particular, that the expected execution times are higher in markets with a high proportion of patient traders. This motivates liquidity providers to submit more aggressive orders and to lower the inside spread. Market orders are less frequent when the portion of patient traders is high since it is impatient traders who use market orders. New limit orders may shield current best prices by more than one tick, which creates holes in the order book — an effect found in real markets (Biais *et al.*, 1995).

Another finding is that the tick size may increase the average inside spread if the portion of patient traders is small, since they can place even less aggressive limit orders. Also, a lower order arrival rate leads to smaller spreads as liquidity providers strive to shorten the execution times.

Rosu (2009) has expanded the FKK model in that traders can dynamically modify their limit orders. This leads to multi-unit orders and a variable (random) number of traders at any time. This model is still analytically tractable. It describes the distribution of orders in the order book and market impact from orders of different size. Rosu discerns temporary (or instantaneous) and permanent (or subsequent) market impacts. The former is the result of filling a market order and the latter is determined with remaining limit orders that are submitted by strategic makers.

Rosu's model (2009) has a number of interesting predictions. First, higher activity of impatient traders causes smaller spreads and lower price impact. Market orders lead to a temporary price impact that is larger than the permanent price impact (so-called *price overshooting*). Limit orders can cluster outside the market, generating a hump-shaped LOB. In other words, there is a price level inside the LOB where aggregated order size has a maximum. Rosu shows also how trading may widen the bid/ask spread. For example, when a sell market order moves the bid price down, the ask price also falls but by a smaller amount. Another observation is related to the *full* LOB (i.e., when the total cost of limit orders — including the waiting cost — is higher than that of market orders). When the LOB is full, patient traders may submit quick (or *fleeting*) limit orders with the price inside the spread. These orders illustrate traders' attempts to simultaneously gain some cost savings and immediacy.

Goettler *et al.* (2005) offered a more generic model in which traders can submit market orders and multiple limit orders at different prices. This model has no analytic solution and search of the market equilibrium represents a computational challenge. Traders in this model are characterized by their private estimate of the asset value and by their maximum trading size. The LOB is assumed to be open, which allows traders to make rational decisions. Traders arrive sequentially and submit several market orders and limit orders to maximize their expected trading gains. Unfilled limit orders are subject to stochastic cancellation over time when the asset value moves in adverse direction. This model offers a rich set of conditional order dynamics. In particular, it shows that traders with low private values often submit ask orders below the consensus value of the asset. On the contrary, overly optimistic traders submit bid orders above the consensus value. As a result, many market orders yield negative transaction costs, that is, they buy (sell) orders matched below (above) the consensus value. Another finding is that the transaction price is closer to the true value of the asset rather than the midpoint of the bid/ask spread.

3.2 Market Microstructure Models

3.2.1 *Introductory comments*

Analysis of the limit-order market microstructure usually focuses on the specifics of order flows, bid/ask spreads, and the LOB structure (Hasbrouck, 2007; de Jong & Rindi, 2009). Several prominent models have been derived in the market microstructure research. I start this section with the classical Roll's model (1984) for the bid/ask spread. Then, I turn to the Glosten–Harris model (1998) that quantifies the contribution of the adverse selection into the bid/ask spread.

In contrast to the models discussed in Chapter 2 and Section 3.1, some models used for analysis of empirical microstructure are not based on various assumptions on trader behavior. Rather, they represent so-called *structural models*. In general, structural models (as opposed to "purely" statistical models) are used in economic theory for describing how observable "endogenous" variables depend on observable (or unobservable) "explanatory" variables (Reiss & Wolak, 2007). For the market microstructure analysis, this approach was pioneered by Hasbrouck (1991). I continue this section with describing the Hasbrouck's (1991) model and its extension offered by Schmidt (2016). Finally, I provide an overview of some recent empirical findings related to the microstructure of the equity markets.

3.2.2 *Roll's model*

Roll's (1984) model derives the bid/ask spread in terms of transaction prices. Hence, it can be particularly helpful when ask prices and bid prices are not easily available (which was the case at the time of deriving this model). Several assumptions are used in this model. First, transaction (that is, observable) price P_t bounces between bid price and ask price:

$$P_t = P_t^* + 0.5Sq_t. \tag{3.15}$$

In (3.15), S is the bid/ask spread assumed to be constant; q_t is the directional factor that equals 1 for buy orders and -1 for sell orders; P_t^* is the fundamental price that is assumed to follow the random walk and is not affected by trading. Therefore,

$$\Delta P_t^* = P_t^* - P_{t-1}^* = \varepsilon_t. \tag{3.16}$$

In (3.16), $\varepsilon_t = N(0, \sigma^2)$. Another assumption is that the probabilities for buying and selling are equal and independent of past transactions:

$$Pr(q_t = 1) = Pr(q_t = -1) = Pr(q_t = q_{t-1}) = 0.5 \quad \text{for all } t. \tag{3.17}$$

Roll's idea is to calculate covariance $\text{Cov}(\Delta P_t, \Delta P_{t-1})$, which ultimately yields an estimate of the bid/ask spread. Note that if $S = 0$, then $\Delta P_t = \Delta P_t^*$ and $\text{Cov}(\Delta P_t, \Delta P_{t-1}) = \text{Cov}(\varepsilon_t, \varepsilon_{t-1}) = 0$.

Consider now $\text{Cov}(\Delta P_t, \Delta P_{t-1})$ for the case with non-zero spread. Possible transaction price paths between two consecutive time periods are depicted in Fig. 3.1. Note that P^* within Roll's model is fixed. Hence, if P_{t-1} is bid price, ΔP_t can be either 0 or $+S$, and if P_{t-1} is ask price, ΔP_t can be either 0 or $-S$. The corresponding probability distribution of price changes is given in Table 3.1.

Transaction at $t-1$ can be on the bid side or the ask side with the same probability. The joint probability distribution for successive price changes ΔP_t and ΔP_{t+1} is presented in Table 3.2.

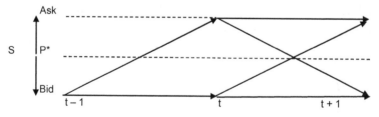

Fig. 3.1.   Possible transaction price paths in Roll's model.

Table 3.1. Probability distribution for price changes ΔP_t and ΔP_{t+1} in Roll's model.

		ΔP_{t-1} at the bid		ΔP_{t-1} at the ask	
		ΔP_t		ΔP_t	
		0	S	$-S$	0
	$-S$	0	0.25	0	0.25
ΔP_{t+1}	0	0	0.25	0.25	0.25
	S	0.25	0	0.25	0

Table 3.2. Joint probability distribution for price changes ΔP_t and ΔP_{t+1} in Roll's model.

		ΔP_t		
		$-S$	0	S
	$-S$	0	0.125	0.125
ΔP_{t+1}	0	0.125	0.25	0.125
	S	0.125	0.125	0

As a result,

$$\text{Cov}(\Delta P_t, \Delta P_{t-1}) = 0.125(-S^2 - S^2) = -0.25S^2. \qquad (3.18)$$

Hence,

$$S = 2\sqrt{-\text{Cov}(\Delta P_t, \Delta P_{t-1})}. \qquad (3.19)$$

Obviously, the relation (3.19) makes sense only if empirical covariance is negative. While this is generally the case, several assumptions made in Roll's model may look simplistic. In particular, empirical data in both equity (Hasbrouck, 2007) and FX (Hashimoto *et al.*, 2008) markets show that q_t can be correlated (so-called *runs*), that is, buys (sells) follow buys (sells). These runs may be caused by optimal execution protocols (see Chapter 15). Fortunately, if

$$Pr(q_t = q_{t-1}) = q \neq 0.5, \qquad (3.20)$$

Roll's formula (3.19) can be easily modified (de Jong & Rindi, 2009):

$$S = q^{-1}\sqrt{-\text{Cov}(\Delta P_t, \Delta P_{t-1})}. \qquad (3.21)$$

Trading within Roll's model does not affect bid price and ask price. Hence, within this framework, the realized spread (1.4) equals the effective spread (1.3): $S^R = S^E$.

3.2.3 The Glosten–Harris model

The Glosten–Harris model (1998) expands Roll's model in that it treats the bid/ask spread as a dynamic variable and splits it into the transitory, C_t, and the adverse selection, Z_t, components

$$S_t = 2(C_t + Z_t). \tag{3.22}$$

Hence the observable transactional price equals

$$P_t = P_t^* + (C_t + Z_t)q_t. \tag{3.23}$$

This implies that the fundamental price is now affected by the adverse selection component

$$P_t^* = P_{t-1}^* + Z_t q_{t+}\varepsilon_t. \tag{3.24}$$

Glosten & Harris (1998) assume in the spirit of Kyle's model that the both components of the bid/ask spread are linear upon the trading size V_t:

$$C_t = c_0 + c_1 V_t, \quad Z_t = z_0 + z_1 V_t. \tag{3.25}$$

It follows from (3.22)–(3.25) that the price change equals

$$\Delta P_t = c_0(q_t - q_{t-1}) + c_1(q_t V_t - q_{t-1}V_{t-1}) + z_0 q_t$$
$$+ z_1 q_t V_t + \varepsilon_t. \tag{3.26}$$

Now, let's calculate price change for the round-trip transaction of a sale immediately following a purchase of the same asset size. Namely, let's put $q_t = 1$ and $q_{t-1} = -1$ into (3.26). Then (neglecting ε_t),

$$\Delta P_t = 2C_t + Z_t. \tag{3.27}$$

In fact, ΔP_t is a measure of the effective spread that is conditioned on the round-trip transaction. It differs from the unconditional quoted spread (3.22) that is observable to uninformed traders.

The model coefficients c_0, c_1, z_0, and z_1 in (3.26) can be estimated using empirical market data. Glosten & Harris (1998) made such estimates with transactional data for 20 NYSE stocks. Their results confirm the prediction made using the information-based microstructure models (see Section 2.3) that the adverse-selection spread component grows with increasing trade size.[6]

3.2.4 *Structural models*

Both the Roll and Glosten–Harris models depart from the EMH paradigm in that the observable transaction prices are not treated as martingales anymore. One can argue that the bid/ask bounces described in Roll's model are small short-lived frictions in otherwise efficient market, and the mid-price equated with the asset fundamental value still follows the random walk. However, Glosten & Harris (1998) went further by offering the price discovery Eq. (3.24) in which trading volume of informed investors can result in a (possibly long-lived) market impact.

The information-based market impact may have lagged components related to quote revisions and past trades. Hasbrouck (1991) suggested that the information-based price impact can be separated from the inventory-based price impact since the former remains persistent at intermediate time intervals while the latter is transient.[7] For describing this idea, Hasbrouck (1991) offered a structural model in which it is assumed that the expectation of the quoted mid-price conditioned on public information I_t available at time t approaches the true asset value P_T at some future time T:

$$E[(p_t^a + p_t^b)/2 - P_T|I_t] \to 0 \text{ as } t \to T. \tag{3.28}$$

In (3.28), p_t^a and p_t^b are ask price and bid price at time t, respectively. Let's introduce the mid-price revision:

$$r_t = 0.5[(p_t^a + p_t^b)/2 - (p_{t-1}^a + p_{t-1}^b)/2]. \tag{3.29}$$

In the general case, r_t can be represented in the following generic form:

$$r_t = a_1 r_{t-1} + a_2 r_{t-2} + \cdots + b_0 x_t + b_1 x_{t-1} + \cdots + \varepsilon_{1,t}. \tag{3.30}$$

In (3.30), a_i and b_i are the coefficients, $\varepsilon_{1,t}$ is a random shock caused by new public information, x_t is the signed order flow (positive for buy orders, and negative for sell orders) that is described as

$$x_t = c_1 r_{t-1} + c_2 r_{t-2} + \cdots + d_1 x_{t-1} + d_2 x_{t-2} + \cdots + \varepsilon_{2,t}.$$

(3.31)

It should be noted that the term *order flow* employed in the market microstructure research often refers to trading (i.e., transactional) volumes. However, equating trading volumes and order flows neglects limit orders that are not immediately filled. This distinction is particularly important in the limit-order markets where market orders are not permitted. Transactional data available for academic research generally do not specify what side of the market initiated transactions. It is usually assumed that a buy (sell) order initiated a transaction if its price is higher (lower) than the bid/ask mid-price.

The specific of Hasbrouck's model (1991) is that the equation for r_t (3.30) has the contemporaneous term, $b_0 x_t$, while the equation for x_t (3.31) has only lagging terms. This implies that the price revision follows trading impact immediately but the order flow does not reflect instantly the change in price. Hasbrouck (1991) assumed also that random innovations have zero means and are not serially correlated:

$$E(\varepsilon_{1,t}) = E(\varepsilon_{2,t}) = 0; E(\varepsilon_{1,t}\,\varepsilon_{1,s}) = E(\varepsilon_{1,t}\,\varepsilon_{2,s}) = E(\varepsilon_{2,t}\,\varepsilon_{2,s})$$
$$= 0 \quad \text{for} \quad t \neq s.$$

(3.32)

The system (3.30)–(3.32) is an example of bivariate *vector autoregression* (VAR).[8] Assuming that $x_0 = \varepsilon_{2,0}$ and $\varepsilon_{1,t} = 0$, the long-term price impact can be estimated using the *cumulative impulse response* (CIR):

$$\alpha_m(\varepsilon_{2t}) = \sum_{t=0}^{m} E[r_t | \varepsilon_{2,0}].$$

(3.33)

CIR in equity markets was studied by Engle & Patton (2004), Mizrach (2008), and Hautsch & Huang (2012). It follows from (3.28) that as m approaches T, CIR (3.33) converges to the revision of the efficient price. Hence, CIR can serve as a measure of the price impact due to the new information.

Hasbrouck (1991) offered a more specific example of a structural model that is formulated in terms of efficient price M_t, bid/ask mid-price p_t, and signed trading size x_t:

$$M_t = M_{t-1} + \varepsilon_{1,t} + z\varepsilon_{2,t}, \tag{3.34}$$

$$p_t = M_t + a(p_t - M_t) + bx_t, \tag{3.35}$$

$$x_t = -c(p_{t-1} - M_{t-1}) + \varepsilon_{2,t}. \tag{3.36}$$

The value of x_t is positive (negative) if a trade is initiated by a buyer (seller). The random shocks $\varepsilon_{1,t}$ and $\varepsilon_{2,t}$ satisfy (3.32) and are related to non-trading and trading information, respectively; z is intensity of the latter, and a, b, and c are the model coefficients that satisfy the following conditions:

$$0 < a \le 1, \quad b > 0, \quad c > 0. \tag{3.37}$$

The coefficient a is responsible for inventory control (which is imperfect when $a < 1$). Indeed, say $p_t = p_0$ at $t = 0$ and $x_1 > 0$. Then the market maker encourages traders to sell by raising p_t. On the contrary, demand is controlled by the negative sign in the first term in (3.36). While the efficient price is unobservable, the system (3.34)–(3.36) can be expressed in terms of observable variables x_t and $r_t = p_t - p_{t-1}$. The case with $a < 1$ yields an infinite VAR[9]:

$$r_t = (z + b)x_t + [zbc - (1 - a)b]x_{t-1} + a[zbc - (1 - a)b]x_{t-2} + \cdots$$
$$+ \varepsilon_{1,t}, \tag{3.38}$$

$$x_t = -bcx_{t-1} - abcx_{t-2} - a^2bcx_{t-3} + \cdots + \varepsilon_{2,t}. \tag{3.39}$$

Since $a < 1$, the coefficients of higher terms decrease and regressions can be truncated at some lag with acceptable accuracy. Then the cumulative impulse response (3.33) has a rather fast convergence.

3.2.5 *Modeling of trading impact*

Now, let's discuss impact of trading on security price (often called *market impact*) in more details as it is an important concept that is widely used in the models of optimal execution (Almgren & Chriss, 2000; Kissell, 2020).

It is usually assumed that market impact has a permanent component. The roots of this assumption may be traced to a typical behavior of monopolistic dealer who is primarily concerned with maintaining preferable bid/offer spread (Amihud & Mendelson, 1980; see also

Section 2.2). Namely, when a large buy order wipes out entire inventory at the best ask price, the spread widens and the dealer responds to increase of demand by lifting the best bid price. However in modern limit-order markets, multiple traders use market making strategy and fiercely compete for occupying top of the LOB. This competition may result in filling the liquidity gap on the ask side, which reduces market impact (see Fig. 3.2). Indeed, empirical findings in equity markets by Bouchaud *et al.* (2006) and in an institutional FX market by Schmidt (2010a) indicate that market impact has a power-law decay.

Schmidt (2015) offered an extension to Hasbrouck's (1991) model for describing dynamics of market impact in an institutional FX market (which can be used for equity markets, too). Namely, the Hasbrouck's bivariate regression (3.30)–(3.31) (denoted further as VAR2) is expressed in the following form:

$$r_t = H_r(r, x) + \varepsilon_{r,t}, H_r(r, x) = \sum_{k=1}^{n_r} a_{r,k} r_{t-k} + \sum_{k=0}^{n_x} a_{x,k} x_{t-k}, \quad (3.40)$$

$$x_t = H_x(r, x) + \varepsilon_{x,t}, H_x(r, x) = \sum_{k=1}^{n_r} b_{r,k} r_{t-k} + \sum_{k=1}^{n_x} b_{x,k} x_{t-k}. \quad (3.41)$$

In Schmidt's (2015) model, two additional variables are chosen to characterize the LOB effects. The first one is the signed order volume at best price, V_1 (the signed LOB top's volume). The second variable

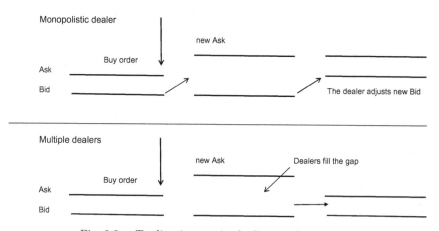

Fig. 3.2.   Trading impact in the limit-order market.

is the signed LOB bulk's volume that excludes inventory at best price, V_b. A four-variable model, VAR4(r, x, V_1, V_b), has the following equation for r_t:

$$r_t = H_r(r, x) + W_r(V_1, V_b) + \varepsilon_{r,t},$$

$$W_r(r, x) = \sum_{k=1}^{n_{i_1}} a_{i_1,k} V_{1,t-k} + \sum_{k=0}^{n_{i_5}} a_{i_1-5,k} V_{b,t-k}. \qquad (3.42)$$

Finally, the five-variable model, VAR5(r, x, V_1, V_b, V_{in}), includes also the signed aggregated volume V_{in} of all orders that were submitted within the time interval $[t{-}1, t]$ inside the market (i.e., with prices that at time $t{-}1$ are lower than the best ask price and higher than the best bid price)

$$r_t = H_r(r, x) + W_r(V_1, V_b) + U_r(V_{in}) + \varepsilon_{r,t}, U_r(V_{in})$$

$$= \sum_{k=0}^{n_u} a_{u,k} V_{in,t-k} \qquad (3.43)$$

Note that (3.43) contains the contemporaneous term $V_{in,t-k}$ with $k = 0$.

The VAR equations for x, V_1, V_b, and V_{in} have a similar form

$$z_t = H_z(r, x) + W_z(V_1, V_b) + U_z(V_{in}) + \varepsilon_{z,t}. \qquad (3.44)$$

The shocks $\varepsilon_{z,t}$ are assumed to have zero means and jointly and serially uncorrelated. When the contributions of V_1 and V_b were qualitatively similar, the model VAR4(r, x, V_{10}, V_{in}) where $V_{10} = V_1 + V_b$ was used instead of VAR5(r, x, V_1, V_b, V_{in}). In all VAR models, CIR (3.33) was calculated for the shock of $x_0 = 1$ assuming that $V_{1,0} = V_{b,0} = V_{in} = 0$.

The structural model (3.42)–(3.44) demonstrates a power-law decay of impact of trading in an institutional FX market (see Fig. 3.3). However, this decay is much slower than the empirical one (Schmidt, 2010a). Such a discrepancy may be explained with that the linear VAR models have limited accuracy for describing nonlinear market impact.

For the most liquid FX rate EUR/USD, the structural model (3.42)–(3.44) describes two subtle effects: the LOB top's "push" and the LOB bulk's "pull." Somewhat paradoxical effect of the LOB

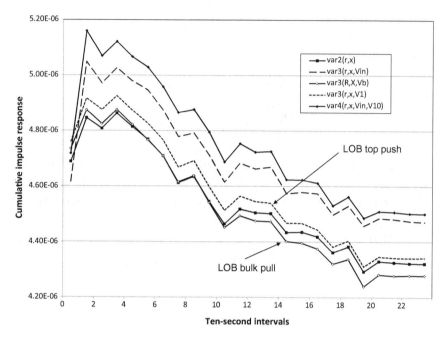

Fig. 3.3. Cumulative impulse response for EUR/USD in 2011.

bulk's volume V_b is that it actually decreases CIR. While growing LOB top's volume V_1 "pushes" price across the bid/offer spread, growing LOB bulk volume "pulls" price outside the market.[10] The LOB top's "push" is actually described in the market microstructure literature. It is often worded in the following form: growing order volume at the best bid price increases probability that the next buyer submits a market order and hence fills the order at the best offer price (Parlour, 1998; see Section 3.1). Indeed, impatient traders may prefer "to pay the spread" for immediacy of execution and submit marketable limit bid orders, which depletes inventory on the ask side of the market and widens the bid/ask spread. The LOB bulk's "pull" implies an opposite behavioral effect: if patient buyers expect price to go down, they submit limit orders below the current best bid price. This may motivate the traders having their orders at the best bid price resubmit their orders at a lower price.

For a less liquid FX rate EUR/JPY, the LOB effects are negligible. However, the inside-market signed order flow V_{in} may add about 15% to the total CIR (see Fig. 3.4).

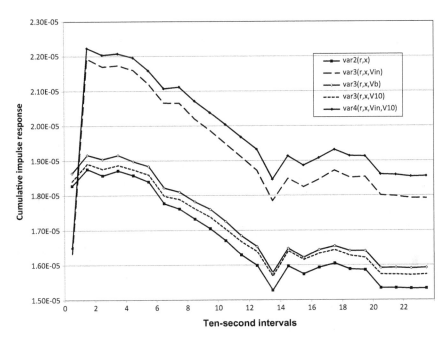

Fig. 3.4. Cumulative impulse response for EUR/JPY in 2011.

3.3 Empirical Findings

3.3.1 *Intraday patterns*

The intraday patterns of trading volumes and bid/ask spreads are well documented (see reviews by Emrich, 2009; Malinova & Park, 2009). In the past, intraday US equity trading volumes were U-shaped. Since 2008, the end-of-day turnover of S&P constituents has significantly increased and the intraday volume pattern has become closer to J- (or even reverse-L-) shaped. London stock exchange and some Asian markets, too, have reverse-L intraday trading volume patterns.

Several theoretical models have been offered to explain the intraday trading volume patterns. Admati & Pfleiderer (1988) have shown that if some liquidity traders have discretion with regard to trading timing (i.e., trade strategically), they concentrate their trading at times when the market is thick and this concentration grows with the increasing number of informed traders.

Hong & Wang (2000) explain the U-shaped pattern by assuming that increasing trading in the morning is caused by risk-averse investors willing to hedge their assets while the high-volume trading in the end of the day is dominated by informed speculators. The latter approach is corroborated by Schiereck & Voigt (2008). On the contrary, according to Hora (2006), the intraday trading pattern can be caused by risk-averse execution strategies with time constraints widely used in algorithmic trading (see Chapter 15). Proliferation of algorithmic trading has also significantly affected an average trade size: for S&P 500 constituents, it has fallen between 2004 and 2009 from about 1,000 shares to below 300 shares (Emrich, 2009).

The intraday bid/ask spreads in equity markets usually have an L-shaped pattern. However, this pattern flattens for illiquid stocks with wide average spreads. Heston *et al.* (2010) offer analysis of intraday patterns in conjunction with predictability of returns.

3.3.2 *Order flows and market impact*

Hasbrouck & Seppi (2001) analyzed market data for 30 Dow stocks and demonstrated that signed order flows and returns are characterized by common factors. Commonality in the order flows explains roughly half of the commonality of returns. On the contrary, commonality in the bid/ask spreads is small.

Long-range autocorrelations in signed order flows in equity markets have been reported in several studies (Farmer *et al.*, 2006; Bouchaud *et al.*, 2006). These autocorrelations with values of approximately 0.05 or higher may last up to 100 5-min intervals. Mimetic contagion of chartists (see Chapter 6) and slicing large orders into small pieces (see Chapter 15) may be the source of such autocorrelations. Bouchaud *et al.* (2006) attempted to reconcile these autocorrelations with the random-walk behavior of returns. Namely, it was suggested that the random walk, being a simple diffusional process (i.e., the Brownian motion; see Chapter 4), results from two opposite but compensating processes. The first one is super-diffusion, which manifests with long autocorrelations in order flows (caused by takers). Another process is sub-diffusion, which manifests with a power-law decay of the market impact (facilitated by market makers).

Fig. 3.5.   Impact of a buy market order.

As I indicated above, impact of trading on price (or market impact) is a key effect addressed in optimal execution strategies. An example of market impact is shown in Fig. 3.5. In this case, a buy market order of 1000 shares completely wipes out inventory at two lowest LOB ask levels and fills a part of the third LOB level. Thus, market impact in this case equals two ticks.

Weber & Rosenow (2005) reported that market impact in equities grows with trading volume as a power law with the exponent lower than one. The *realized* market impact is generally estimated as a function of trading volume. However, the *expected* market impact (estimated by parsing the LOB for some time and averaging its inventory) is much higher than the realized one. This may be explained with that traders avoid placing their orders at times of low liquidity when market impact is expected to be high.

Notes

1. Taker who submits a maker (limit) order is not called market maker since he submits an order only on one side of the market.
2. FPT in the equity and FX markets were discussed by Eisler *et al.* (2009) and Schmidt (2010a), respectively.
3. The uniform distribution is described in Appendix A.
4. A detailed description of volatility is given in Chapter 5.
5. FKK consider risk-neutral traders in their model and perceive impatience simply as an emotional component of trader behavior. However, the cost of execution delay has a rational meaning in terms of volatility risk. Hence, this cost implies risk aversion.
6. Actually, Glosten & Harris (1998) are very cautious in their conclusions: they just state that their results "do not reject" the conclusion made using the information-based models.

7. While the information-based market impact may be persistent at intermediate time horizons, Hasbrouck (2007) assumes that the random walk stays in the background of the structural models at longer (e.g., monthly) time intervals.

8. The generic VAR is described in Appendix B.

9. In the case with $a = 1$, trading volume cannot be presented in the autoregressive form.

10. While contrasting the LOB top's "push" and the LOB bulk's "pull," one may find some similarity with physics of fluids: surface tension and bulk pressure act in the opposite directions.

Part II
Market Dynamics

Chapter 4

Dynamics of Returns

4.1 Introduction

I start this chapter by introducing the notion of return. Then, I describe the *efficient market hypothesis* and its relationship with the *random walk*. In particular, I define three types of the random walk and address the problem of predictability of returns. Further, I offer an overview of recent empirical findings and models describing the distributions of the US equity returns. I also discuss corrections in the US equity markets. Finally, I introduce the concept of fractals and its applications in finance.

4.2 Prices and Returns

Let's start with the basic definitions. The logarithm of price P denoted further as $p = \log(P)$ is widely used in quantitative finance. One practical reason for this is that simulation of random price variations can move price into the negative region, which does not make sense. On the contrary, the negative logarithm of price (which always yields positive price) is perfectly acceptable. Log price is closely related to *return*, which is a measure of investment efficiency. Its advantage is that some important statistical properties, such as *stationarity* and *ergodicity*[1] are better applicable to returns than to prices (Campbell *et al.*, 1997). The single-period return (or *simple return*) $R(t)$ between two subsequent moments t and $t-1$ is defined as[2]

$$R(t) = P(t)/P(t-1) - 1. \tag{4.1}$$

Note that return is sometimes defined as the absolute difference $[P(t) - P(t-1)]$. Then, $R(t)$ in (4.1) is supposed to be called *rate of return*. However, (4.1) is overwhelmingly used as the definition of return in the economics and finance literature.

Multi-period returns that are usually called *compounded returns* define returns between the times t and $t - n$:

$$R(t, n) = P(t)/P(t-n) - 1. \tag{4.2}$$

Log returns are defined as

$$r(t) = \log[R(t) + 1] = p(t) - p(t-1). \tag{4.3}$$

Calculation of the continuous compounded log returns is reduced to simple summation:

$$r(t, n) = r(t) + r(t-1) + \cdots + r(t-n). \tag{4.4}$$

The *arithmetic average* of compounded return equals

$$\bar{r} = r(t, n)/n. \tag{4.5}$$

A popular performance measure in investing is the *geometric average* of compounded return

$$\bar{r}_{\text{geom}} = \left(\prod_{i=1}^{n} (1 + r_i) \right)^{\frac{1}{n}} - 1. \tag{4.6}$$

Returns being time-ordered sequences of random variables represent *time series* (Hamilton, 1994; Tsay, 2005). I introduce the major concepts of time series analysis including statistical distributions and the autoregressive moving-average (ARMA) model in Appendices A and B, respectively.

4.3   The Efficient Market Hypothesis

The *efficient market hypothesis* (EMH) states that markets instantly incorporate all new information into securities prices. Since news generally come unexpectedly, prices change unpredictably.[3] In other words, markets are informationally efficient. As a result, any attempt to forecast future price using new information does not produce better results than a forecast that neglects this information. The very notion of hypothesis implies an explanation of some empirical facts, which has yet to be proven correct. The empirical background of the EMH is multiple observations of securities price dynamics that follow the random walk, which is unpredictable (see Section 4.4 for details). These observations have led to the *random walk hypothesis*. Namely, returns are *independent* of each other and *identically distributed* (IID), and returns lack trends that are needed for forecasting.

The EMH, however, is more than the trivial consequence of the random walk hypothesis. The EMH is also based on the notion of rational investors (introduced in Section 1.2) who immediately incorporate all new information into the fair asset prices.

The evolution of the EMH paradigm, starting with the Bachelier's pioneering work on the random walk price dynamics back in 1900 to the formal definition of EMH by Fama (1970) and its expansion by multiple followers is well publicized (see, e.g., Lo & MacKinlay, 1999; Malkiel, 2003). The EMH implies two unfortunate for investors consequences. First, various opportunistic investing strategies are ineffective.[4] Second, investors should not expect earnings exceeding the total market return. Now, let's get into the EMH specifics.

Three forms of the EMH are discerned in the modern economic literature. In the *weak form* of the EMH, current price reflects all information on past prices. Then, the technical analysis that is often used for forecasting future price direction (see Chapter 11) must be ineffective. The weak EMH form still allows for the possibility that the value investing based on the fundamental analysis in the spirit of Graham & Dodd (2008) may yield excess returns. The *semi-strong form* of the EMH states that prices reflect all publicly available information. If this is true, fundamental analysis cannot systematically produce excess returns either. Finally, the *strong form* of the EMH implies that prices instantly reflect not only all public but also private (insider) information.

While the EMH remains a powerful concept in classical finance, its criticism has been offered on several fronts. First, human actions cannot be reduced to rational optimization of some universal utility function. Even if investors are always rational, they may have heterogeneous beliefs in terms of both expected returns and perceived risk.[5] In fact, investors are often driven by human emotions, such as greed and fear, rather than by rational expectations (see a popular account on the Keynesian concept of *animal spirits* by Akerlof & Shiller, 2010). The Internet bubble in 1999–2000 and the global financial crisis in 2008–2009 have dealt serious blows to the ideal world of the EMH.

The EMH has several other methodological difficulties. In particular, the famous Grossman & Stiglitz (1980) paradox states that if the market is informationally efficient, investors have no rationale for collecting and analyzing economic information (let alone paying for it). However, the asset management firms keep hiring analysts to do just that. Pedersen (2015) calls the markets "efficiently inefficient," which implies that the markets are "inefficient enough" to justify compensation and expenses of professional asset managers.

Also, it has been shown that the random walk hypothesis is, in fact, neither a necessary nor sufficient condition for rationally functioning efficient markets. Finally, careful statistical analysis of price dynamics demonstrates that the random walk hypothesis does not always hold (Lo & MacKinlay, 1999).

To address the conflict between the EMH and empirical findings, Lo (2004) has proposed the *adaptive market hypothesis*, according to which modern equity markets represent an ecological system in which its agents (mutual funds, hedge funds, and individual investors) compete for scarce resources (profits). Market prices reach their new efficient values not instantly but over some time, during which the agents adapt to new information by trial and error. In a highly liquid and competitive market (e.g., the US Treasury market), price quickly attains its efficient value. On the contrary, a market with few competitors may be less efficient (e.g., antiques). Since many agents have limited resources for optimizing their decisions, they are not able to collect and/or process all available information, i.e., investors exhibit *bounded rationality* and therefore may leave profit opportunities for more capable (or fortunate) competitors. These profit opportunities are limited but when they are exhausted, new information may stimulate novel trading ideas.

The adaptive market hypothesis is an attractive concept that encourages everlasting learning and offers some hopes for "beating the market." However, it does not address an important pragmatic argument of unabated defenders of the EMH: no individual or institution has yet demonstrated the capacity to *consistently* produce excess market returns (Malkiel, 2003). Therefore, the practical problem for ambitious investors is whether returns are at least partially predictable. I discuss this problem below.

4.4   Random Walk and Predictability of Returns

Three models of the random walk are discussed in the modern economic literature (Campbell *et al.*, 1997; Fabozzi *et al.*, 2007). In the first one (called here RW1), the dynamics of log prices are described using the following equation:

$$p_t = p_{t-1} + \mu + \varepsilon_t. \tag{4.7}$$

In (4.7), μ is the expected drift, and noise $\varepsilon_t = \text{IID}(0, \sigma^2)$, which implies that random price innovations are independently and identically distributed with zero mean and variance σ^2. In other words,

$$E[\varepsilon_t] = 0; \ E[\varepsilon_t^2] = \sigma^2; \ E[\varepsilon_t \varepsilon_s] = 0, \ \text{if } t \neq s. \tag{4.8}$$

This form of innovations is called *strict white noise*. RW1 is a discrete stochastic process in which time is not included explicitly since the value of the time lag is not defined. When ε_t has the normal distribution $N(0, \sigma^2)$, its continuous differential form coincides with the *Brownian motion*

$$dp_t = \mu_t dt + \sigma_t dW_t. \tag{4.9}$$

In (4.9), W_t is the *standard Brownian motion* (also called the *Wiener process*) with random innovations being $\text{IID}(0, 1)$. When σ_t is not constant, it is called *instantaneous volatility*. RW1 with non-zero drift has *non-stationary* conditional mean

$$E[p_t|p_0] = p_0 + \mu t. \tag{4.10}$$

In (4.10), p_0 is log price at $t = 0$. Also, RW1 has non-stationary conditional variance

$$Var[p_t \,|\, p_0] = \sigma^2 t. \tag{4.11}$$

Importantly, expectations and higher moments of RW1 are unpredictable. Hence, trading strategies that employ forecasts based on historical data described with RW1 can be profitable only by luck.

In a more generic form of the random walk called RW2, ε_t has independent but not identical innovations. In other words, innovations can be drawn from different distributions. RW2 is based on the *martingale* model, which is rooted in the gambling theory. Note that a stochastic process X_t is a martingale if

$$E[X_t \,|\, X_{t-1}, X_{t-2}, \ldots] = X_{t-1}. \tag{4.12}$$

The martingale difference represents the outcome of *fair game*

$$E[X_t - X_{t-1}|X_{t-1}, X_{t-2}, \ldots] = 0. \tag{4.13}$$

Hence, the expected future value of a martingale equals its current value. This property has a close connection with the weak form of the efficient market. While forecasting of the expected values is impossible for RW2, its higher moments may be predictable (Fabozzi *et al.*, 2007).

RW2 can be relaxed further, so that innovations remain uncorrelated (i.e., $\mathrm{Cov}(\varepsilon_t, \varepsilon_{t-k}) = 0$) yet higher moments (in particular, variance) can be dependent (i.e., $\mathrm{Cov}(\varepsilon_t^2, \varepsilon_{t-k}^2) \neq 0$). In this case, higher moments are forecastable. Such a model (RW3) is also called *white noise* (but not the strict one). RW3 exhibits *conditional heteroscedasticity*, which is well supported with empirical data on volatility and will be described in details in Chapter 5. RW3 does not permit linear forecasting of expectations but nonlinear forecasting, for example, with neural nets, may be possible (Gencay *et al.*, 2001).

Comprehensive statistical analysis of various financial time series has shown that the random walk hypothesis may be sometimes rejected. In particular, Lo and MacKinlay (1999) have found that daily returns may exhibit slight serial correlations. In this case, RW3 should be rejected. But since RW3 is the weakest form of the random walk, its rejection implies also rejection of RW1 and RW2. Hence, financial markets are predictable to some degree. Alas, this does not guarantee noticeable (let alone persistent) excess returns. Various market imperfections, such as the bid/ask spread, trading expenses, and limited liquidity can completely absorb potential profits expected from simple predictive models. Still, there are many instances when investors outperform the market. I describe several popular trading strategies, as well as the approaches to testing their efficiency in Part IV.

4.5 Empirical Findings

As I indicated above, the random walk hypothesis is based on the early empirical research and still enjoys great popularity in classical finance. Another (practical) reason for the popularity of the random walk approximation is that it often significantly simplifies tractability of statistical models. In fact, a hypothesis remains what it is: a hypothesis. This implies that the assumption that returns follow the strict random walk with the normal distribution of noise must be tested for each asset, and for every time period and timescale. Here, I describe the main stylized facts for daily returns that have been accumulated in recent years.

Statistical properties of daily stock returns demonstrate notable deviations from the normal distribution (see, e.g., the review by Taylor, 2005). Generally, daily returns have low (if any) serial correlations. Also, it is known that the conditional expected daily returns are close to zero. This leads to the martingale hypothesis and makes forecasting of returns very difficult. Therefore, mathematical description of the return dynamics can be based on the random walk that is less restrictive than the strict white noise.

Another important finding is that the squared (or absolute) returns are clearly correlated. This implies that while returns are practically uncorrelated, they are not independent. Volatility of returns may vary over time (see Chapter 5). Volatility can also be clustered, that is, large returns (of any sign) follow large returns (conditional heteroscedasticity). These facts lead to even greater relaxation of the strict random walk model.

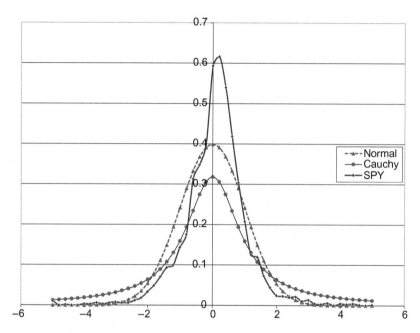

Fig. 4.1. Distribution of the SPY returns in 2007–2009.

Empirical distributions of returns may differ significantly from the Gaussians. In particular, these distributions may have high kurtosis, *fat tails* (which implies that the distribution asymptotic decay is slower than the exponential one), and asymmetrical shape. An example of the distribution of returns for the ETF[6] SPY that mimics the S&P 500 Index in comparison with the normal and Cauchy distributions is given in Fig. 4.1.

Importance of long-range effects in the financial time series was greatly emphasized by Mandelbrot (1997). Early research in this field was based on the *stable distributions* called *Levy flights* (see Appendix A). This approach, however, has an important drawback: Levy flights have infinite variance. Such uncertainty of the volatility measure is unacceptable for financial applications. The truncated Levy flights that satisfy the requirement for finite volatility are sometimes used as a way around (Mantegna & Stanley, 2000; Bouchaud & Potters, 2000).

Gabaix *et al.* (2003) indicated that the asymptotic distributions of returns in equity markets at the timescales varying from one minute to several days in 1984–1996 followed the power law with an index close to three. At longer timescales, distributions of returns slowly approached the Gaussian form. The presence of fat tails in distributions of returns implies that financial crises are less improbable than one might expect from the normal distribution. This certainly has important implications for risk management.

In general, power-law distributions describe *scale-free processes*. Scale invariance implies that the distribution has similar shape on different scales of the independent variable. Namely, function $f(x)$ is scale-invariant to the transformation $x \rightarrow \alpha x$ if there is such a parameter L that

$$f(x) = Lf(\alpha x). \tag{4.14}$$

The solution to (4.14) has a power-law form

$$f(x) = x^n. \tag{4.15}$$

In (4.15), $n = -\ln(L)/\ln(\alpha)$. The function $f(x)$ is scale-free since the ratio $f(x)/f(ax) = L$ does not depend on x.

Several theoretical models offered in explanation of the power-law distributions in finance are reviewed by Gabaix (2009). One such model derived by Gabaix *et al.* (2003) is based on two observations:

1. The distribution of trading volumes obeys the power law with an index of about 1.5.
2. The distribution of the number of trades is a power law with an index of 3 (in fact, it was close 3.4).

Two other assumptions are made in this model:

1. Price movements are caused primarily by activity of large mutual funds whose size distribution is the power law with an index of one (so-called *Zipf's law*).
2. Mutual fund managers trade in an optimal way.

The mathematical transformations based on these rules yield a power-law return distribution with the index of 3.

In another approach, LeBaron (2001) has shown that power-law distributions can be generated by a mix of normal distributions with different timescales. Namely, fitting a combination of Gaussians with a half-life of about 2.7 years, 2.5 weeks, and one day to the Dow returns for 100 years (from 1900 to 2000), yields the power-law index in the range between 2.98 and 3.33 for the timescales in the range between 1 and 20 days. The rationale for three different Gaussians reflects various time horizons for investors: from buy-and-hold strategy to day trading.

While studying power-law distributions, it is important to remember the comments on spurious scaling laws made by Lux (2001a). There may be a problem with extracting the scaling index from not sufficiently long data samples if the true distribution has the form

$$f(x) = x^{-\alpha}L(x). \tag{4.16}$$

In (4.16), $L(x)$ is a slowly varying function that determines the behavior of the distribution in the short-range region. In other words, the power law may be valid only asymptotically. Obviously, the universal scaling exponent $\alpha = -\log[f(x)]/\log(x)$ is as accurate as $L(x)$ is close to a constant.

4.6 Corrections in the US Equity Markets

4.6.1 *The model*

Corrections in the US equity markets are defined as declines of the S&P 500 Index (^GSPC) by more than 10% (but less than 20%) from its most recent peak (see, e.g., Schwab Center for Financial Research, 2018; Yardeni *et al.*, 2020). Corrections exceeding 20% are called *bear markets*. The problem with this definition is that the notion of "most recent peak" is ambiguous. Indeed, say the trough B that follows the peak A is followed by a notably smaller peak C < A that in turn is followed by a deeper trough D < B (see Fig. 4.2). Are there two corrections (A to B and C to D) or only one (A to D)?

A related definition of the *maximum drawdown*[7] (MDD), which is the maximum peak-to-trough decline of asset price during given period, registers drawdown only when the preceding peak fully recovers (see, e.g., Magdon-Ismail & Atiya, 2004). In the example in Fig. 4.2, this implies that the trough B is MDD only if the peak C is not lower than the peak A. But then, according to the MDD definition, the NASDAQ (^IXIC) bear market in 2007–2009 was just a continuation of the dot-com market crash in 2000–2002. Indeed, the

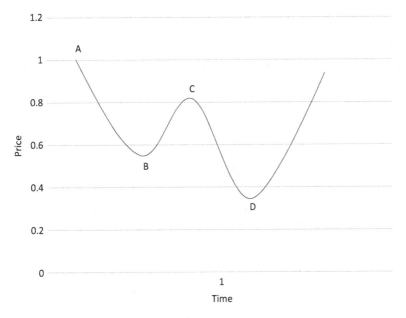

Fig. 4.2.   An example of market correction.

highest NASDAQ price in 2000 recovered only in 2015. Hence, the MDD definition is too restrictive for describing market corrections.

Fabozzi & Francis (1977) defined bull (bear) markets in terms of "substantial" up (down) price movements. Namely, monthly stock returns were assumed substantial when they exceeded one half of standard deviation of the return distribution. As Lunde & Timmermann (2004) indicated, this definition does not reflect long-run dependencies in stock prices and ignores information about the trend in stock price levels.

Pagan & Sossounov (2003) proposed a two-threshold filter $H_{\text{down}}/H_{\text{up}}$ that registers correction when price falls from its peak by more than H_{down} percent and then recovers from the trough by more than H_{up} percent (see also Lunde & Timmermann, 2004; Kole & van Dijk, 2017). Schmidt (2020a) suggested using a symmetric H/H filter that depends on the asset volatility. The daily volatility, σ_d, for the ^GSPC returns during the period 1950–2018 was 1.0%. Hence, to adapt the conventional ^GSPC threshold H of 10%, Schmidt (2020a) proposed a formula

$$H = 10\sigma_d. \tag{4.17}$$

Note that if the asset returns follow the random walk (as is generally assumed), volatility for a period of T days is proportional to $\sqrt{T}$. Therefore, the factor of 10 in (4.17) relates to the 100-day volatility or, providing that an average month has 21 trading days, to about five-month volatility. This approach enables consistent comparison of corrections in different markets.

Market corrections are characterized using the following parameters: peak-to-trough loss (relative decline of price P between the peak A and the trough B that is lower than A by at least the value of H), peak-to-trough duration (PTD, the number of days between the peak A and the trough B), trough-to-the-next-peak duration (TNPD, the number of days between the trough B and the peak C that is higher than B by at least the value of H), and first-peak-recovery duration (FPRD, the number of days between the trough B and the day R when the price of the peak A recovers)

$$\text{Loss} = (P_A - P_B)/P_A, \tag{4.18}$$

$$\text{PTD} = t_B - t_A, \tag{4.19}$$

$$\text{TNPD} = t_C - t_B, \tag{4.20}$$

$$\text{FPRD} = t_R - t_B. \tag{4.21}$$

Schmidt (2020a) used the ARMA-GARCH model[8] for describing dynamics of daily returns. Market corrections were described with the binary variables for the mean (D_m) and for the variance (D_v) that are equal to unity during the peak-to-trough price declines and equal to zero at all other times

$$D_m = D_v = \begin{cases} 1, \text{ market in correction state} \\ 0, \text{ otherwise.} \end{cases} \tag{4.22}$$

4.6.2 *Corrections in major US equity indexes*

Schmidt (2020a) found that the H/H filter yields 50 corrections for ^GSPC in 1950–2018 excluding the correction that started in September 2018 and had not recovered by February 2019 (when the market data for this work were compiled). The period 2007–2009 is usually treated as a single ^GSPC bear market (see, e.g., Yardeni *et al.*, 2020). However, according to the H/H filter, this period had five distinct corrections, three of which exceeded 20%. Hence the H/H filter demonstrates that the bear market in 2007–2009 was not in a monotonic decline; it offered some short-term buying opportunities.

Since volatility of ^IXIC, has notably increased in recent years, the average losses during the ^IXIC corrections have become significantly higher than those of ^GSPC. On the contrary, the average PTDs and TNPDs of ^GSPC have become much closer to that of ^IXIC. The FPRDs for both ^GSPC and ^IXIC have notably increased in recent years (cf. Tables 4.1 and 4.2).

Comparison of corrections in the S&P 500 Growth Index (^SGX) and S&P 500 Value Index (^SVX) reveals another interesting result. While the statistics of the losses before and after 2007 is not very reliable in terms of p-values (each sub-sample has only eight data points), the losses of ^SGX during the market corrections before 2007 were mostly higher than the losses of ^SVX. However, this is not the case since 2007 (see Table 4.3 and Fig. 4.3). This can be explained with that the bear market of 2000–2002 was the burst of the dot-com bubble while the bear market in 2007–2009 was caused by the problems in the financial industry. As a result, switching investments during market corrections from a market-wide growth portfolio to a market-wide value portfolio might not decrease the losses in recent years.

4.6.3 *Corrections for the US equity sector ETFs*

Schmidt (2020a) studied corrections in nine major US equity sector SPDR ETFs: Materials (XLB), Energy (XLE), Financials (XLF), Industrials (XLI), Technology (XLK), Consumer Staples (XLP), Utilities (XLU), Healthcare (XLV), and Consumer Discretionary (XLY) in comparison with the S&P 500 SPDR ETF (SPY). Their statistics is listed in Table 4.4.

The correlation between the ETF correction thresholds, H, and the number of the ETF corrections is very weak: 0.04. This implies that the number of corrections in the US equity sector ETFs is determined by the sector-specific trends rather than by their price volatility. XLF and XLP had the highest and the lowest values of volatility (and hence H), respectively. XLV and XLU had the highest and the lowest number of corrections, respectively. XLP and XLV had the lowest average losses while XLF and XLK had the highest

Table 4.1. Statistics of the corrections for ^GSPC and ^IXIC during 2/6/1971–1/31/2019.

	Correction threshold (%)	Number of corrections	Loss (%)		PTD (days)		TNPD (days)		FPRD (days)	
			Mean	Median	Mean	Median	Mean	Median	Mean	Median
^GSPC	11	33	19.6	17.1	130	95	31	22	533	163
^IXIC	12	49	21.9	18.7	88	70	39	32	854	160
p-value[a]	NA	NA	0.24	0.16	0.12	0.24	0.32	0.39	0.21	0.79

[a]*p*-Values from *t*-tests and Wilcoxon tests for means and medians, respectively.

Table 4.2. Statistics of the corrections for ^GSPC and ^IXIC during 1/2/1993–1/31/2019.

	Correction threshold (%)	Number of corrections	Loss (%)		PTD (days)		TNPD (days)		FPRD (days)	
			Mean	Median	Mean	Median	Mean	Median	Mean	Median
^GSPC	11	18	20.4	19.3	97	96	26	13	712	233
^IXIC	15	20	26.7	23.8	94	70	27	14	1215	276
p-value[a]	NA	NA	0.02	0.04	0.86	0.82	0.86	0.61	0.30	1.00

[a]p-Values from t-tests and Wilcoxon tests for means and medians, respectively.

Table 4.3.   Losses of ˆSVX and ˆSGX before and after 2007.

	Loss in 1995–2006, %		Loss in 2007–2018, %	
	Mean	Median	Mean	Median
ˆSVX	18.7	16.4	25.0	22.0
ˆSGX	24.8	25.9	21.0	18.9
p-value[a]	0.10	0.19	0.41	0.44

[a]p-Values from t-tests and Wilcoxon tests for means and medians, respectively.

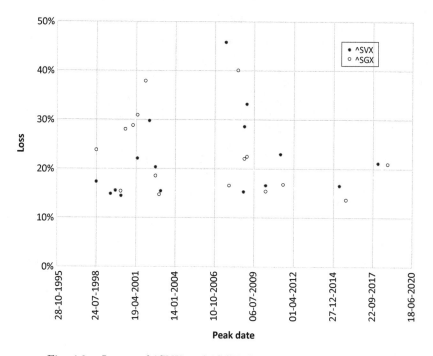

Fig. 4.3.   Losses of ˆSVX and ˆSGX during market corrections.

average losses. In terms of the sum PTD+TNPD, XLP and XLU had the shortest and the longest average durations of their corrections, respectively. XLK had the longest average time to recover (FPRD). XLU was the only ETF that did not have corrections in 2018.

Table 4.4. Statistics of the corrections in the US equity ETFs during 1999–2018.

ETF	Correction threshold, (%)	Number of corrections	Loss (%)		PTD (days)		TNPD (days)		FPRD (days)	
			Mean	Median	Mean	Median	Mean	Median	Mean	Median
SPY	10	14	22.1	19.1	121	114	24	17	593	249
XLB	15	17	24.8	24.7	111	102	36	28	441	164
XLE	17	15	26.9	26.5	131	112	37	25	361	136
XLF	19	17	29.8	25.3	118	92	29	15	755	446
XLI	13	15	24.0	22.1	106	101	25	13	468	246
XLK	16	14	30.3	25.3	118	114	30	15	1925	736
XLP	9	16	16.1	14.3	82	73	27	13	436	214
XLU	12	12	22.2	16.6	146	93	67	34	436	211
XLV	11	20	17.1	15.5	96	68	37	26	408	217
XLY	14	16	23.8	21.8	94	73	30	18	285	171
mean	14	16	23.7	21.1	112	94	34	20	611	279
median	14	16	23.9	22.0	115	97	30	18	439	216

Fig. 4.4.   Sierpinski triangle.

4.7   Fractals in Finance

The fractal theory and its first applications in finance were developed by Mandelbrot (1997). Since then, the fractal theory has become a popular tool for analysis of financial market data (Peters, 1996). In natural sciences, fractals denote the geometric objects whose defining property is *self-similarity*, that is, they can be constructed by repeating some geometric pattern at a smaller and smaller scale. The Sierpinski triangle is a classic example of a two-dimensional fractal (see an example in Fig. 4.4). It can be derived using the following rules:

1. Start with a triangle in a plane.
2. Shrink the triangle to one-half width and one-half height, and position the three shrunken triangles into the original triangle so that each shrunken triangle touches the two other triangles at a corner.
3. Repeat step 2 multiple times.

Self-similarity of an object implies its isotropic properties. This concept is not applicable for time series in which dependent (price, return) and independent (time) variables are measured with different units. In this case, the notion of *self-affinity* is used instead.

Let's introduce the *fractional Brownian motion* $B_H(t)$. This random process satisfies the following condition for all t and T:

$$E[B_H(t+T) - B_H(t)] = 0, \qquad (4.23)$$

$$E[B_H(t+T) - B_H(t)]^2 = T^{2H}. \qquad (4.24)$$

The fractional Brownian motion is reduced to the regular Brownian motion when $H = 0.5$. It can be shown that the correlation between the past average $E[B_H(t) - B_H(t-T)]/T$ and the future average $E[B_H(t+T) - B_H(t)]/T$ equals

$$C = 2^{2H-1} - 1. \qquad (4.25)$$

Note that this correlation does not depend on T. If $0.5 < H < 1$, then $C > 0$ and it is said that $B_H(t)$ is a *persistent process*. Namely, if $B_H(t)$ grew (fell) in the past, most probably it will grow (fall) in the immediate future. In other words, persistent processes maintain trend. In the opposite case ($C < 0$ when $0 < H < 0.5$), the process is called *anti-persistent*. It is also said that anti-persistent processes demonstrate *mean reversion*; that is, if the recent trend was positive, then the immediate future trend will most probably be negative, and vice versa.

The Hurst exponent of a time series sample can be estimated using the *rescaled range* (R/S) *analysis*. Consider a data set x_i ($i = 1, \ldots, N$) with mean m_N and the standard deviation σ_N. In this method, the partial sums S_k must be calculated at first:

$$S_k = \sum_{i=1}^{k} (x_i - m_N), \quad 1 \leq k \leq N. \qquad (4.26)$$

The rescaled range equals

$$R/S = [\max(S_k) - \min(S_k)]/\sigma_N, \quad 1 \leq k \leq N. \qquad (4.27)$$

The value of R/S is always greater than zero since $\max(S_k) > 0$ and $\min(S_k) < 0$. The Hurst exponent for a given R/S can be estimated using the relation

$$R/S = (aN)^H. \qquad (4.28)$$

In (4.28), a is a constant. Hence, when $\log(R/S)$ and $\log(N)$ are plotted against each other, the slope of the line determines H.

The R/S analysis is superior to many other methods of determining the long-range dependencies and hence can be useful in trading. Obviously, confirming current trend is important for choosing trend-based trading strategies (see Chapter 11). It should be noted that the R/S analysis has some shortcomings, particularly, high sensitivity to the short-range memory (Campbell *et al.*, 1997).

A more complex, *multifractal theory* has recently drawn the attention of economists (Lux, 2001b; Calvet & Fisher, 2002). In a nutshell, the multifractal theory describes the objects defined with a generic relationship

$$X(ct) = M(c)X(t). \qquad (4.29)$$

A general multifractal process (4.29) is reduced to the fractional Browning motion when

$$M(c) = c^H, H = \text{const.} \qquad (4.30)$$

Notes

1. The notions of stationarity and ergodicity are defined in Appendix A.
2. The definition (4.1) neglects possible dividend payments during the interval $[t-1, t]$.
3. Price may react unpredictably even in the case of "expected" news. For example, if a good company's performance report is widely expected, it can be priced into the stock value prior to the reporting date. Then, the adage "buying on gossips, selling on news" may play out after the report is published.
4. Opportunistic trading strategies are discussed in Part IV.
5. Recall the concept of risk aversion outlined in Section 2.3.
6. Exchange trading fund (ETF) is a security that represents a basket of stocks that is often based on some equity index. ETFs are traded the same way as single stocks.
7. A formal definition of MDD is given in Section 14.2.
8. The ARMA and GARCH models are described in Appendix B and Section 5.3, respectively.

Chapter 5

Price Volatility

5.1 Introduction

I start this chapter with the definition of volatility and practical methods of its estimation. Then, I provide an overview of the conditional heteroscedastic models that were derived for describing volatility clustering observed in financial markets. Further, I introduce the integrated volatility (IV) that has been drawing attention in the current econometric research of high-frequency financial data. Finally, I describe the volatility-based measures, *value at risk* (VaR) and *expected tail loss* (ETL), widely used in market risk management.

5.2 Basic Notions

Volatility is a measure of price variability. It is directly related to the concept of market risk. While investing strategies may benefit from a directional price change, it is uncertainty of price variation that makes investing risky. Standard deviation of returns is generally used for quantifying volatility. Usually, returns are calculated on a homogeneous time grid. For a data sample with N returns r_i at $i = 1, 2, \ldots, N$ and mean $\bar{r}$, *realized volatility* (called also *historical volatility*) is defined as

$$\sigma = \left[\frac{1}{N} \sum_{i=1}^{N} (r_i - \bar{r})^2 \right]^{1/2} . \qquad (5.1)$$

For financial reporting, volatility is often calculated as the annualized percentage, that is,

$$\sigma_{\text{ann}} = 100\sigma\sqrt{T}. \tag{5.2}$$

In (5.2), T is the annual period. For example, in the cases of daily returns and monthly returns, $T = 252$ (which is the average yearly number of trading days) and $T = 12$, respectively. Note that the square root in (5.2) is based on the assumption that returns follow the random walk (see (4.11)).

Formulas for calculating volatility on the inhomogeneous time grids that may be useful for tick data[1] in the HFT environment are offered by Dacorogna *et al.* (2001).

Usage of very long data samples for calculating historic volatility may not be such a good idea: in general, volatility may be non-stationary, so that the recent returns reflect current volatility better than the older data. Then, only the last n data points are used for calculating recent historical volatility:

$$\sigma_t = \left(\frac{1}{n} \sum_{i=t-n+1}^{t} r_i - \bar{r} \right)^{1/2}. \tag{5.3}$$

In this case, volatility estimates are based on the rolling windows with n data points. Poon & Granger (2003) describe several practical approaches used for forecasting volatility. The simplest forecast in the spirit of the martingale hypothesis is referred to as the *random walk forecast*: $\hat{\sigma}_t = \sigma_{t-1}$. Other popular linear forecasting methods are as follows:

- *Simple moving average* (SMA):

$$\hat{\sigma}_t = (\sigma_t + \sigma_{t-1} + \cdots + \sigma_{t-T})/T. \tag{5.4}$$

- *Exponential moving average* (EMA):

$$\hat{\sigma}_t = (1 - \beta)\sigma_t + \beta\hat{\sigma}_{t-1}, \quad 0<\beta<1. \tag{5.5}$$

Note that the value of $\hat{\sigma}_{t-1}$ for $t = 1$ is not defined in (5.5). It is often assumed that $\hat{\sigma}_1 = \sigma_1$; sometimes, SMA for a few initial values of σ_t is used instead.

- *Exponentially weighed moving average* (EWMA), which is a truncated version of EMA:

$$\hat{\sigma}_t = \sum_{i=1}^{n} \beta^i \sigma_{t-i} \bigg/ \sum_{i=1}^{n} \beta^i. \tag{5.6}$$

It can be shown by comparing EMA and EWMA that the smoothing parameter in the limit of high n equals

$$\beta = 2/(n+1). \tag{5.7}$$

SMA and EMA with the relation (5.7) are widely used in technical analysis (see Chapter 11).

As indicated in Section 4.4, the concept of *conditional volatility* appears in random walk RW3 in which return innovations are uncorrelated but not independent. Forecasting volatility using conditional heteroscedasticity models is widely used in financial research. This topic is addressed in Section 5.3.

An alternative to the realized volatility is the so-called *implied volatility*. It is based on the Black–Scholes theory of option pricing (see, e.g., Hull, 2006). In this theory, volatility is one of the parameters that determine price of an option. Hence, reverse calculation of volatility is possible when the true market option prices are available.

Finally, there is a concept of *stochastic volatility* (Shephard, 2005; Taylor, 2005). Within this framework, price dynamics is not a covariance-stationary[2] and volatility is described as an independent stochastic process.

Traditionally, estimates of volatility are made using daily or even monthly returns. However, with the proliferation of publicly available high-frequency market data, there has been a growing interest in the analysis of the IV (see Section 5.4).

5.3 Conditional Heteroscedasticity

Noticeable autocorrelations in the squared asset returns imply that large returns (either positive or negative) follow large returns of the opposite sign (see an example for SPY in 2005–2012 in Fig. 5.1). In this case, it is said that the volatility of returns is clustered.[3]

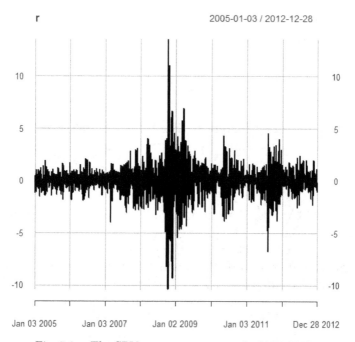

Fig. 5.1.   The SPY percentage returns in 2005–2012.

The effect of volatility clustering is also named *autoregressive conditional heteroscedasticity* (ARCH). Several mathematical models in which past shocks contribute to the current volatility have been developed (see, e.g., Alexander, 2001; Taylor, 2005; Tsay, 2005). Generally, these models are rooted in the ARCH(m) model offered by Engle (1982), where conditional variance is a weighed sum of m squared lagged return *residuals* (see Appendix section B.1.1):

$$\sigma^2(t) = \omega + a_1 \varepsilon^2(t-1) + a_2 \varepsilon^2(t-2) + \cdots + a_m \varepsilon^2(t-m). \quad (5.8)$$

In (5.8), $\varepsilon(t) = N(0, \sigma^2(t))$, $\omega > 0$, and $a_1, a_2, \ldots, \geq 0$.

Unfortunately, application of the ARCH(m) process to modeling the financial time series often requires polynomials with a very high order m. A more efficient model is the *generalized ARCH* (GARCH) process. The GARCH(m, n) process combines the ARCH(m) process with the autoregressive AR(n) process for lagged variance:

$$\sigma^2(t) = \omega + a_1 \varepsilon^2(t-1) + a_2 \varepsilon^2(t-2) + \cdots + a_m \varepsilon^2(t-m)$$
$$+ b_1 \sigma^2(t-1) + b_2 \sigma^2(t-2) + \cdots + b_n \sigma^2(t-n). \quad (5.9)$$

A simple GARCH(1, 1) model is widely used in financial applications:

$$\sigma^2(t) = \omega + a\varepsilon^2(t-1) + b\sigma^2(t-1). \tag{5.10}$$

Equation (5.10) can be transformed into

$$\sigma^2(t) = \omega + (a+b)\sigma^2(t-1) + a[\varepsilon^2(t) - \sigma^2(t-1)]. \tag{5.11}$$

The last term in (5.11) being conditioned on information available at time $(t-1)$ has zero mean and can be treated as a shock to volatility. Therefore, the unconditional expectation of volatility for the GARCH(1, 1) model equals

$$E[\sigma^2(t)] = \omega/(1-a-b). \tag{5.12}$$

This indicates that the GARCH(1, 1) process is weakly stationary when $a + b < 1$. The advantage of the GARCH(1, 1) model is that it can be easily used for forecasting. Namely, the conditional expectation of volatility at time $(t+k)$ equals

$$E[\sigma^2(t+k)] = (a+b)^k[\sigma^2(t) - \omega/(1-a-b)] + \omega/(1-a-b). \tag{5.13}$$

The GARCH(1, 1) model (5.10) can be rewritten as

$$\sigma^2(t) = \omega/(1-b) + a(\varepsilon^2(t-1) + b\varepsilon^2(t-2) + b^2\varepsilon^2(t-3) + \cdots). \tag{5.14}$$

Equation (5.14) implies that the GARCH(1, 1) model is equivalent to the infinite ARCH model with exponentially weighed coefficients. This explains why the parsimonious GARCH(1, 1) model is more efficient than the multi-lag ARCH models.

Several other GARCH models have been derived for addressing the specifics of various economic and financial time series. One popular GARCH(1, 1) model, in which $a + b = 1$, is named *integrated* GARCH (IGARCH). This model has the *unit root*.[4] Hence, volatility in this case follows the random walk. IGARCH can be presented in the form

$$\sigma^2(t) = \omega + (1 - \lambda)\varepsilon^2(t - 1) + \lambda\sigma^2(t - 1). \qquad (5.15)$$

In (5.15), $0 < \lambda = 1 - b < 1$. It can be shown that in the case with $\omega = 0$, IGARCH has the EWMA form (5.6)

$$\sigma^2(t) = (1 - \lambda)\sum_{i=1}^{n} \lambda^{i-1}\varepsilon^2(t - i). \qquad (5.16)$$

For IGARCH, the forecast (5.13) is reduced to

$$E[\sigma^2(t + k)] = \sigma^2(t) + k\omega. \qquad (5.17)$$

Hence, the IGARCH variance grows linearly with time.

The GARCH models discussed so far are symmetric in that the sign of price innovations does not affect the resulting volatility. In practice, however, negative price shocks often influence volatility more than the positive shocks. An example of the GARCH model that describes such an asymmetric effect is the *exponential GARCH* (EGARCH). It has the form

$$\log[\sigma^2(t)] = \omega + \beta\log[\sigma^2(t - 1)]$$
$$+ \lambda z(t - 1) + \gamma(|z(t - 1)| - \sqrt{2/\pi}). \qquad (5.18)$$

In (5.18), $z(t) = \varepsilon(t)/\sigma(t)$. Note that $E[z(t)] = \sqrt{2/\pi}$; therefore, the last term in (5.18) is mean deviation of $z(t)$. When the EGARCH parameters satisfy the conditions $\gamma > 0$ and $\lambda < 0$, the negative price shocks lead to higher volatility than the positive shocks.

Another popular asymmetric model, GJR-GARCH (Glosten *et al.*, 1993), has the following form:

$$\sigma_i^2(t) = \omega_i + \alpha_{i,1}\varepsilon_i^2(t - 1) + \alpha_{i,2}\varepsilon_i^2(t - 2) + \beta_{i,1}\sigma_i^2(t - 1)$$
$$+ \gamma_{i,1}I_i(t - 1)\varepsilon_i^2(t - 1). \qquad (5.19)$$

In (5.19), $I_i(t-1) = 0$ if $\varepsilon_i(t-1) \geq 0$ and $I_i(t-1) = 1$ if $\varepsilon_i(t-1) < 0$.

5.4 Integrated Volatility

Realized volatility is usually calculated using historical data for daily returns. Such a measure, however, does not reflect intraday price dynamics. Indeed, if opening and closing daily prices are the same, various intraday price fluctuations remain unaccounted for and all days with zero returns look alike. This is not helpful for deriving the HFT strategies. Therefore, there has been growing interest in IV, which is calculated using intraday returns.

Consider the Brownian motion $X(t)$ with trend $\mu(t)$, instantaneous variance $\sigma(t)$, and the Wiener process $dW(t)$ that was introduced in Section 4.4,

$$dX = \mu(t)dt + \sigma(t)dW. \tag{5.20}$$

The IV is defined as

$$\text{IV} = \int_0^T \sigma^2(t)dt. \tag{5.21}$$

It is a natural measure for variance of the process (5.20) within the interval $[0, T]$. IV equals the *quadratic variation* (QV) for any sequence of the partitions $t_0 = 0 < t_1 < \cdots < t_{N-1} = T$ with $\sup(t_i - t_{i-1})- > 0$ as $N \to \infty$ (Andersen *et al.*, 2000):

$$\text{QV} = p \lim \sum_{i=1}^{N-1} (X(t_i) - X(t_{i-1}))^2$$

$$N \to \infty. \tag{5.22}$$

In practice, empirical data are available on a discrete grid with spacing $\tau = T/N$, and IV is estimated as

$$\text{IV} = \sum_{i=1}^{N-1} (X(t_i) - X(t_{i-1}))^2. \tag{5.23}$$

It can be shown that IV $\to$ QV as $N \to \infty$ (Barndorff-Nielsen & Shephard, 2002). Hence, IV can be used as a practical measure of intraday volatility. Obviously, if the process $X(t)$ within the period

$[0, T]$ follows random walk with zero trend and stationary σ, IV should not depend on N or τ:

$$IV = \sigma^2 T. \qquad (5.24)$$

In the general case with non-stationary instantaneous volatility $\sigma(t)$, the dependence $IV(\tau)$ is called the *volatility signature* (Andersen *et al.*, 2000). Then, one might expect that IV calculated at the smallest time interval available is the most accurate estimate for the IV. However, the market microstructure effects (such as ask-bid bounce and liquidity gaps) add additional noise $\varepsilon(t)$, so that the observable variable is $Y(t) = X(t) + \varepsilon(t)$ rather than the process $X(t)$. The microstructure noise induces autocorrelations in returns. As a result, the observable sum has the following form (Zhang *et al.*, 2005):

$$\sum_{i=1}^{N-1} (Y(t_i) - Y(t_{i-1}))^2 = 2NE[\varepsilon^2] + O(N^{0.5}). \qquad (5.25)$$

This implies that realized volatility may not approach IV at the highest sample frequency. Indeed, the typical volatility signature has a maximum at the smallest available τ, which decays to some plateau expected from (5.23). It is reasonable to estimate IV at the highest frequencies where the microstructure effects are not important. Several methods have been offered for reducing the microstructure effects. In a nutshell, they can be partitioned into such smoothing techniques as combining calculations on different timescales (Ait-Sahalia *et al.*, 2005) and moving averages (Hansen *et al.*, 2008). Another promising approach for filtering out high-frequency noise is designing realized kernel estimators[5] (Barndorff-Nielsen *et al.*, 2008).

Schmidt (2009b) found that the volatility signatures for very busy days in the institutional FX market do not follow the typical IV pattern. In particular, $IV(\tau)$ may have maxima at larger timescales. Since the smoothing techniques did not remedy this problem, Schmidt (2009b) suggested that price micro-trends caused by automated trading might yield unconventional IV patterns. Indeed, detrending of the original time series recovered volatility signatures with a pronounced plateau at intermediate timescales (see Fig. 5.2).

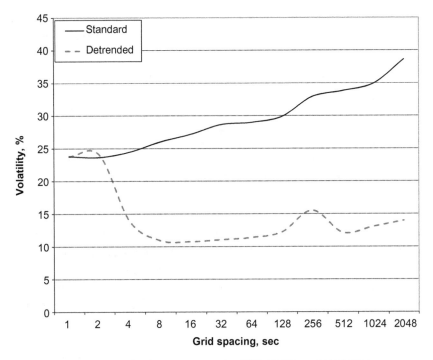

Fig. 5.2. Volatility signature for USD/JPY on 8/16/2007.

5.5 Market Risk Measurement

Several possible causes of financial losses are described in the literature (Jorion, 2000). First, there is *market risk* resulting from unexpected changes in the market prices, interest rates, or foreign exchange rates. Other types of financial risk include *liquidity risk*, *credit risk*, and *operational risk*. Liquidity risk being closely related to market risk is determined by a finite number of assets available at best market price. Hence, it may be impossible to liquidate an asset at this price. Another form of the liquidity risk (so-called *cash flow risk*) refers to the inability to pay off debt on time. Credit risk arises when one of the counterparts involved in a financial transaction does not fulfill its obligation. Finally, operational risk is a generic notion for unforeseen human and technical problems, such as fraud, accidents, and so on. In this book, I focus exclusively on market risk.

Historical volatility σ calculated using the daily returns is the most straightforward measure of market risk. In equities, the parameter beta

$$\beta_i = \text{Cov}(R_i, R_p)/\text{Var}(R_p) \tag{5.26}$$

is also used for measuring market risk. In (5.26), $R_i = r_i - r_f$ and $R_p = r_p - r_f$ are the excess returns of a stock i and entire market portfolio, respectively; r_f is a risk-free asset return. The definition of beta stems from the classical *Capital Asset Pricing Model* (CAPM), according to which (e.g., Bodie & Merton, 1998)

$$E[r_i] = r_f + \beta_i(E[r_p] - r_f). \tag{5.27}$$

Usually, the S&P 500 Index and three-month US Treasury bills are used as proxies to the market portfolio and the risk-free asset, respectively. Beta defines sensitivity of the risky asset i to the market dynamics. That is to say, $\beta_i > 1$ means that the asset is more volatile than the entire market, while $\beta_i < 1$ implies that the asset has lower sensitivity to the market movements. Note that the CAPM is valid only if $\beta_i \geq 0$; otherwise, investment in a risky asset does not make sense. Hence, the CAPM is not applicable in a bear market. I shall describe CAPM in greater detail in Chapter 10.

The classical performance measure that is rooted in the CAPM combines excess return with volatility risk into a single parameter. It is usually called the *Sharpe ratio* (or the *risk-adjusted return*):

$$\text{SR} = (E[r_i] - r_f)/\sigma_i. \tag{5.28}$$

Arguably, the risk measure most widely used in asset management is VaR (Jorion, 2000; Dowd, 2002). VaR refers to the maximum amount of an asset that is likely to be lost over a given period at a specific confidence level α. This implies that the probability density function for *profit and loss*[6] (P&L) is known. It is often assumed that the P&L distribution is normal and hence is completely determined with mean μ and standard deviation σ. Then,

$$\text{VaR}(\alpha) = -\sigma z_\alpha - \mu. \tag{5.29}$$

Note that VaR is defined as a positive value for losses, hence the minus signs in the right-hand side of (5.29). The value of z_α can be determined from the cumulative distribution function for the standard normal distribution

$$\Pr(Z \le z_\alpha) = \int_{-\infty}^{z_\alpha} \frac{1}{\sqrt{2\pi}} \exp[-z^2/2]dz = 1 - \alpha. \qquad (5.30)$$

Since $z_\alpha < 0$ when $\alpha > 50\%$, the relation (5.30) implies that positive values of VaR point to loss. In general, VaR(α) grows with the confidence level α. Sufficiently high values of the mean value μ (that satisfy the condition $\mu > -\sigma z_\alpha$) move VaR(α) into the negative region, which implies profit for a given α rather than loss. The values of z_α for frequently used confidence levels of $\alpha = 95\%$ and $\alpha = 99\%$ are given in Fig. 5.3.

The advantage of VaR is that it is a simple and universal measure that can be used for determining the risks of different financial assets and entire portfolios. Yet, VaR has several drawbacks (Dowd, 2002). First, the accuracy of VaR is completely determined by the model assumptions. Also, VaR provides an estimate for losses within a given confidence interval α, but says nothing about possible outcome outside this interval. A somewhat paradoxical feature of VaR is that

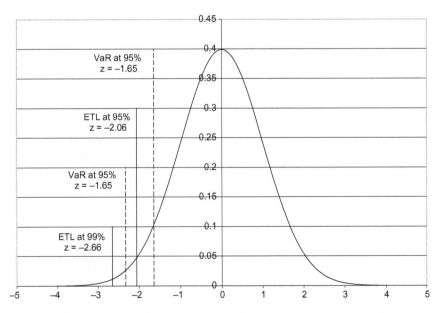

Fig. 5.3. An example of VaR and ETL for normal P/L distribution.

it can discourage investment diversification. Indeed, adding volatile
assets to a portfolio may move VaR above the chosen risk threshold.
Another problem with VaR is that it can violate the sub-additivity
rule for portfolio risk. According to this rule, the risk measure ρ must
satisfy the condition

$$\rho(A + B) \leq \rho(A) + \rho(B). \tag{5.31}$$

Obviously, the risk of owning the sum of two assets must not be
higher than the sum of the individual risks of these assets. The condition (5.31) yields an upper estimate of combined risk. Violation
of the sub-additivity rule may provoke investors to establish separate accounts for every asset they have. Unfortunately, VaR satisfies
(5.31) only if the probability distribution for P&L is normal or, more
generally, elliptical (Dowd, 2002).

The generic criterions for the risk measures that broadly satisfy the requirements of the modern risk management include the
following conditions:

$$\rho(\lambda A) = \lambda\rho(A), \lambda > 0 \,(\text{homogeneity}), \tag{5.32}$$

$$\rho(A) \leq \rho(B), \text{ if } A \leq B \,(\text{monotonicity}), \tag{5.33}$$

$$\rho(A + C) = \rho(A) - C \,(\text{translation invariance}). \tag{5.34}$$

In (5.34), C is a risk-free amount. Adding this amount to a risky
portfolio should decrease the total risk, since this amount is not subject to potential losses. The risk measures that satisfy the conditions
(5.32)–(5.34) are named *coherent risk measures* (Artzner *et al.*, 1999).
It can be shown that any coherent risk measure represents the maximum of the expected loss on a set of generalized scenarios where
every such scenario is determined with its value of loss and probability of occurrence. This result yields a coherent risk measure named
the expected tail loss[7] (ETL):

$$\text{ETL} = E[L|L > \text{VaR}]. \tag{5.35}$$

While VaR is an estimate of loss within a given confidence level,
ETL is an estimate of loss within the remaining tail (i.e., an average
worst-case scenario). For a given probability distribution of P&L and
a given α, ETL is always higher than VaR (see Fig. 5.3). As a simple
example of comparing VaR and ETL, consider a sample with 100

P&L values. Say the chosen confidence level is 95%. Then, VaR is the sixth smallest number in the sample, while ETL is the average of the five smallest numbers within the sample.

Notes

1. Tick data are time-stamped records of all market events: order arrivals and cancellations, and transactions.
2. Weak stationarity implies that the mean and variance of the stochastic process do not change with time. However, higher moments of the process, such as *skewness* and *kurtosis* (see Appendix A), may be not stationary.
3. Small autocorrelations in squared returns do not necessarily mean that there is no volatility clustering. If there are outliers in the sample that lead to high values of skewness and kurtosis, they may lower autocorrelations. If these outliers are removed from the sample, volatility clustering may become apparent (Alexander, 2001).
4. The notion of unit root is described in Appendix B.
5. Kernel regression estimators are a popular technique for smoothing various noisy data. In particular, they were used in a sophisticated analysis of technical trading strategies (Lo *et al.*, 2000).
6. The term *profit and loss* (P&L) is generally used in risk management for referring to returns of institutional portfolio.
7. ETL is sometimes called *expected shortfall* or *conditional VaR*.

Chapter 6

Agent-Based Modeling of Financial Markets

6.1 Introduction

The main idea behind the agent-based modeling in various fields is that agents' actions affect or even determine the environment in which they function. This framework is similar to the methodology of statistical physics where macroscopic properties of a continuum are calculated using averaging over interactions among the particles that form the continuum. A noted expansion of the microscopic modeling methodology into the social systems is a *minority game* (Challet *et al.*, 2001). Its development was inspired by the famous El Farol's bar problem (Arthur, 1994). This problem considers a number of patrons N willing to attend a bar with a number of seats N_s. It is assumed that $N_s < N$ and every patron prefers to stay at home if he expects that the number of people attending the bar will exceed N_s. There is no communication among patrons and they make decisions using only information on past attendance and different predictors (e.g., attendance today is the same as yesterday, or is an average of past attendances).

The minority game is a simple binary choice problem in which players have to choose between two sides, and those on the minority side win. Similarly to El Farol's bar problem, there is no communication among players in the minority game and only a given set of forecasting strategies defines players' decisions. The minority game is an interesting stylized model that has some financial implications (Challet *et al.*, 2001).

Here, I focus on the agent-based models that have become very popular in economics and finance (see the reviews by Hommes, 2006; LeBaron, 2006; Chiarella *et al.*, 2009; Hommes & LeBaron, 2018).

The notion of agents (traders) is used in various models of the dealer markets discussed in Chapter 2. However, the two approaches differ significantly in their assumptions and in the object of research. Namely, the current market microstructure theory is focused primarily on the properties of the order book in equilibrium. In this theory, it is usually assumed that all investors are rational, prices are (partly) exogenous, and returns follow the random walk in the spirit of the EMH.[1] On the contrary, the main goal of agent-based market modeling is to describe how the asset price dynamics is affected by investors' behavior. The deterministic component in the agent-based models implies that financial markets are at least partially predictable, which directly contradicts to the EMH.

The agent-based models are capable of describing several stylized facts observed in financial markets. One of the first agent-based models of financial markets was offered by Beja & Goldman (1980). In this work, two major trading strategies, value investing and trend following, were considered. Beja & Goldman (1980) have shown, in particular, that the system equilibrium may become unstable as the number of trend followers grows. Since then, multiple agent-based models of financial markets have been offered. Some of these models describe, at least qualitatively, market cycles, booms, and crashes (Levy *et al.*, 2000) and reproduce such important empirical properties of returns as power-law scaling in price distributions, and volatility clustering (Lux & Marchesi, 2000).

Current agent-based models of financial markets differ in various ways. Schmidt (2004) discerns two major groups of these models depending on how the process of price discovery is formulated. In the first group that is called the *adaptive equilibrium models*, agents adapt their heterogeneous beliefs using past returns. Price in these models is derived from the supply-demand equilibrium (see, e.g., Brock & Hommes, 1998; Chiarella & He, 2001; LeBaron *et al.*, 1999; Levy *et al.*, 2000). In the second group, the assumption of the equilibrium price is not employed. Instead, price is a dynamic variable determined via its empirical relation to excess demand (Lux, 1998; Farmer & Joshi, 2002). Therefore, this group is called the *non-equilibrium price models*.

In the following two sections, I introduce the main concepts used in deriving both groups of the agent-based models. Then, I describe a parsimonious non-equilibrium price model that is derived exclusively in terms of observable variables (Schmidt, 1999). Finally, I offer two examples of how the agent-based models can be used for describing market liquidity effects. Namely, I formulate a model of birth of a two-sided market (Schmidt, 2000) and a model of the possible effects of technical trading (Schmidt, 2002).

6.2 Adaptive Equilibrium Models

Here, I mostly follow the work of Chiarella & He (2001) for describing the framework of the adaptive equilibrium models. According to this approach, agents can invest either in a risk-free asset or in a risky asset. The risk-free asset is assumed to have an infinite supply and a constant interest rate. Agents are rational and use some risk aversion criterion for maximizing their wealth. Agents may predict future returns using past returns. The solution to the wealth maximization problem yields the agents' demand for the risky asset, which, in turn, determines the asset price in equilibrium.

Specifically, return on a risky asset at time t equals

$$\rho_t = (p_t - p_{t-1} + y_t)/p_{t-1}. \tag{6.1}$$

In (6.1), p_t and y_t are the ex-dividend price and dividend of one share of the risky asset, respectively. The wealth dynamics of agent i is given by

$$W_{i,t+1} = R(1 - \pi_{i,t})W_{i,t} + \pi_{i,t}W_{i,t}(1 + \rho_{t+1})$$
$$= W_{i,t}[R + \pi_{i,t}(\rho_{t+1} - r)]. \tag{6.2}$$

In (6.2), r is the interest rate of the risk-free asset, $R = 1 + r$, and $\pi_{i,t}$ is the proportion of wealth of agent i invested in the risky asset at time t. Every agent is assumed to be a taker of the risky asset at the price that is established in the demand-supply equilibrium. Let's denote $E_{i,t}$ and $V_{i,t}$ as the *beliefs* of trader i at time t regarding the conditional expectation of wealth and the conditional variance of wealth, respectively. It follows from (6.2) that

$$E_{i,t}[W_{i,t+1}] = W_{i,t}[R + \pi_{i,t}(E_{i,t}[\rho_{t+1}] - r)], \qquad (6.3)$$

$$V_{i,t}[W_{i,t+1}] = \pi_{i,t}^2 W_{i,t}^2 V_{i,t}[\rho_{t+1}]. \qquad (6.4)$$

Within this framework, every agent i believes that return of the risky asset is normally distributed with mean $E_{i,t}[\rho_{t+1}]$ and variance $V_{i,t}[\rho_{t+1}]$. The latter is usually assumed to be constant: $V_{i,t}[\rho_{t+1}] = \sigma^2$. Agents choose to invest in the risky asset such a proportion $\pi_{i,t}$ of their wealth that maximizes the utility function U:

$$\max\{E_{i,t}[U(W_{i,t+1})]\}, \pi_{i,t}. \qquad (6.5)$$

The CARA and CRRA utility functions described in Chapter 3 are generally used in the adaptive equilibrium models. In the former case,

$$U(W_{i,t+1}) = E_{i,t}[W_{i,t+1}] - \frac{a}{2}V_{i,t}[W_{i,t+1}]. \qquad (6.6)$$

In (6.6), a is the risk aversion constant. For the constant conditional variance $V_{i,t} = \sigma^2$, the CARA function yields the following demand:

$$\pi_{i,t} = \frac{E_{i,t}[\rho_{t+1}] - r}{a\sigma^2}. \qquad (6.7)$$

The number of shares of the risky asset that corresponds to demand $\pi_{i,t}$ equals

$$N_{i,t} = \pi_{i,t}W_{i,t}/p_t. \qquad (6.8)$$

Since the total number of shares is assumed to be fixed ($\sum N_{i,t} = N = \text{const}$), the market-clearing price equals

$$p_t = \frac{1}{N}\sum \pi_{i,t}W_{i,t}. \qquad (6.9)$$

So far this approach remains within the framework of the classical asset pricing theory. The novelty in adaptive equilibrium models is in that the agents may have heterogeneous beliefs.[2] These beliefs can be described using the following generic form:

$$E_{i,t}[\rho_{t+1}] = f_i(\rho_t, \dots, \rho_{t-Li}). \qquad (6.10)$$

The deterministic function f_i in (6.10) must be specified for describing various trading strategies. Usually, this function depends on past returns with lags up to L_i and may vary for different agents. In many models, the agent type is represented by a single trading strategy. First, there are *fundamentalists* who use analysis of the risky asset fundamentals for forecasting its risk premium. In simple models, the risk premium $\delta_F > 0$ is a constant:

$$E_{F,t}[\rho_{t+1}] = r + \delta_F. \tag{6.11}$$

In the general case, risk premium can be a function of time and/or variance.

Another major strategy is momentum trading (see Chapter 11). Investors who use it are often called *chartists*. They use the history of past returns for making their forecasts. In the general (yet linear) case, their strategy can be described as

$$E_{M,t}[\rho_{t+1}] = r + \delta_M + \sum_{k=1}^{L} a_k \rho_{t-k}. \tag{6.12}$$

In (6.12), $\delta_M > 0$ is a constant component of the momentum risk premium that is responsible for the asset intrinsic value; $a_k > 0$ are the weights of past returns ρ_{t-k}.

Finally, some agents may be *contrarians* who expect market reversal and hence act in the way that is opposite to chartists. The contrarian strategy is formally similar to the momentum strategy (6.12) but has negative weights a_k.

Agents in the adaptive equilibrium models are able to analyze the performance of different strategies and choose the most efficient one. Obviously, these strategies have limited accuracy due to the linear form of forecast and finite number of lags L. Sometimes, such a constrained adaptability is called *bounded rationality*.

Brock & Hommes (1998) offer a discrete analog of the Gibbs probability distribution for the fraction of traders with the strategy i in the limiting case of infinite number of agents

$$N_{i,t} = \exp[\beta(\Phi_{i,t-1} - C_i)]/Z_t, Z_t = \sum_i \exp[\beta(\Phi_{i,t-1} - C_i)]. \tag{6.13}$$

In (6.13), $C_i \geq 0$ is the cost of the strategy i, the parameter β is called the intensity of choice, and $\Phi_{i,t}$ is the fitness function that characterizes the efficiency of strategy i. The natural choice for the fitness function is

$$\Phi_{i,t} = \gamma\Phi_{i,t-1} + \varphi_{i,t}, \quad \varphi_{i,t} = \pi_{i,t}(W_{i,t} - W_{i,t-1})/W_{i,t-1}.$$

$$(6.14)$$

In (6.14), $0 \leq \gamma \leq 1$ is the memory parameter that retains part of past performance in the current strategy.

Adaptive equilibrium models have been studied in several directions. Extensive computational modeling was performed by LeBaron *et al.* (1999) and Levy *et al.* (2000). In the meantime, the system stability and routes to *chaos* have been discussed by Brock & Hommes (1998) and Chiarella & He (2001).

The presence of chaos implies that very small changes in the initial conditions or parameters of a nonlinear dynamical system can lead to drastic changes in its behavior. In the chaotic regime, the system solutions stay within the phase space region named *strange attractor*. These solutions never repeat themselves; they are not periodic and they never intersect. Thus, a system in the chaotic regime is unpredictable (see, e.g., Hilborn, 2000). While it is generally believed that the investor reaction to news is the main cause of price fluctuations (see Chapter 4), it is reasonable to suggest that the intrinsic complexity of financial markets can be partly responsible for the price randomness. If this was the case, it would be another argument in defense of partial price predictability.

While the adaptive equilibrium models may yield strange attractors, there has been little (if any) evidence of chaos in financial and economic time series (LeBaron, 1994; Lux, 1998; Peters, 2000). It should be noted that the adaptive equilibrium models are discrete, i.e., they do not include time explicitly (so-called *maps*). This implies that the interval between the time moments t and $t-1$ is arbitrary. It is known that a single nonlinear map, e.g., a popular *logistic equation*, can produce chaos (Hilborn, 2000; Peters, 2000; Schmidt, 2004). On the contrary, continuous models, including the non-equilibrium price models described in Section 6.3, need at least three coupled equations in order to generate strange attractors. As a result, the same nonlinear dynamical process may exhibit chaos within the discrete framework while its continuous model is perfectly predictable. Hence, some exotic discrete solutions may be the model artifacts rather than manifestations of true events that may happen in the real-world processes.

6.3 Non-Equilibrium Price Models

The basic assumption in the adaptive equilibrium models that the security price is instantly determined by market clearing is a serious simplification. In fact, the number of shares involved in trading varies with time, and prices may deviate from their equilibrium (fair) values for a long time. A reasonable alternative to instant market clearing is a model of price formation that is based on the empirical relation between price change and excess demand (Beja & Goldman, 1980).[3]

Here, I outline an elaborate model offered by Lux (1998). In this model, two groups of agents, chartists and fundamentalists, are considered. Agents can compare the efficiency of different trading strategies and switch from one strategy to another. Therefore, the numbers of chartists, $n_c(t)$, and fundamentalists, $n_f(t)$, vary with time while the total number of agents in the market N is assumed constant. The chartist group, in turn, is subdivided into optimistic (bullish) and pessimistic (bearish) traders with the numbers $n_+(t)$ and $n_-(t)$, respectively:

$$n_c(t) + n_f(t) = N, n_+(t) + n_-(t) = n_c(t). \qquad (6.15)$$

Lux (1998) considers several patterns of trader behavior. First, chartists are influenced by the peer opinion (so-called *mimetic contagion*). Second, traders switch strategies while seeking optimal performance. Finally, traders may exit and reenter markets. As a result, the bullish chartist dynamics is formalized in the following way:

$$dn_+/dt = \text{"mimetic contagion"} + \text{"strategy change"}$$
$$+ \text{"market entry/exit"}$$
$$= (n_- p_{+-} - n_+ p_{-+})(1 - n_f/N)$$
$$+ n_f n_+ (p_{+f} - p_{f+})/N + (b - a)n_+. \qquad (6.16)$$

In (6.16), p_α denotes the probability of transition from group β to group α, and the probabilities of market entry and exit satisfy the relation $bn_c = aN$. The bearish chartist dynamics is described similarly

$$dn_-/dt = (n_+p_{-+} - n_-p_{+-})(1 - n_f/N) + n_f n_-(p_{-f} - p_{f-})/N$$
$$+ (b - a)n_-. \qquad (6.17)$$

It is assumed that traders enter the market using the chartist strategy. Therefore, constant total number of traders yields the relation $b = aN/n_c$. Equations (6.15)–(6.17) describe the dynamics of three trader groups (n_f, n_+, n_-) assuming that all transfer probabilities $p_{\alpha\beta}$ are determined.

Conversion of the bullish chartists into the bearish chartists is given by the following relation:

$$p_{+-} = 1/p_{-+} = \nu_1 \exp(-U_1), U_1 = \alpha_1(n_+ - n_-)/n_c$$
$$+ (\alpha_2/\nu_1)dP/dt. \qquad (6.18)$$

In (6.18), ν_1, α_1, and α_2 are the model parameters, P is price. Conversion of fundamentalists into bullish chartists and back is described with the relations

$$p_{+f} = 1/p_{f+} = \nu_2 \exp(-U_{21}),$$
$$U_{21} = \alpha_3((r + \nu_2^{-1}dP/dt)/P - R - s|(P_f - P)/P|). \qquad (6.19)$$

In (6.19), ν_2 and α_3 are the model parameters, r is the stock dividend, R is the average revenue of economy, s is a discounting factor $0 < s < 1$, and P_f is the fundamental price of the risky asset assumed to be an input parameter. Similar relations are used to describe the conversion of fundamentalists into bearish chartists, p_{-f}

$$p_{-f} = 1/p_{f-} = \nu_2 \exp(-U_{22}),$$
$$U_{22} = \alpha_3(R - (r + \nu_2^{-1}dP/dt)/P - s|(P_f - P)/P|). \qquad (6.20)$$

As was pointed out earlier, price dynamics in the non-equilibrium price models is described with an empirical relation between the price change and the excess demand[4]

$$dP/dt = \beta D. \qquad (6.21)$$

In the Lux (1998) model, excess demand equals

$$D = t_c(n_+ - n_-) + \gamma n_f(P_f - P). \qquad (6.22)$$

The first and second terms in the right-hand side of (6.22) describe excess demands of chartists and fundamentalists, respectively; β, t_c, and γ are the model parameters.

The Lux (1998) model has rich dynamic properties. Depending on the input parameters, its solutions may include stable equilibrium, periodic patterns, and chaotic attractors. Lux & Marchesi (2000) extended this model for describing arrival of news, which affects the fundamental price. Namely, the news arrival process was modeled with the Gaussian random variable $\varepsilon(t)$ so that

$$\ln P_f(t) - \ln P_f(t-1) = \varepsilon(t). \tag{6.23}$$

This allows for describing such stylized market facts as power-law scaling in the price distribution and volatility clustering.

6.4   The Observable Variables Model

One may notice that there is a degree of arbitrariness in agent-based modeling as the number of different agent types and their behavior can vary upon the modeler's imagination. This is not that innocuous since some interesting model properties (e.g., chaos) can be artifacts of the model's complexity that are irrelevant to real market dynamics (Schmidt, 2004).

Schmidt (1999) has offered a parsimonious approach to choosing variables in agent-based modeling of financial markets. Namely, Schmidt (1999) suggested that only observable variables should be used in deriving the agent-based models. The observable variables in finance are defined as those that can be retrieved or calculated from the records of market events. They include traders' order submissions and cancellations, and transactions.[5] The numbers of agents of different types generally are not observable. Indeed, one cannot discern chartists and fundamentalists in such a typical situation when price is growing (falling) being lower (higher) than the fundamental one. In this case, all traders (let alone contrarians) would rather buy (sell) than sell (buy). Only price and the total numbers of buyers and sellers are always observable. Whether a trader becomes a buyer or seller can be defined by mixing different behavior patterns in the individual trader decision-making rules.

A simple non-equilibrium price model derived along these lines has a constant number of traders, N, including buyers $N_+(t)$ and sellers $N_-(t)$:

$$N_+(t) + N_-(t) = N. \tag{6.24}$$

The dynamics of scaled numbers of buyers, $n_+(t) = N_+(t)/N$, and sellers, $n_-(t) = N_-(t)/N$, is described with the following equations:

$$\frac{dn_+}{dt} = v_{+-}n_- - v_{-+}n_+, \tag{6.25}$$

$$\frac{dn_-}{dt} = v_{-+}n_+ - v_{+-}n_-. \tag{6.26}$$

The factors v_{+-} and v_{-+} characterize the probabilities for transfer from seller to buyer and back, respectively:

$$v_{+-} = 1/v_{-+} = \nu \exp(U), \quad U = \alpha p^{-1}\frac{dp}{dt} + \beta(1-p). \tag{6.27}$$

In (6.27), price $p(t)$ is given in units of its fundamental value. The first term in the utility function U characterizes the chartist behavior, while the second term describes the fundamentalist pattern. The factor ν has the sense of the frequency of transitions between the seller and buyer behavior. Since $n_+(t) = 1-n_-(t)$, the system (6.25)–(6.26) is reduced to the equation

$$\frac{dn_+}{dt} = v_{+-}(1 - n_+) - v_{-+}n_+. \tag{6.28}$$

The price formation equation is assumed to have the following form:

$$\frac{dp}{dt} = \gamma D. \tag{6.29}$$

In (6.29), the excess demand, D, is proportional to the excess number of buyers.

$$D = d(n_+ - n_-) = d(2n_+ - 1). \tag{6.30}$$

6.4.1 *Modeling price–demand relationship*

The model described above is defined with two observable variables: $n_+(t)$ and $p(t)$. In equilibrium, the number of buyers and sellers are equal, and price equals the fundamental values:

$$n_+ = n_- = 0.5, \quad p = 1. \tag{6.31}$$

The necessary stability condition for this model is (Schmidt, 1999)

$$\theta = \alpha\delta\gamma\nu \leq 1 + \varepsilon. \tag{6.32}$$

In the continuous limit, $\varepsilon = 0$. However, the numerical solution on a finite-difference grid leads to some computational noise characterized with a finite ε. Violation of the condition (6.32) leads to system instability, which can be interpreted as a market crash.

When the condition (6.32) is satisfied, weak perturbations to the equilibrium values quickly decay (see an example in Fig. 6.1).

Lower values of α and g suppress oscillations of price and facilitate relaxation of the initial perturbations. On the contrary, raising α, which controls the strength of the chartist behavior, increases price volatility.

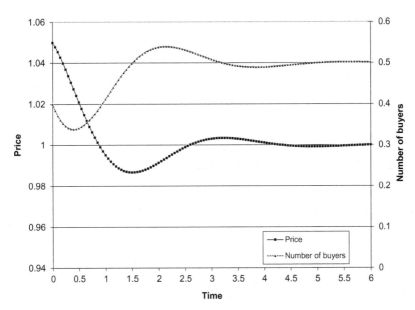

Fig. 6.1. Decay of perturbations to equilibrium state in the observable-variables model with $\alpha = 1$, $\beta = 10$, $\gamma = 0.2$, and $\delta = 1$.

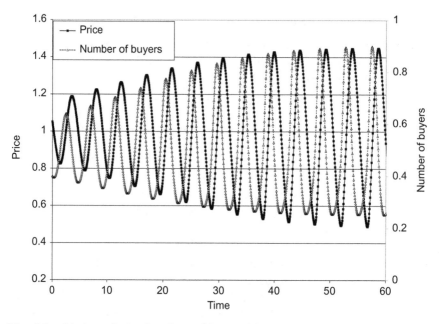

Fig. 6.2. Limit cycle in the observable-variables model with $\alpha = 1.05$, $\beta = 1$, $\gamma = 1$, and $\delta = 1$.

When the value of θ is close to violation of the condition (6.32), price oscillations do not decay; rather, they exhibit the so-called *limit cycle* (Schmidt, 2004). An example of such behavior is shown in Fig. 6.2. Further growth of θ leads to ever-growing oscillation amplitudes, which may be interpreted as a market crash.

6.4.2 *Why technical trading may be successful*

Various technical strategies will be reviewed in Chapter 11. In this section, I offer an application of the observable variables model that shows how trader behavior can affect profitability of technical trading (Schmidt, 2002).

Consider a system with the fixed number of traders N that consists of regular traders N_R and technical traders N_T. The regular traders N_R are divided into buyers, $N_+(t)$, and sellers, $N_-(t)$:

$$N_T + N_R = N = \text{const}, \quad N_+ + N_- = N_R = \text{const}. \quad (6.33)$$

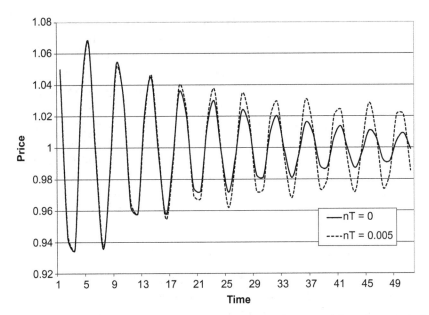

Fig. 6.3. Price dynamics for the observable-variables model with technical traders with $\alpha = \gamma = 1 = \delta = 1$, and $\beta = 4$.

The scaled numbers of regular traders, $n_+(t) = N_+(t)/N$ and $n_-(t) = N_-(t)/N$, and price discovery are described with Eqs. (6.25)–(6.29). The excess demand in this model includes also the technical traders $n_T = N_T/N$

$$D = \delta(n_+ - n_- + Fn_T). \qquad (6.34)$$

In (6.34), the function F defines the technical trader strategy. Schmidt (2002) considered a simple technical rule: *buying on dips–selling on tops*. Namely, technical traders buy at the moment when the price starts rising and sell when the price starts falling

$$F(k) = 1, \quad \text{when} \quad p(k) > p(k-1) \quad \text{and} \quad p(k-1) < p(k-2)$$

$$= -1, \quad \text{when} \quad p(k) < p(k-1) \quad \text{and} \quad p(k-1) > p(k-2)$$

$$= 0, \quad \text{otherwise.} \qquad (6.35)$$

Figure 6.3 shows that the inclusion of the "technical" traders in the model strengthens price oscillations, which increases return on their strategy. Indeed, if technical traders decide that price is going to fall, they sell and thus decrease the excess demand. Due to the selling pressure, price does fall, and the chartist component in the regular traders' behavior motivates them to sell, too. This suppresses price further until the fundamentalist component in the regular traders' behavior becomes overwhelming. The opposite effect occurs if the technical traders decide that it is time to buy: they increase demand and price starts to grow until it notably exceeds its fundamental value. Then, regular traders start selling. In other words, if the concerted actions of technical traders produce a noticeable market impact, they can provoke the regular traders to amplify this trend. As a result, price moves in the direction favorable to the technical strategy.

6.4.3   *Modeling the birth of a two-sided market*

The founders of a new market face many challenges. In particular, they must attract both buyers and sellers immediately at the opening their market for trading. This may be a real problem since investors are used to trade in well-established markets. Indeed, right after opening a new market, its order book is empty. A casual buyer may submit an order. But if he does not see sellers for some time, he cancels his order and places it elsewhere. Then a seller may show up — and leave with the same outcome. In short, trading cannot start until sufficient number of traders is present on both sides of the market. Schmidt (2000) offered a model describing the birth of a two-sided market[6]:

$$\frac{dn_+}{dt} = v_{+-}n_- - v_{-+}n_+ + \sum_i R_{+i} + \rho_+, \qquad (6.36)$$

$$\frac{dn_-}{dt} = v_{-+}n_+ - v_{+-}n_- + \sum_i R_{-i} + \rho_-. \qquad (6.37)$$

Here, $R_{ki}(k = +, -; i = 1, 2, \ldots, M)$ and ρ_k are the deterministic and stochastic rates of entering and exiting the market, respectively. Three deterministic effects defining the total number of traders are considered in this model, i.e., $M = 3$. First, some traders stop trading immediately after completing a trade since they have limited resources and/or need some time for making new decisions:

$$R_{+1} = R_{-1} = -bn_+n_-, \quad b > 0. \qquad (6.38)$$

Second, some traders currently present in the market will enter the market again and possibly will bring in some newcomers (mimetic contagion). Therefore, the inflow of traders is proportional to the number of traders present in the market:

$$R_{+2} = R_{-2} = a(n_+ + n_-), \quad a > 0. \tag{6.39}$$

And finally, some unsatisfied traders leave the market. Namely, it is assumed that those traders who are not able to find the trading counterparts within some time exit the market:

$$R_{+3} = -c(n_+ - n_-) \quad \text{if} \quad n_+ > n_-$$

$$= 0, \quad \text{if} \quad n_+ \leq n_-, \tag{6.40}$$

$$R_{-3} = -c(n_- - n_+) \quad \text{if} \quad n_- > n_+$$

$$= 0, \quad \text{if} \quad n_- \leq n_+. \tag{6.41}$$

The parameter $c > 0$ in (6.40) and (6.41) is called the *impatience factor*. To simplify the model, Schmidt (2000b) neglected stochastic rates and transfers from seller to buyer and back. Hence,

$$\rho_+ = \rho_- = v_{+-} = v_{-+} = 0. \tag{6.42}$$

If the initial state has imbalance of buyers and sellers, i.e.,

$$n_+(0) - n_-(0) = \delta > 0, \tag{6.43}$$

then Eqs. (6.36), (6.37), and (6.43) can be transformed into the following:

$$\frac{dn_+}{dt} = a(n_+ + n_-) - bn_+n_- - c(n_+ - n_-), \tag{6.44}$$

$$\frac{dn_-}{dt} = a(n_+ + n_-) - bn_+n_-. \tag{6.45}$$

It follows from (6.44) and (6.45) that the equation for the total number of traders $n = n_+ + n_-$ has the Riccati form and can be transformed into the Schrodinger equation with the Morse-type potential[7] (Schmidt, 2000b)

$$\frac{dn}{dt} = 2an - 0.5bn^2 + 0.5b\delta^2 \exp(-2ct) - c\delta \exp(-ct). \tag{6.46}$$

Equation (6.46) has the following asymptotic stationary solution at $t \to \infty$:

$$n_\infty = 4a/b. \tag{6.47}$$

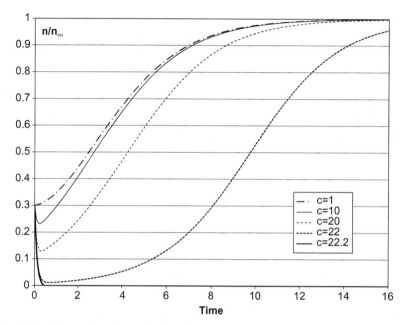

Fig. 6.4. Dynamics of the birth of a two-sided market for $a = 0.25$, $b = 1$, $n(0) = 0.3$, $\delta = 0.1$, $\tau = 0.1$, and different values of the impatience factor, c.

A finite-difference solution to Eq. (6.46) in units of n_∞ with the time step τ of 0.1 is shown in Fig. 6.4 for $a = 0.25$, $b = 1$, $n(0) = 0.3$, $\delta = 0.1$, and different values of the impatience factor, c. Obviously, the higher is impatience, the deeper is the minimum of $n(t)$, which delays the birth of a liquid market. At sufficiently high values of c, the finite-difference solution to (6.46) falls to zero. For the latter parameter set, this happens at $c > 22$. The analytic solution, however, never reaches zero and always approaches the asymptotic value (6.47) after passing the minimum. This points to the drawback of the continuous model: by choosing a sufficiently high value of the impatience factor, one may get a minimum of $n(t)$ smaller than one trader and still approach non-zero asymptotic solution (6.47), which does not make sense. Obviously, we expect from the model to yield the zero solution (i.e., failed birth of a liquid market) in the case with highly impatient traders. Therefore, a discrete analog of (6.46) along with a constraint on the minimal value of $n_\pm(t)$ is preferable.

Notes

1. Some structural models do permit persistent impact of trading on price. See, however, note 7 for Chapter 3.
2. Importance of heterogeneous beliefs is sometimes reflected in the model's name: *heterogeneous agent model.*
3. Similar assumption is used in some market microstructure models (e.g., Kyle, 1985) for describing impact of trading (see Chapter 2).
4. Log price in the left-hand side of (6.21) might be a better choice in order to avoid possible negative price values that may occur in simulations (Farmer & Joshi, 2002).
5. Observable financial market variables may not necessarily be publicly available due to the privacy regulations.
6. A similar model can be used for describing the mating dynamics where only agents of the opposite sex interact and deactivate each other, at least temporarily.
7. The Morse potential has the following form (Landau & Livshitz, 1989): $U(x) = 2C \exp(-2cx) - C \exp(-cx)$.

Part III
Portfolio Management

Chapter 7

Mean–Variance Portfolio Theory

7.1 Introduction

I begin this chapter with the basic ideas used in portfolio selection. First, I consider a combination of two risky assets and a combination of a risky asset and a risk-free asset. Then, I introduce the classical mean–variance portfolio theory in Section 7.3. I describe two approaches to the problem of portfolio diversification, namely, replacement of Pearson's correlations with partial correlations and so-called diversity booster in Section 7.4. Finally, I conclude this chapter by discussing the concept of the ESG optimal portfolios in Section 7.5.

7.2 Portfolio Selection

Investing is an important real-life problem that has been translated into several mathematical theories.[1] In general, opportunities for investing include financial assets (such as equities, bonds, foreign currency) and physical assets (so-called *real assets*). The latter include real estate, land, commodities, infrastructure, and antique, among others. Here, I consider portfolios that contain only financial assets.

There is no single strategy for selection of investor portfolio since there is always a trade-off between the expected return on portfolio and the risk of portfolio losses. Risk-free assets such as the US Treasury bills and bank CDs guarantee some return, but it is generally believed that stocks provide higher returns in the long run. Unfortunately, the notion of "long run" is doomed to bear an element of uncertainty. Alas, a decade of market growth may end up with a market crash that evaporates significant part of the equity wealth of entire generation. Hence, risk aversion (that is generally well correlated with investor's age) is a very important factor in investment strategies.[2] It is well known that diversification of investments mitigates their risk. Therefore, implementing optimal portfolios that satisfy investor's sensitivity to both risk and reward is an essential topic in portfolio management.

Portfolio selection has two major steps (e.g., Bodie & Merton, 1998; Elton *et al.*, 2009). First, it is the selection of a combination of one risky and one risk-free assets. And second, it is the selection of risky assets. Let's start with the first step.

7.2.1 *Portfolio with one risky asset and one risk-free asset*

If the portion of the risky asset in the portfolio is $w \leq 1$, then the expected portfolio return equals

$$E[R_p] = wE[R_r] + (1 - w)R_f = R_f + w(E[R_r] - R_f). \quad (7.1)$$

In (7.1), R_f and R_r are rates of returns of the risk-free and risky assets, respectively. In the classical portfolio theory, risk is measured with portfolio volatility[3] that is characterized by the standard deviation of portfolio return σ_p. Since no risk is associated with the risk-free asset, portfolio risk in this case equals

$$\sigma_p = w\sigma_r. \quad (7.2)$$

Substituting α from (7.2) into (7.1) yields

$$E[R_p] = r_f + \sigma_p(E[R_r] - R_f)/\sigma_r. \quad (7.3)$$

The dependence of expected return on portfolio risk is called *risk-return trade-off line* or *capital allocation line* (CAL). The slope of the straight line (7.3), s, is a measure of return in excess of the risk-free return per unit of risk

$$s = (E[R_r] - R_f)/\sigma_r. \quad (7.4)$$

Recall that (7.4) represents the definition of the Sharpe ratio (5.28). Obviously, investing in a risky asset makes sense only if $s > 0$, that is, $E[R_r] > R_f$. In general, the mean–variance portfolio theory is not applicable to bear markets.

Investor's decisions may be driven by the mean–variance utility function with a coefficient of risk aversion λ

$$U = E[R_p] - 0.5\lambda\sigma_p^2. \tag{7.5}$$

The utility function (7.5) is closely related to the CRRA function (see Section 2.3), which follows from the utility approximation offered by Levy & Markowitz (1979)

$$E[U(1 + R_p)] \approx E[R_p] + U(1 + R_p) + 0.5U''(1 + E[R_p])\text{var}(R_p). \tag{7.6}$$

In (7.6), U'' denotes the second derivative of the utility function. The optimal weight that maximizes the utility function (7.5) for a portfolio with one risky and one risk-free asset equals

$$w_{\text{opt}} = (E[R_r] - R_f)/(\lambda\sigma_r^2). \tag{7.7}$$

Utility functions are sometimes called *indifference curves* as they indicate that investor with a chosen level of risk aversion and utility value may accept various combinations of portfolio risk and return. Another related concept is the utility *certainty equivalent*: the risk-free return that yields the chosen utility value (Ang, 2014). In the σ_p–R_p plane, the certainty equivalent is the intercept of the indifference curve at $\sigma_p = 0$.

The most commonly accepted measures of the coefficient of risk aversion lie between 1 and 3, but there is a wide range of estimates in the literature — from as low as 0.2 to 10, and even higher (Gandelman & Hernández-Murillo, 2014). Ang (2014) offers an estimate of $\lambda = 2.8$ for a popular 60%/40% stock/bond portfolio ratio.

7.2.2 *Portfolio with two risky assets*

On the second step of portfolio selection, consider portfolio that consists of two risky assets with returns R_1 and R_2, and the standard deviations σ_1 and σ_2, respectively. If the weight of the risky asset 1 in the portfolio is $w \leq 1$, then portfolio return and its variance equal,

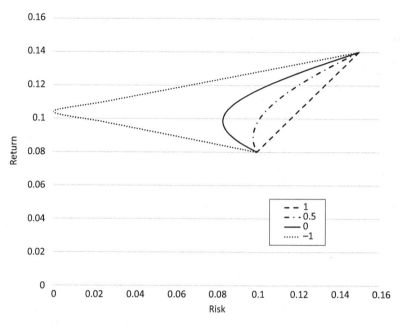

Fig. 7.1. Mean–variance frontier for two-asset portfolio with various asset correlations ρ_{12}.

respectively,

$$E[R_p] = wE[R_1] + (1 - w)E[R_2], \tag{7.8}$$

$$\sigma_p^2 = w^2\sigma_1^2 + (1 - w)^2\sigma_2^2 + 2w(1 - w)\sigma_{12}. \tag{7.9}$$

In (7.9), σ_{12} is covariance between returns of asset 1 and asset 2 that can be expressed in terms of the correlation coefficient ρ_{12}

$$\sigma_{12} = \rho_{12}\sigma_1\sigma_2. \tag{7.10}$$

Markowitz (1952) suggested that investors should choose portfolio with minimum variance (i.e., with minimum risk) among all possible portfolios located on the risk-return trade-off line. This idea is the bedrock of the MVPT that is sometimes called *modern portfolio theory*. The risk-return trade-off curve for a *mean–variance portfolio* (MVP) with risky assets is also called *mean–variance frontier*. It is usually convex to the left (unless the portfolio assets are perfectly correlated and its tip corresponds to the minimum variance portfolio (see Fig. 7.1 for various ρ_{12}). The locus of the mean–variance frontier with expected returns higher than that of the minimum-variance portfolio (MinVP) is called *efficient frontier*. It represents the highest expected returns at given risk levels.

Now, assume for simplicity that the asset returns are uncorrelated, that is, $\sigma_{12} = 0$. Then the value of w that yields minimal risk for this portfolio equals

$$w_m = \sigma_2^2/(\sigma_1^2 + \sigma_2^2). \tag{7.11}$$

This value yields the minimal portfolio risk σ_{pm}

$$\sigma_{pm}^2 = \sigma_1^2\sigma_2^2/(\sigma_1^2 + \sigma_2^2). \tag{7.12}$$

Consider an example with $E[R_1] = 0.1$, $E[R_2] = 0.2$, $\sigma_1 = 0.15$, $\sigma_2 = 0.3$. Then $w_m = 0.8$, $\sigma_{pm} \approx 0.134 < \sigma_1 < \sigma_2$ and $E[R_p] = 0.12 > E[R_1]$. Hence, adding a more risky asset 2 with higher return to asset 1 decreases portfolio risk and increases portfolio return. This somewhat surprising outcome demonstrates the advantage of portfolio diversification. Obviously, when $\sigma_{12} < 0$, the benefits of diversification become even more transparent.

In the case of portfolio with N uncorrelated assets, portfolio variance equals

$$\sigma_p^2 = \sum w^2\sigma_i^2 = \frac{1}{N^2}\sum \sigma_i^2 = \frac{1}{N}\bar{\sigma}_p^2, \tag{7.13}$$

where $\bar{\sigma}_p^2$ is the average of the portfolio asset variances that does not depend on N. Hence, portfolio variance decreases with growing N, and inclusion of uncorrelated assets in portfolio reduces its risk.

Investors often prefer portfolios with maximum Sharpe to minimum variance portfolio. For portfolio with two risky assets, the maximum of (7.4) yields the following weight of asset 1

$$w_{\text{max\_s}} = \frac{(E[r_1] - r_f)\sigma_2^2 - (E[r_2] - r_f)\sigma_{12}}{(E[r_1] - r_f)\sigma_2^2 + (E[r_2] - r_f)\sigma_1^2}. \tag{7.14}$$
$$-(E[r_1] - r_f + E[r_2] - r_f)\sigma_{12}$$

7.2.3 *Portfolio with two risky assets and one risk-free asset*

Finally, let's combine risk-free asset with portfolio that contains two risky assets. The optimal combination of a risky asset portfolio and a risk-free asset can be found at the tangency point between the

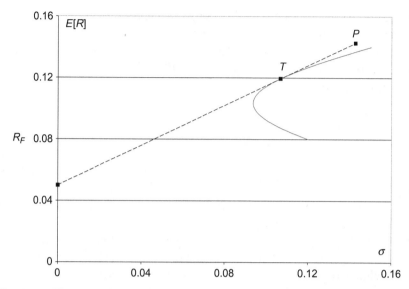

Fig. 7.2.   The capital allocation line for portfolio with risk-free asset (dashed line) and risky assets (solid line).

straight CAL with the intercept $E[R_p] = R_f$ and the risk-return trade-off curve for the risky asset portfolio (see Fig. 7.2). For portfolio with two risky uncorrelated assets, the weight of the asset 1 at the tangency point T equals

$$w_T = (E[R_1] - R_f)\sigma_2^2/\{(E[R_1] - R_f)\sigma_2^2 + (E[R_2] - R_f)\sigma_1^2\}. \tag{7.15}$$

Substituting w_T from (7.15) into (7.8) and (7.9) yields the coordinates of the tangency point (denoted as $E[R_{pT}]$ and σ_{pT}, respectively). Portfolio at the tangency point T is called *super-efficient portfolio*. A similar approach can be used in the general case with an arbitrary number of risky assets.

Return $E[R_{pT}]$ for portfolio with risk σ_{pT} is "as good as it gets." Is it possible to have returns higher than $E[R_{pT}]$ while investing in the same portfolio? In other words, is it possible to reach say point P on the risk-return trade-off line depicted in Fig. 7.2? Yes, if you *borrow* money at rate R_f and invest it in the portfolio with $w = w_T$. However, the investment risk is then higher than σ_{pT}.

7.3 The Markowitz Model

According to the MVPT, the optimization problem for MVP with N risky assets can be formulated in the following way

$$\min_{w_i \in Q} \left[U_{\text{MVPT}} = 0.5\lambda \sum_{i,j=1}^{N} w_i w_j \sigma_{ij} - \sum_{i=1}^{N} w_i r_i \right]. \quad (7.16)$$

In (7.16), w_i and r_i are portfolio weights and expected returns, respectively, λ is coefficient of risk aversion, and σ_{ij} is covariance. The first and the second terms in U_{MVPT} are related to portfolio variance and expected return, respectively,

$$\sigma_p^2 = \sum_{i,j=1}^{N} w_i w_j \sigma_{ij}, \quad (7.17)$$

$$E[r_p] = \sum_{i=1}^{N} w_i r_i. \quad (7.18)$$

U_{MVPT} in (7.16) has the sign opposite to that of in (7.5) because it is used for formulation of the minimization problem. Q is a subset of admissible values of the portfolio weights w_i that satisfy the constraint

$$\sum_{i=1}^{N} w_i = 1. \quad (7.19)$$

Since it is not easy to estimate individual investor's risk aversion, the MVP problem is usually formulated in terms of a target portfolio return μ

$$\min_{w_i \in Q} \sum_{i,j=1}^{N} w_i w_j \sigma_{ij}, \quad (7.20)$$

$$\text{subject to} \sum_{i=1}^{N} w_i r_i = \mu. \quad (7.21)$$

This implies that $\lambda = E[r_p]/\mu$. The linear problem (7.19)–(7.21) can be solved analytically using the Lagrange multiplier method (see, e.g., Luenberger, 1998). The Lagrangian in this case equals

$$L = \sum_{i,j=1}^{N} w_i w_j \sigma_{ij} - \alpha \left(\sum_{i=1}^{N} w_i r_i - \mu \right) - \beta \left(\sum_{i=1}^{N} w_i r_i - 1 \right) = 0.$$

$$(7.22)$$

In (7.22), α and β are the Lagrange multipliers to be calculated along with N values of w_i. Taking derivatives $\delta L/\delta w_i$ and equating them to zero yields N equations

$$\sum_{j=1}^{N} w_j \sigma_{ij} - \alpha r_i - \beta = 0, \quad i = 1, 2, \ldots, N. \qquad (7.23)$$

These equations along with the constraints (7.19) and (7.21) can be used for calculating α, β, and portfolio weights.

If portfolio contains N risky assets and a risk-free asset with return r_f, the constraint (7.19) is not necessary and the minimization problem (7.20) is subject to the condition

$$\left(1 - \sum_{i=1}^{N} w_i \right) r_f + \sum_{i=1}^{N} w_i r_i = \mu. \qquad (7.24)$$

In this case, the optimal Sharpe portfolio is at the tangency point between the CAL and the risky asset efficient frontier (see Fig. 7.2). Hence, the optimal Sharpe portfolio with risky and risk-free assets does not depend on investor's risk aversion.

The solution to the mean–variance problem (7.20) and (7.24) can be expressed in the following matrix form

$$\boldsymbol{w}_{\min} = \gamma \sum^{-1} (\boldsymbol{r} - r_f \mathbf{1}), \quad \gamma = \sigma_{\min}^2/(\mu - r_f), \qquad (7.25)$$

where $\boldsymbol{r}$ is $N \times 1$ vector of $\{r_i\}$, $\mathbf{1}$ is $N \times 1$ vector of ones, $\sum$ is covariance matrix, and $\sigma_{\min}^2$ is the minimized variance

$$\sigma_{\min}^2 = \frac{(\mu - r_f)^2}{(\boldsymbol{r} - r_f \mathbf{1})' \sum^{-1} (\boldsymbol{r} - r_f \mathbf{1})}. \qquad (7.26)$$

Various constraints, including the limits on transaction costs, regulatory and discretionary exposure constraints may be imposed by portfolio manager (see for a review, Kolm *et al.*, 2014). Some popular constraints include (but are not limited to)

- Long-only constraint for avoiding (sometimes extreme) short positions.

$$w_i \geq 0. \qquad (7.27)$$

Jagannathan & Ma (2003) show that the long-only constraints are equivalent to reducing the estimated stock covariance with other stocks. Also, implementing short positions requires borrowing assets from broker, which may significantly increase portfolio losses if the market moves in adverse direction. Therefore, portfolio managers often impose long-only constraints.
- Holding constraints for avoiding overly concentrated portfolios:

$$w_M \geq w_i \geq w_m. \qquad (7.28)$$

In (7.28) w_M and w_m are the preferred maximum and minimum portfolio weights, respectively.
- Tracking error (TE) minimization constraint:

$$\text{var}(r_P - r_B) \leq \sigma_{\text{TE}}^2. \qquad (7.29)$$

In (7.29), r_B is return of a benchmark portfolio (e.g., S&P 500 Index).

If all MVP constraints are linear in terms of w_i, (7.20) represents a *quadratic problem* that can be solved using standard numerical optimization software packages. Non-linear constraints may need more sophisticated methods (see Fabozzi *et al.*, 2007). In general, the optimal solutions that satisfy various constraints can be found by comparing portfolio variances and/or Sharpe ratios computed for various values of μ.

While the MVPT has become a textbook material, its practical application is complicated with its high sensitivity to estimation errors of covariance matrix and expected returns. Chopra & Ziemba (1993) have shown that the MVP performance is much more sensitive (up to ten times higher) to the estimation errors in expected returns. Several robust optimization techniques can be used to mitigate this problem (see Section 8.4).

Another drawback with MVPs is that they are not well diversified (Green & Hollifield, 1992). As a result, equal-weight portfolios (EWPs) sometimes outperform MVPs (DeMiguel *et al.*, 2009;

Duchin & Levy, 2009; Tu & Zhou, 2009).[4] However, portfolios with a few assets may have a very high variance, and portfolio diversification is a common practice for reducing portfolio risk.[5] I discuss this topic the next section.

7.4   Portfolio Diversification

7.4.1   *Introductory comments*

Poor diversity of MVPs is associated with another problem: MVPs with unconstrained weights can have extreme (sometimes greater than 100%) long and short positions (Jacobs *et al.*, 2013). This is the result of the implicit assumption of the persistent momentum that is made in the mean–variance optimization protocol. Namely, the assets that outperformed (underperformed) in the recent past will continue to outperform (underperform) in the future. Hence, implementation of MVPs with unconstrained weights often implies buying a small subset of original portfolio assets that significantly outperformed in the recent past and shorting the assets that underperformed in the recent past.[6] While momentum can sometimes generate notable profits (see Chapter 11), it doesn't last forever. That is why diversification is very useful for mitigating market risk.

Here, I describe two approaches for increasing diversity of long-only MVPs. The first one is based on replacing Pearson's correlations with partial correlations conditioned on the state of the economy that is mimicked for the US equity market by the S&P 500 SPDR ETF SPY (Nadler & Schmidt, 2014a).

In the second approach, the mean–variance minimizing objective function U_{MVPT} is expanded with additional terms that explicitly strengthen diversification. In particular, Meucci (2009) introduced the diversification distribution, i.e., the distribution of the uncorrelated bets in the portfolio and then used the entropy of this distribution as an additional term in U_{MVPT}. Here I focus on the idea to expand U_{MVPT} with the term similar to the Herfindahl–Hirschman index that I call *diversity booster* (Bouchaud *et al.*, 1997; Schmidt, 2018).

7.4.2   *Partial correlations-based mean variance*

Before discussing the economic motivation for using partial correlations in portfolio theory, let's start with an instructive example from statistical physics. The term "like-charge attraction" sounds like an oxymoron since the classical Coulomb's law states that like charges repel each other. However, the Coulomb's law is valid in vacuum (or, more generally, in a dielectric continuum). If like-charged particles are immersed in an electrolyte, their charges may become completely screened by the electrolyte counter-ions. This effect can appear in the case of large particles with small charges and/or multi-valent electrolyte counter-ions. As a result, the particles effectively interact as if they are neutral (see for a review, Schmidt, 2003). The obvious lesson from this digression is that in order to describe *true* particle interactions, one should filter out the collective effects caused by particle interactions with the medium.

By the same token, in order to describe true correlations between asset returns, one may want to filter out market trend that affects price dynamics of individual stocks. Indeed, according to the capital asset pricing model[7] (CAPM), one may expect that in a trending market, most of equity prices follow the trend, which increases their Pearson's correlations with each other. On the contrary, partial correlations between individual assets that are conditioned on the market return describe co-movements of the excess asset returns unaffected by market momentum. As a result, partial correlations are lower than the corresponding Pearson's correlations, and partial correlation based MVPs (PaMVPs) are more diversified than Pearson's correlation based MVPs (PeMVPs). This is the motivation to modify the Markowitz model by replacing Pearson's correlations with partial correlations.

It should be noted that the idea of substituting Pearson's correlations in the MVPT with other measures of co-movements of returns is not novel: DeMiguel *et al.* (2013), and Gerber *et al.* (2015) used implied volatility and so-called robust co-movement measure, respectively, instead of Pearson's correlations. Partial correlations were used also in other financial applications (Kenett *et al.*, 2010, 2012, 2015; Tumminello *et al.*, 2010).

Partial covariances and correlations are defined with formulas (A.17)–(A.19) in Appendix A. Portfolio variance in terms of partial covariance $\sigma_{ij|m}$ equals

$$\sigma_p^2 = \sum_{i,j=1}^{N} w_i w_j \sigma_{ij|m}. \tag{7.30}$$

Index m in $\sigma_{ij|m}$ refers to the market return on which returns of securities i and j are conditioned. Therefore, Eq. (7.30) should be used instead of (7.17) for deriving PaMVP.

Nadler & Schmidt (2014a) considered a portfolio formed with 12 major US equity sector ETFs (denoted further as 12USETF) and found that Pearson's correlations between these ETFs and SPY are strongly positive. However, the corresponding partial correlations conditioned on SPY are not only notably weaker but even can be negative (see Tables 7.1 and 7.2).

The differences between the Pearson's correlations and partial correlations can be visualized using financial correlation-based networks (Tumminello *et al.*, 2010). In these networks, financial assets are the nodes and the network edges are assigned the weights being some functions of correlations between the assets. Various definitions of the network edge weights are used in the literature (Mantegna & Stanley, 2000). Nadler & Schmidt (2014a) have chosen the Pearson's distance

$$d = 1 - \rho. \tag{7.31}$$

In (7.31), ρ is either ρ_{ij} or $\rho_{ij|k}$ for the Pearson's and partial correlation networks, respectively.

Correlation-based networks for the 12USETF returns in 2013 are plotted in Figs. 7.3 and 7.4 for Pearson's and partial correlations, respectively. Only the edges with statistically significant correlations whose p-values satisfy the condition $p < 0.1$ are shown. The edges with positive and negative correlations are drawn using the thick and thin lines, respectively. Pearson's correlation-based networks had the same structure each year during the period 2007–2015. However, partial correlation-based networks may vary significantly from year to year. Some ETFs might have only negative partial correlations with all other ETFs, e.g., the Technology ETF, XLK, in 2013 (see Fig. 7.4).

Further in this chapter, I discuss the maximum Sharpe MVPs. The data in Table 7.3 for the 12USETF portfolio show that PaMVPs are much more diversified than PeMVPs with the exclusion of the bear market of 2008.

Performance of MVPs out of sample is very sensitive to the model calibration window used for estimating portfolio weights (lookback period) and to rebalancing period (look-ahead period).[8] In a nutshell,

Table 7.1. Pearson's correlations between returns of the US equity sector ETFs and SPY.

ETF		Pearson's correlations with SPY								
Ticker	Sector	2007	2008	2009	2010	2011	2012	2013	2014	2015
XHB	Homebuilders	0.68	0.71	0.85	0.84	0.92	0.74	0.75	0.72	0.78
XLY	Consumer Discretionary	0.89	0.87	0.92	0.94	0.96	0.9	0.92	0.90	0.93
XRT	Retail	0.82	0.77	0.84	0.84	0.9	0.82	0.82	0.74	0.81
XLP	Consumer Staples	0.79	0.83	0.77	0.87	0.91	0.79	0.79	0.77	0.88
XLE	Energy	0.8	0.84	0.89	0.92	0.92	0.87	0.84	0.68	0.72
XLF	Finance	0.89	0.85	0.89	0.92	0.94	0.9	0.93	0.91	0.93
XLV	Healthcare	0.86	0.84	0.71	0.86	0.94	0.87	0.85	0.85	0.86
XLI	Industrial	0.9	0.91	0.92	0.96	0.98	0.92	0.92	0.92	0.94
XLB	Materials	0.87	0.85	0.89	0.90	0.95	0.88	0.86	0.86	0.85
XLK	Technology	0.86	0.93	0.91	0.94	0.95	0.91	0.83	0.92	0.94
XLU	Utilities	0.71	0.83	0.71	0.83	0.84	0.53	0.65	0.41	0.56
RWR	Real Estate	0.77	0.81	0.86	0.86	0.9	0.71	0.68	0.55	0.67

Table 7.2. Statistics of correlations between returns of
the ETFs listed in Table 7.1.

	Pearson's corr.		Partial corr.	
Year	$p^{a} > 0.1$	corr < 0	$p^{a} > 0.1$ (%)	corr < 0 (%)
2007	0	0	53.0	21.2
2008	0	0	30.3	30.3
2009	0	0	33.3	37.9
2010	0	0	34.8	39.4
2011	0	0	37.9	39.4
2012	0	0	37.9	39.4
2013	0	0	43.9	34.8

[a]p-Value for the null hypothesis that correlation is zero.

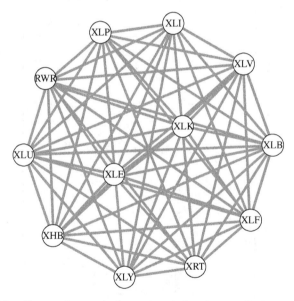

Fig. 7.3. Pearson's correlation network for the 12USETF in 2013.

more frequent rebalancing yields more accurate estimates for portfolio weights and a better performance.

For the 12USETF portfolio, PaMVP outperformed PeMVP and
EWP in 2010–2015 when the 3-year lookback period and 1-month
rebalancing period were chosen (see Table 7.4). Note that I subscribe

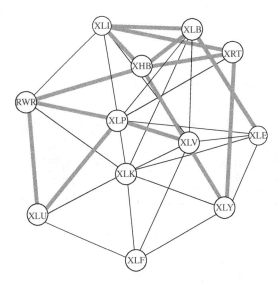

Fig. 7.4. Partial correlation network for the 12USETF in 2013.

to the opinion that the leading MVP performance measure should be the same as the MVP optimization criterion (see also Lee, 2011). Hence, the Sharpe ratio should be chosen as the leading out-of-sample performance measure for the maximum Sharpe MVPs.

Another advantage of PaMVPs is that their weights outside the bear market effects are almost constant while the PeMVP weights fluctuate wildly (cf. Figs. 7.5 and 7.6 for 3-year lookback and 1-month rebalancing periods).

Cai & Schmidt (2020b) compared performance of EWPs, and maximum Sharpe PaMVPs and PeMVPs for portfolios formed with the constituents of five major tradable US equity index SPDR ETFs: S&P 500 (SPY), S&P 500 Growth (SPYG), S&P 500 Value (SPYV), S&P MidCap 400 (MDY), and S&P 600 SmallCap (SLY) in 2006–2018. Survival bias in this work was avoided by including in the EWPs and MVPs only those ETF constituents that were tradable within the 3-year lookback periods and subsequent holding periods. In the case of SPY, PeMVP significantly outperformed SPY, EWP, and PaMVP in terms of the Sharpe ratio at the 6-month and 3-month holding periods. Yet, the differences in performance were statistically insignificant at the 1-month holding period (see Table 7.5).

Table 7.3.   Weights of the 12USETF portfolio.

Year	SPY return	Portfolio	XHB	XLY	XRT	XLP	XLE	XLF	XLV	XLI	XLB	XLK	XLU	RWR	weights >= 1%
2015	0.013	PeMVP	0.00	1.00	0.00	0.00	0.00	0.00	0.00	0.00	0.00	0.00	0.00	0.00	1
		PaMVP	0.00	0.45	0.00	0.22	0.00	0.00	0.11	0.00	0.00	0.22	0.00	0.00	4
2014	0.136	PeMVP	0.00	0.00	0.00	0.00	0.00	0.00	0.09	0.00	0.00	0.00	0.25	0.66	3
		PaMVP	0.01	0.11	0.00	0.11	0.08	0.15	0.13	0.11	0.05	0.21	0.33	0.00	10
2013	0.255	PeMVP	0.00	0.21	0.21	0.00	0.00	0.00	0.52	0.06	0.00	0.00	0.00	0.00	4
		PaMVP	0.00	0.11	0.00	0.11	0.10	0.17	0.13	0.11	0.03	0.21	0.04	0.00	9
2012	0.132	PeMVP	0.55	0.00	0.00	0.00	0.00	0.00	0.45	0.00	0.00	0.00	0.00	0.00	2
		PaMVP	0.00	0.11	0.00	0.13	0.11	0.14	0.13	0.10	0.03	0.22	0.04	0.00	9
2011	0.009	PeMVP	0.00	0.00	0.00	0.00	0.00	0.00	0.00	0.00	0.00	0.00	1.00	0.00	1
		PaMVP	0.00	0.11	0.28	0.07	0.00	0.00	0.18	0.00	0.00	0.04	0.32	0.00	6
2010	0.123	PeMVP	0.00	0.00	0.95	0.05	0.00	0.00	0.00	0.00	0.00	0.00	0.00	0.00	2
		PaMVP	0.00	0.08	0.00	0.13	0.13	0.16	0.11	0.11	0.02	0.22	0.04	0.00	9
2009	0.204	PeMVP	0.00	0.00	0.61	0.00	0.00	0.00	0.00	0.00	0.00	0.39	0.00	0.00	2
		PaMVP	0.01	0.03	0.05	0.11	0.13	0.12	0.17	0.10	0.03	0.20	0.05	0.01	12
2008	−0.45	PeMVP	0.00	0.00	0.00	1.00	0.00	0.00	0.00	0.00	0.00	0.00	0.00	0.00	1
		PaMVP	0.00	0.00	0.00	1.00	0.00	0.00	0.00	0.00	0.00	0.00	0.00	0.00	1
2007	0.052	PeMVP	0.00	0.00	0.00	0.38	0.61	0.00	0.00	0.00	0.00	0.00	0.01	0.00	3
		PaMVP	0.00	0.00	0.00	0.16	0.29	0.00	0.00	0.11	0.11	0.24	0.09	0.00	6
Times included		PeMVP	1	2	3	3	1	0	3	1	0	1	3	1	
		PaMVP	2	7	2	9	6	5	7	6	6	8	7	1	

Table 7.4. Out-of-sample performance of the 12USETF portfolio.[a]

Rebalancing Portfolio	Calibration window: 36 months starting in Jan 2007							
	Monthly				Yearly			
	Return[b]	σ_p^b	Sharpe[b]	MDD	Return[b]	σ_p^b	Sharpe[b]	MDD
EWP	0.108	0.147	1.273	0.033	0.113	0.157	0.860	0.063
PeMVP	**0.130**	**0.146**	1.302	0.033	**0.146**	0.160	**1.097**	0.064
PaMVP	0.108	**0.132**	**1.337**	**0.030**	0.123	**0.142**	0.862	**0.059**

Rebalancing Portfolio	Calibration window: 12 months starting in Jan 2007							
	Monthly				Yearly			
	Return[b]	σ_p^b	Sharpe[b]	MDD	Return[b]	σ_p^b	Sharpe[b]	MDD
EWP	**0.065**	0.193	**0.989**	0.043	0.059	0.210	**0.610**	0.090
PeMVP	0.047	0.170	0.897	0.039	**0.062**	0.216	0.575	0.095
PaMVP	0.043	**0.166**	0.929	**0.038**	0.027	**0.191**	0.596	**0.086**

[a]Best performing measures are in bold. [b]Annualized values.

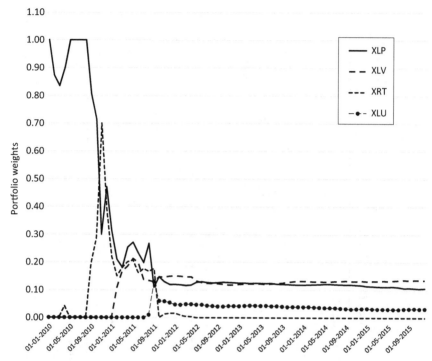

Fig. 7.5.   Highest PaMVP weights for the 12USETF portfolio.

However, when six hyper-growth companies: Facebook, Apple, Amazon, Netflix, Nvidia, and Google (so-called FAANNG) were deleted from the SPY-based portfolio, the differences between performance of PeMVP and PaMVP at the 6-month and 3-month holding periods have become insignificant. Moreover, both EWP and particularly PaMVP significantly outperformed PeMVP at the 1-month holding period (see Table 7.6). The reason for that is that the returns of the highly concentrated FAANNG- based PeMVP could not be matched by returns of more diversified PaMVP and EWP. Nevertheless, in the case of the S&P 500 Growth ETF (that lacks relatively low-performing value stocks), PeMVP did not outperform PaMVP. These results imply that the comparative performance of EWP and MVPs has no simple pattern: it depends on portfolio constituents and holding periods.

For the other US equity index ETFs (SPYV, MDY, and SLY) considered by Cai & Schmidt (2020b), PaMVP always outperformed

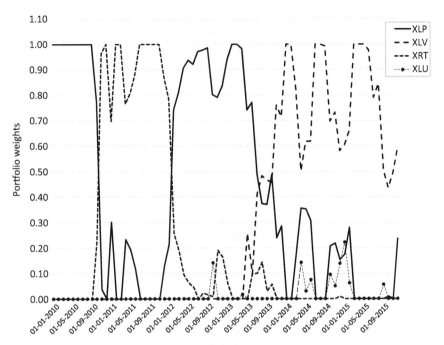

Fig. 7.6.   Highest PeMVP weights for the 12USETF portfolio.

PeMVP, and EWP could outperform PeMVP at shorter holding periods.

7.4.3   *Diversity booster*

As I indicated above, another idea for increasing diversity of MVPs is expanding the MVPT minimizing objective function with an additional term that explicitly controls portfolio diversity. This approach has some similarity with the extension of the standard OLS regression[9] to the (Least Absolute Shrinkage and Selection Operator) *LASSO regression.* Namely, the latter adds to the OLS minimizing function the term that penalizes high number of regressors (see, e.g., James *et al.*, 2013). We, of course, want the opposite, namely, the function that promotes higher number of non-zero portfolio weights. A suitable choice for the diversity booster is

$$DB = \delta \sum_{i=1}^{N} w_i^2. \tag{7.32}$$

Table 7.5. Performance of PeMVP, PaMVP, and EWP for SPY.

Holding period, months	6				3				1			
Portfolio	SPY	EWP	PeMVP	PaMVP	SPY	EWP	PeMVP	PaMVP	SPY	EWP	PeMVP	PaMVP
Ann return	7.8%	9.4%	13.0%	8.2%	7.45%	9.03%	12.62%	7.96%	7.50%	9.06%	11.39%	8.28%
Ann. volatility	16.4%	20.0%	20.8%	14.7%	15.22%	18.16%	19.75%	14.16%	15.39%	18.41%	18.28%	14.25%
Sharpe	0.90	0.86	1.00	0.95	1.02	0.98	1.13	1.06	1.38	1.29	1.32	1.30
p-value[a]	0.00	0.00	NA	0.00	0.00	0.00	NA	0.01	0.22	0.47	NA	0.62

[a]Paired t-test for the differences between given Sharpe ratio and that of PeMVP.

Table 7.6. Performance of PeMVP, PaMVP, and EWP for SPY without FAANNG.

Holding period, months	6				3				1			
Portfolio	SPY	EWP	PeMVP	PaMVP	SPY	EWP	PeMVP	PaMVP	SPY	EWP	PeMVP	PaMVP
Ann return	7.80%	9.17%	11.36%	7.41%	7.45%	8.80%	10.65%	7.10%	7.50%	8.83%	8.67%	7.30%
Ann.volatility	16.43%	19.93%	18.23%	14.38%	15.22%	18.15%	17.30%	13.82%	15.39%	18.40%	17.06%	14.02%
Sharpe	0.90	0.85	0.90	0.89	1.02	0.96	1.02	0.99	1.38	1.26	1.18	1.30
p-value[a]	0.99	0.00	NA	0.24	0.95	0.03	NA	0.13	0.00	0.10	NA	0.01

[a]Paired *t*-test for the differences between given Sharpe ratio and that of PeMVP.

The *DB* parameter δ (*diversity strength*) is investor's choice, similarly to the risk aversion parameter λ. The value of δ may be adjusted to satisfy investor's desire to specify the minimum value of portfolio weights, w_0.

At very high values of δ, *DB* becomes the dominant term in the objective function U_{DMVPT} and yields EWP. Indeed, *DB* decreases with growing number of non-zero portfolio weights and has a minimum when all weights are equal ($w_i = 1/N$). This property stems from the root mean square — arithmetic mean inequality (Bullen *et al.*, 1988)

$$\sqrt{\sum_{i=1}^{N} w_i^2 / N} \geq \sum_{i=1}^{N} w_i / N. \tag{7.33}$$

The inequality (7.33) becomes equality if and only if all w_i are equal. It should be noted that DB has a close relationship to the Herfindahl–Hirschman index that is used as a measure of concentration of firms within industry (Hirschman, 1964). The term (7.32) coincides also with another extension of the OLS regression, namely, with the ridge regression that is used for handling ill-posed problems. I denote the portfolio based on the MVPT objective function expanded with *DB* (U_{DMVPT}) as the *diversified MVP* (DMVP).

The derivation of long-only DMVP represents the following quadratic programming problem:

$$\min_{w_i} \left[U_{\text{DMVPT}} = 0.5 \sum_{i,j=1}^{N} w_i w_j \sigma_{ij} + \delta \sum_{i=1}^{N} w_i^2 \right], \tag{7.34}$$

$$\text{s.t.} \sum_{i=1}^{N} w_i r_i = r_p, \tag{7.35}$$

$$\sum_{i=1}^{N} w_i = 1, \tag{7.36}$$

$$w_i \geq 0; i = 1, 2, \ldots, N. \tag{7.37}$$

For out-of-sample performance analysis, Schmidt (2018) considered the maximum Sharpe 12USETF portfolio in 2009–2015 with 3-year calibration window and monthly rebalancing. The value of

Table 7.7. Annualized out-of-sample performance of MVP($w0$), DMVP(δ), and EWP.

	MVP(0)	MVP(0.02)	DMVP(0.004)	EWP
r_P	0.136	0.138	0.123	0.121
σ_P	0.126	0.124	0.121	0.121
Sharpe	1.473	1.476	1.513	1.405
p-value[a]	NA	0.886	0.06	0.001

[a]t-Test for the differences between given Sharpe ratio and that of MVP(0).

diversity strength $\delta = 0.004$ was chosen for DMVP because it yields for 12USETF practically all weights that are not smaller than 0.02. Performance of this DMVP was compared with that of MVP with the following constraint:

$$w_i \geq w_0; \quad i = 1, 2, \ldots, N. \tag{7.38}$$

Performance measures for MVP with $w_0 = 0$ and $w_0 = 0.02$ (denoted as MVP(0) and MVP(0.02), respectively), and DMVP(0.004) with $\delta = 0.004$ listed in Table 7.7 show that DMVP outperformed MVP out of sample.

Another advantage of DMVP is that, similarly to PaMVP and in contrast to MVP, its weights vary slowly outside the bear markets.

It should be noted that while PaMVP and DMVP are derived using very different ideas, their performance in respect to MVP is quite similar. This can be explained with that both approaches weaken off-diagonal terms of covariance matrix. In PaMVP, it is done explicitly since partial correlations are weaker than Pearson's correlations. In DMVP, the diagonal terms are strengthened with adding to them the diversity strength δ.

7.5 Optimal ESG Portfolios

As we already know, classical finance treats investors as rational agents "who always prefer more wealth to less" (Miller & Modigliani, 1961). Yet, the research in behavioral finance attests that real people are not always rational in a way that classical finance expects them to be (see Statman, 2019, for a review). Sometimes this happens because

Table 7.8. Typical ESG factors.

Environmental	Social	Governance
• Climate change (low-carbon economy) • Resource (energy, water) efficiency • Biodiversity and deforestation • Pollution and waste management	• Human rights • Labor standards • Diversity • Healthcare availability • Income equality • Customer satisfaction • Community relationships	• Board structure • Executive compensation • Bribery and corruption policies • Lobbying and political contributions • Tax strategies

humans may be driven by their cognitive errors and/or emotions. Also, some investors strive for social responsibility and social status besides increasing their wealth.

A case in point is a significant growth of socially responsible and sustainable investing. It is generally denoted as environmental, social, and governance (ESG) investing (see, e.g., Baron, 2009; Benabou & Tirole, 2010; Hart & Zingales, 2017; Oehmke & Opp, 2020; Pastor *et al.*, 2020, among others).

The ESG evaluation of companies is based on multiple factors (see Table 7.8). There are several providers of the ESG ratings that aggregate these factors in different ways and sometimes offer divergent scores for the same companies (Berg *et al.*, 2019; Dimson *et al.*, 2020).

While there are some indications that neglecting so-called "sin-stocks" can decrease portfolio returns (Hong & Kacperczyk, 2009), many studies point at a positive correlation between the corporate ESG scores and financial performance (Friede *et al.*, 2015; Nagy *et al.*, 2016). This, however, does not guarantee outperformance of portfolios that hold shares of companies with high ESG scores. Therefore, a reasonable investing strategy offered by Pedersen *et al.* (2020) and Schmidt (2020b) is simultaneous portfolio optimization in terms of portfolio return, risk, and portfolio ESG value (PESGV).

Pedersen *et al.* (2020) derived analytically an ESG-efficient frontier for a portfolio with long/short weights using risk aversion as a

Table 7.9. The ESG scores based on the MSCI ratings.

MSCI ratings	CCC	BBB	BB	B	A	AA	AAA
linear grid	1	2	3	4	5	6	7
scaled scores	0.143	0.286	0.429	0.571	0.714	0.857	1

controlling parameter and analyzed the empirical ESG-efficient frontier to demonstrate the costs and benefits of responsible investing.

Here, I reproduce an approach offered by Schmidt (2020b). Namely, optimal ESG portfolio is derived using the following optimization problem:

$$\min_{w_i \in Q} [U_{MVPT} + V]. \tag{7.39}$$

In (7.39), U_{MVPT} is defined in (7.16) and the term V is proportional to portfolio ESG value (PESGV), which is assumed to be a linear function of the portfolio constituents' ESG scores δ_i

$$V = \gamma^* \mathrm{PESGV}, \quad \mathrm{PESGV} = \sum_{i=1}^{N} w_i \delta_i. \tag{7.40}$$

In (7.40), γ is the ESG strength parameter that is investors' choice depending on how important for them is PESGV. Schmidt (2020a, 2020b) suggested a new performance measure, the *ESG tilted Sharpe ratio*, Sh_{ESG},

$$Sh_{\mathrm{ESG}} = Sh(1 + \mathrm{PESGV}). \tag{7.41}$$

Sh_{ESG} can better reflect an interest of socially conscious investors in portfolios with high PESGV than the classical Sharpe ratio. Then, the ESG strength parameter γ can be chosen for maximizing Sh_{ESG}.

Schmidt (2020b) considered a long-only portfolio of 29 stocks that constituted DJI in October 2019.[10] The averaged MSCI ESG ratings for 2015–2019 available on the MSCI website https://www.msci.co m/esg-ratings were used in this work. Specifically, the MSCI seven-level literal ratings were mapped on a linear grid and scaled with the maximum value of seven (see Table 7.9).

The weights and performance of the maximum Sharpe portfolio formed with the Dow Jones Index (DJI) constituents are listed in

Table 7.10. Maximum Sharpe ESG portfolio for the DJI Index in 2015–2019.

| | ESG strength | | 0 | | 0.00005 | | 0.0001 | | 0.0005 | | 0.001 | |
| | Correlations | | | | | | | | | | | |
Ticker	Score	Total return	Pearson	Partial	Pearson	Partial	Pearson	Partial	Pearson	Partial	Pearson	Partial
MMM	1.00	22.7%	0.0%	1.4%	0.0%	0.0%	0.0%	12.0%	0.0%	12.3%	0.0%	19.7%
MSFT	0.97	275.4%	19.4%	6.1%	37.7%	45.3%	66.3%	56.4%	100.0%	87.7%	100.0%	80.3%
CAT	0.83	90.3%	0.0%	3.2%	0.0%	8.0%	0.0%	10.0%	0.0%	0.0%	0.0%	0.0%
PG	0.83	61.1%	0.0%	1.8%	9.1%	0.0%	0.8%	1.6%	0.0%	0.0%	0.0%	0.0%
IBM	0.80	1.7%	0.0%	2.8%	0.0%	0.0%	0.0%	0.0%	0.0%	0.0%	0.0%	0.0%
INTC	0.80	88.5%	0.0%	2.6%	0.0%	0.0%	0.0%	0.0%	0.0%	0.0%	0.0%	0.0%
AXP	0.77	44.5%	0.0%	2.3%	0.0%	0.0%	0.0%	0.0%	0.0%	0.0%	0.0%	0.0%
NKE	0.77	127.7%	0.0%	3.0%	5.2%	8.3%	6.0%	8.5%	0.0%	0.0%	0.0%	0.0%
CSCO	0.74	100.3%	0.0%	2.6%	0.0%	0.0%	0.0%	0.0%	0.0%	0.0%	0.0%	0.0%
KO	0.74	54.4%	0.0%	5.6%	0.0%	0.0%	0.0%	0.0%	0.0%	0.0%	0.0%	0.0%
AAPL	0.71	190.2%	4.2%	6.5%	4.3%	10.3%	2.9%	6.4%	0.0%	0.0%	0.0%	0.0%
MRK	0.71	85.3%	0.0%	2.6%	1.0%	5.6%	0.0%	3.4%	0.0%	0.0%	0.0%	0.0%
UTX	0.71	46.6%	0.0%	3.5%	0.0%	0.0%	0.0%	0.0%	0.0%	0.0%	0.0%	0.0%
BA	0.57	187.7%	10.0%	2.0%	8.5%	7.8%	8.5%	1.7%	0.0%	0.0%	0.0%	0.0%
HD	0.54	135.2%	1.7%	5.0%	0.0%	1.8%	0.0%	0.0%	0.0%	0.0%	0.0%	0.0%
TRV	0.54	45.2%	0.0%	2.5%	0.0%	0.0%	0.0%	0.0%	0.0%	0.0%	0.0%	0.0%
V	0.54	195.7%	7.4%	7.0%	0.0%	0.9%	0.0%	0.0%	0.0%	0.0%	0.0%	0.0%
CVX	0.51	30.6%	0.0%	4.2%	0.0%	0.0%	0.0%	0.0%	0.0%	0.0%	0.0%	0.0%
DIS	0.46	64.5%	0.0%	3.2%	0.0%	0.0%	0.0%	0.0%	0.0%	0.0%	0.0%	0.0%
JPM	0.46	152.9%	1.2%	4.9%	0.0%	7.8%	0.0%	0.0%	0.0%	0.0%	0.0%	0.0%

MCD	0.43	142.5%	31.2%	2.4%	19.5%	0.0%	6.3%	0.0%	0.0%	0.0%	0.0%	0.0%
PFE	0.40	48.7%	0.0%	4.8%	0.0%	0.0%	0.0%	0.0%	0.0%	0.0%	0.0%	0.0%
VZ	0.37	63.5%	0.0%	1.7%	0.0%	0.0%	0.0%	0.0%	0.0%	0.0%	0.0%	0.0%
WBA	0.37	−13.5%	0.0%	1.7%	0.0%	0.0%	0.0%	0.0%	0.0%	0.0%	0.0%	0.0%
WMT	0.37	57.5%	0.0%	1.6%	0.0%	0.0%	0.0%	0.0%	0.0%	0.0%	0.0%	0.0%
UNH	0.34	215.4%	25.0%	4.4%	14.7%	4.1%	9.3%	0.0%	0.0%	0.0%	0.0%	0.0%
GS	0.31	27.4%	0.0%	3.8%	0.0%	0.0%	0.0%	0.0%	0.0%	0.0%	0.0%	0.0%
JNJ	0.29	59.5%	0.0%	3.2%	0.0%	0.0%	0.0%	0.0%	0.0%	0.0%	0.0%	0.0%
XOM	0.29	−9.2%	0.0%	4.0%	0.0%	0.0%	0.0%	0.0%	0.0%	0.0%	0.0%	0.0%
# of weights >= 0.1%			8	29	8	10	6	8	1	2	1	2
Ann volatility			14.7%	13.5%	15.4%	17.8%	19.0%	18.6%	23.3%	21.7%	23.3%	20.8%
Ann return			23.8%	15.2%	23.8%	24.6%	27.0%	23.1%	29.2%	26.4%	29.2%	24.7%
Ann max Sharpe ratio Sh_m			1.61	1.13	1.54	1.39	1.42	1.25	1.25	1.22	1.25	1.19
PESGV			0	0	0.70	0.79	0.82	0.91	0.97	0.97	0.97	0.98
Ann ESG tilted Sharpe ratio Sh_{mESG}			1.61	1.13	2.63	2.49	2.58	2.38	2.47	2.41	2.47	2.35

Table 7.10. For zero PESGV ($\gamma = 0$), PeMVP has only eight weights higher than 0.1%, i.e., 27.6% out of 29 DJI constituents. On the contrary, PaMVP has all 29 weights higher than 1%. With increasing PESGV, both PeMVP and PaMVP become less diversified and their maximum Sharpe ratios decrease. This is caused by that the correlation between the DJI constituents' total returns in 2015–2019 and their averaged ESG scores was very low (0.17). However, the ESG tilted Sharpe ratio (7.41) has a maximum for the ESG strength parameter γ in the vicinity of 0.0005. Hence, Sh_{ESG} is a reasonable performance measure for optimal ESG portfolios.

Notes

1. While the expression "theory" is widely used in finance, I subscribe to the opinion that the theories in finance are merely models that often "behave badly" (Derman, 2011).
2. The concept of risk aversion is introduced in Section 2.3.
3. See Chapter 5 for price volatility.
4. In general, comparative performance of MVPs and EWPs depends on portfolio composition and rebalancing frequency (Kritzman *et al.*, 2010; Cai & Schmidt, 2020b).
5. Macroeconomic risks are non-diversifiable. Market impact of these risks will be discussed in Section 13.3.
6. The definition of "recent past" is a subject of interpretation. The lookback periods for which portfolio mean returns and covariances are estimated may vary from 100 days to 1250 days (Litterman & Wilkenmann, 1998). From my experience, the lookback periods shorter than one year are insufficient for robust estimates.
7. The CAPM is described in Chapter 10.
8. Importance of rebalancing was discussed by Booth & Fama (1992), and Willenbrock (2011), among others.
9. An example of the ordinary least square method (OLS) for the linear regression is given in Appendix B.1.3.
10. One constituent, Dow Chemical for which prices prior to its merger with DuPont in 2015 were not available, was excluded from the DJI portfolio.

Chapter 8

Portfolio Optimization

8.1 Introduction

As I indicated in Chapter 7, high sensitivity of MVPs to possible estimation errors in their inputs (covariance matrix and mean returns) complicates their usage in practice. This problem can be addressed using two different portfolio optimization techniques (Fabozzi *et al.*, 2007; Kolm *et al.*, 2014; Yin *et al.*, 2021). The first involves obtaining better estimates of the MVP input parameters using the shrinkage and Bayesian operators, either by applying them to expected returns (Jorion, 1986; Black & Litterman, 1990) or to a covariance matrix (Ledoit & Wolf, 2003, 2004).

The second technique is based on accounting of the input parameter uncertainty directly within the MVP optimization framework by adding additional constraints. In this chapter, I outline both these approaches.

8.2 Shrinkage in Portfolio Theory

The idea of shrinkage in statistical science is based on the fact that some biased estimators may yield more accurate estimates than the unbiased ones. In particular, for a multivariate n-dimensional normal distribution $N(\boldsymbol{\mu}, \Sigma)$, the sample mean $\hat{\boldsymbol{\mu}}$ is inferior to the so-called *James-Stein shrinkage estimator* of the population mean $\boldsymbol{\mu}$ in terms of the quadratic loss function

$$L(\boldsymbol{\mu}, \hat{\boldsymbol{\mu}}) = (\boldsymbol{\mu} - \hat{\boldsymbol{\mu}})'\Sigma^{-1}(\boldsymbol{\mu} - \hat{\boldsymbol{\mu}}). \tag{8.1}$$

The James–Stein shrinkage estimator has the following form

$$\hat{\boldsymbol{\mu}}_{\text{JS}} = (1 - w)\hat{\boldsymbol{\mu}} + w\mu_0 l, \qquad (8.2)$$

$$w = \min\left(1, \frac{n - 2}{T(\hat{\boldsymbol{\mu}} - \mu_0 l)'\Sigma^{-1}(\hat{\boldsymbol{\mu}} - \mu_0 l)}\right). \qquad (8.3)$$

In (8.2) and (8.3), l is $1 \times n$ vector of ones, μ_0 is an arbitrary number, and T is the number of observations. The vector $\mu_0 l$ and the weight w are called the *shrinkage target* and the *shrinkage intensity* respectively.

Using this idea, Jorion (1986) proposed the following shrinkage estimator for expected returns

$$\mu_0 l = \frac{l'\Sigma^{-1}\hat{\boldsymbol{\mu}}}{l'\Sigma^{-1}l}, \qquad (8.4)$$

$$w = \frac{n + 2}{n + 2 + T(\hat{\boldsymbol{\mu}} - \mu_0 l)'\Sigma^{-1}(\hat{\boldsymbol{\mu}} - \mu_0 l)}. \qquad (8.5)$$

Similar approach can be used for covariance matrix. The variance of the Bayes–Stein estimator for the expected returns equals

$$var(\hat{\boldsymbol{\mu}}_{\text{JS}}) = \Sigma\left(1 + \frac{1}{T + \tau}\right) + \frac{\tau}{T(T + \tau + 1)}\frac{ll'}{l'\Sigma^{-1}l}. \qquad (8.6)$$

In (8.6), τ is a parameter that describes the confidence in the estimate of the covariance matrix Σ that can be approximated with the sample covariance matrix $\hat{\Sigma}$

$$\Sigma = \frac{(T - 1)\hat{\Sigma}}{T - n - 2}. \qquad (8.7)$$

Ledoit & Wolf (2003, 2004) suggested the Sharpe's (1963) single-factor matrix or the *constant correlation model* as the shrinkage target for covariance matrix. The latter one has a comparable performance but is much easier to implement. Namely, the shrinkage estimator has the following form:

$$\widehat{\Sigma_{LW}} = w\widehat{\Sigma_{CC}} + (1 - w)\hat{\Sigma}. \qquad (8.8)$$

In (8.8), $\hat{\Sigma}$ is the sample covariance matrix, and $\widehat{\Sigma_{CC}}$ is the sample covariance matrix with constant correlation. In order to calculate the latter, the sample covariance matrix is decomposed

$$\hat{\Sigma} = \Lambda C \Lambda', \tag{8.9}$$

where Λ is a matrix of return correlations with the terms

$$\rho_{ij} = \sigma_{ij}/(\sigma_{ii}\sigma_{jj}), \tag{8.10}$$

and C is the constant correlation matrix in which all off-diagonal terms are equal to the average of all off-diagonal terms in Λ

$$c_{ij} = \hat{\rho}, i \neq j, \hat{\rho} = \frac{2}{n(n-1)} \sum_{i=1}^{n} \sum_{j=i+1}^{n} \rho_{ij}. \tag{8.11}$$

The shrinkage weight w in (8.8) is estimated by minimizing the quadratic loss function

$$L(w) = ||w\widehat{\Sigma_{CC}} + (1-w)\hat{\Sigma} - \hat{\Sigma}||. \tag{8.12}$$

Ledoit & Wolf (2014) found that their shrinkage estimator is superior to the sample covariance matrix, a statistical factor model based on the first five principal components, and a factor model based on the 48 industry factors defined by Fama & French (1997).

8.3 The Black–Litterman Model

The Black–Litterman model (BLM) enables investors to combine their personal (and, hence, subjective) views on future asset returns with the market equilibrium theory (e.g., the CAPM described in Chapter 10). While the BLM is based on the Bayesian framework,[1] its expected return can be interpreted as a shrinkage estimator where market equilibrium is the shrinkage target and the shrinkage intensity is determined by the investor views (Fabozzi *et al.*, 2007). Within the Bayesian framework, investors derive the *posterior distribution* of their portfolio returns using the *prior distribution* of equilibrium

market returns. Namely, in terms of notations used by Satchell &
Scowcroft (2000),

$$\text{pdf}(E(\boldsymbol{r})|\boldsymbol{\pi}) = \frac{\text{pdf}(\boldsymbol{\pi}\,|\,E(\boldsymbol{r}))\text{pdf}(E(\boldsymbol{r}))}{\text{pdf}(\boldsymbol{\pi})}. \tag{8.13}$$

In (8.13), pdf(.) denotes probability density function; $\text{pdf}(E(\boldsymbol{r}))$
expresses investor's views on portfolio returns $\boldsymbol{r}$, both $\boldsymbol{r}$ and $\boldsymbol{\pi}$
are $n \times 1$ vectors where n is the number of portfolio constituents,
$\text{pdf}(\boldsymbol{\pi}\,|\,E(\boldsymbol{r}))$ is the conditional pdf of equilibrium returns given
investor's expectations of the equilibrium returns, $\text{pdf}(\boldsymbol{\pi})$ is the
marginal pdf of the equilibrium returns (which is canceled out in
the final results).

Within the CAPM,

$$\boldsymbol{\pi} = \beta(\mu_m - r_f) = \delta\boldsymbol{w}_m\sum, \tag{8.14}$$

where $\beta = \text{cov}(\boldsymbol{r}, \boldsymbol{r}'\boldsymbol{w}_m)/\sigma_m^2$, μ_m is total market return, r_f is risk-free
return, $\delta = (\mu_m - r_f)/\sigma_m^2$, $\boldsymbol{w}_m$ is the vector of the market weights,
and $\sum = \text{cov}(\boldsymbol{r}, \boldsymbol{r}')$.

Let investor have k beliefs ($k \leq n$). Consider $k \times n$ matrix $\boldsymbol{P}$ and
a known $k \times 1$ vector of beliefs $\boldsymbol{q}$. Within the BLM, the $k \times 1$ vector
$\mathbf{y} = \boldsymbol{P}E(\boldsymbol{r})$ is assumed to be normally distributed: $\mathbf{y} \sim N(\boldsymbol{q}, \boldsymbol{\Omega})$
where $\boldsymbol{\Omega}$ is a $k \times k$ diagonal matrix with diagonal elements ε_{ii} that
characterizes uncertainty of investor's beliefs. For example, consider a
portfolio with three assets named A, B, and C for which investor has
the following views: A will outperform B by 5% and C will outperform
B by 2%. Then $k = 2$, and investor's views can be expressed as

$$\begin{pmatrix} 1 & -1 & 0 \\ 0 & -1 & 1 \end{pmatrix} \begin{pmatrix} E(r_A) \\ E(r_B) \\ E(r_C) \end{pmatrix} = \begin{pmatrix} 0.05 \\ 0.02 \end{pmatrix} + \begin{pmatrix} \varepsilon_{11} \\ \varepsilon_{22} \end{pmatrix}, \tag{8.15}$$

where ε_{11} and ε_{22} characterize uncertainties of these views.

It is assumed in the BLM that the $\text{pdf}(\boldsymbol{\pi}|E(\boldsymbol{r}))$ is $N(E(\boldsymbol{r}), \tau\sum)$
where τ is a scaling factor often set to 1. This assumption means that
the market equilibrium excess returns conditional upon investor's
forecast equal the investor's forecast on average. This conditioning
implies that if all investors hold homogenous beliefs and invest in a
market described by the CAPM, then $\boldsymbol{\pi}$ represents the equilibrium

returns conditional upon the investor's common beliefs (Satchell & Scowcroft, 2000).

Given all assumptions listed above, the BLM yields the normal distribution $\text{pdf}(E(\boldsymbol{r})|\boldsymbol{\pi}) = N(\hat{\boldsymbol{\mu}}_{\text{BLM}}, \sum_{BLM})$ where

$$\hat{\mu}_{\text{BLM}} = [(\tau\Sigma)^{-1} + \mathbf{P}'\mathbf{\Omega}^{-1}\mathbf{P}]^{-1}[(\tau\Sigma)^{-1}\boldsymbol{\pi} + \mathbf{P}'\mathbf{\Omega}^{-1}\mathbf{q}], \quad (8.16)$$

$$\sum_{BLM} = [(\tau\Sigma)^{-1} + \mathbf{P}'\mathbf{\Omega}^{-1}\mathbf{P}]^{-1}. \quad (8.17)$$

Kolm & Ritter (2017) offer a comprehensive review of the Bayesian interpretation of the BLM.

8.4 Robust Portfolio Optimization

Application of the robust optimization techniques in the MVPT implies that uncertainty in the portfolio input parameters is directly incorporated into the MVP optimization protocol. The mean variance optimization problem described in Chapter 7 may be presented in the following vector form

$$\max_{\boldsymbol{w}}(\boldsymbol{\mu}'\boldsymbol{w} - \lambda\boldsymbol{w}'\boldsymbol{\Sigma}\boldsymbol{w}) \quad \text{so that } \boldsymbol{w}'\boldsymbol{l} = 1. \quad (8.18)$$

Two types of uncertainty specification, box and quadratic, are described in the literature (see for a recent review, Yin *et al.*, 2021). The former one implies that the estimation error of the expected returns $\boldsymbol{\mu}$ approximated by the sample mean $\hat{\boldsymbol{\mu}}$ does not exceed some threshold $\boldsymbol{\delta}$ and has the following form:

$$U_{\mu} = \{\boldsymbol{\mu}||\mu_i - \hat{\mu}_i| \leq \delta_i\}. \quad (8.19)$$

For example, if portfolio asset returns are assumed to follow the normal distribution, then a 95% confidence interval for μ_i can be obtained by setting $\delta_i = 1.96\,\sigma_i\sqrt{T}$, where T is the sample size (Fabozzi *et al.*, 2007). Incorporation of the box uncertainty set into the mean variance optimization problem yields

$$\max_{\boldsymbol{w}}(\boldsymbol{\mu}'\boldsymbol{w} - \boldsymbol{\delta}'|\boldsymbol{w}| - \lambda\boldsymbol{w}'\boldsymbol{\Sigma}\boldsymbol{w}) \quad \text{so that } \boldsymbol{w}'\boldsymbol{l} = 1. \quad (8.20)$$

One can define the worst-case scenario portfolio when the inequality (8.19) is saturated (i.e., the equality is achieved):

$$\max_{w}(\boldsymbol{\mu}'\boldsymbol{w} - k\max|w_i| - \lambda\boldsymbol{w}'\boldsymbol{\Sigma}\boldsymbol{w}) \quad \text{so that} \quad \boldsymbol{w}'\boldsymbol{l} = 1, \quad (8.21)$$

where $k = \sum_i^n \delta_i$.

The quadratic uncertainty specification is a more sophisticated approach in which the uncertainty of $\boldsymbol{\mu}-\hat{\boldsymbol{\mu}}$ follows the normal distribution with zero mean and variance $\sum_{\mu}$.

$$U_{\mu} = \left\{\boldsymbol{\mu}|(\boldsymbol{\mu} - \hat{\boldsymbol{\mu}})'\sum\nolimits_{\mu^{-1}}|(\boldsymbol{\mu} - \hat{\boldsymbol{\mu}}) \leq \delta^2\right\}. \quad (8.22)$$

In this case, the robust portfolio optimization can be formulated as follows:

$$\max_{w}\left(\min_{\mu \in U_{\mu}}(\boldsymbol{w}'\boldsymbol{\mu}) - \lambda\boldsymbol{w}'\boldsymbol{\Sigma}\boldsymbol{w}\right), U_{\mu} = (\boldsymbol{\mu} - \hat{\boldsymbol{\mu}})'\sum\nolimits_{\mu^{-1}}(\boldsymbol{\mu} - \hat{\boldsymbol{\mu}}) \leq \delta^2. \quad (8.23)$$

The solution to (8.23) can be obtained in two steps (Fabozzi *et al.*, 2007). The first one is solving the inner problem, namely, fixing the portfolio weights $\boldsymbol{w}$ and finding the worst-case expected portfolio return from the confidence region derived from the uncertainty set $\mathbf{U}_{\mu}$

$$\min_{\mu}(\boldsymbol{w}'\boldsymbol{\mu} - \lambda\boldsymbol{w}'\boldsymbol{\Sigma}\boldsymbol{w}) \quad \text{so that}$$

$$(\boldsymbol{\mu} - \hat{\boldsymbol{\mu}})'\sum\nolimits_{\mu^{-1}}(\boldsymbol{\mu} - \hat{\boldsymbol{\mu}}) \leq \delta^2. \quad (8.24)$$

The Lagrangian of this problem has the form

$$L(\boldsymbol{\mu}, \gamma) = \mathbf{w}'\boldsymbol{\mu} - \lambda\mathbf{w}'\boldsymbol{\Sigma}\mathbf{w} - \gamma\left[\delta^2 - (\boldsymbol{\mu} - \hat{\boldsymbol{\mu}})'\sum\nolimits_{\mu^{-1}}(\boldsymbol{\mu} - \hat{\boldsymbol{\mu}})\right], \quad (8.25)$$

where γ is the Lagrange multiplier. Differentiating $L(\boldsymbol{\mu}, \gamma)$ with respect to $\boldsymbol{\mu}$ yields the optimal value for $\boldsymbol{\mu}$

$$\boldsymbol{\mu}^* = \hat{\boldsymbol{\mu}} - \frac{1}{2\gamma}\sum\nolimits_{\mu}\boldsymbol{w}. \quad (8.26)$$

Then the Lagrangian has the form

$$L(\boldsymbol{\mu}, \gamma) = \boldsymbol{w}'\boldsymbol{\mu} - \lambda\boldsymbol{w}' - \lambda\boldsymbol{w}\text{'}\boldsymbol{\Sigma}\boldsymbol{w} - \frac{1}{4\gamma}\mathbf{w}'\sum\boldsymbol{w} - \delta\gamma^2 \quad (8.27)$$

which yields the following optimal γ:

$$\gamma^* = \frac{1}{2\delta}\sqrt{\boldsymbol{w}'\sum\nolimits_\mu \boldsymbol{w}}. \quad (8.28)$$

On the second step, plugging the optimal value of γ^* into the Lagrangian yields the robust optimization problem

$$\max_{\boldsymbol{w}} \left(\boldsymbol{w}'\boldsymbol{\mu} - \lambda\boldsymbol{w}'\sum\boldsymbol{w} - \delta\sqrt{\boldsymbol{w}'\sum\nolimits_\mu \boldsymbol{w}} \right) \quad \text{so that} \quad \boldsymbol{w}'\boldsymbol{l} = 1.$$
$$(8.29)$$

Further developments in portfolio robust optimization are discussed by Kolm *et al.* (2014) and Yin *et al.* (2021).

Note

1. Elements of Bayesian framework are introduced in Section 2.5 for describing the Glosten–Milgrom model. See also Note 10 for Chapter 2.

Chapter 9

Risk-Based Asset Allocation

9.1 Introduction

The problem with high MVP sensitivity to the input errors, particularly in estimating expected returns, motivated development of risk-based asset allocation strategies that do not depend explicitly on forecasts of returns. In this chapter, I describe four such strategies: equal weight, minimum variance, maximum diversification, and risk parity. The latter has two flavors: equal risk budget and equal risk contribution (De Carvalho et al., 2012). It can be shown that all these risk-based methodologies are special cases of a generic function defined by two parameters: the first one controls the intensity of regularization and the second one determines the tolerance for total risk (Jurczenko et al., 2013). None of the risk-based asset allocation strategies is a clear winner across all performance measures (return, volatility, Sharpe ratio, maximum drawdown,[1] and turnover) for all portfolios, time periods, and international markets (see, e.g., Lee, 2011; De Carvalho et al., 2012; Jurczenko et al., 2013; Reigneron et al., 2019, and references therein). It should be noted that while the Sharpe ratio is arguably the most widely used performance criterion, risk-based portfolios are rarely compared with the maximum Sharpe mean variance portfolios.

9.2 Equal Weight Portfolio

In EWP that was already introduced in Chapter 7, all asset weights are equal to $1/N$ (where N is the number of portfolio assets).

EWP is the simplest diversification idea based on our belief that neither future returns nor risk can be predicted. Ironically, equal-weight diversification was described about 1500 years ago in the Babylonian Talmud according to which "A man should always place his money, one third in land, a third into merchandise, and keep a third in hand" (Duchin & Levy, 2009). However, the proponents of the axiomatic approach can treat EWP as the limiting case in the DMVPT quadratic problem (7.36)–(7.39)

$$\sigma_p^2 = \sum_{i,j=1}^{N} w_i w_j \sigma_{ij}, \tag{9.1}$$

$$\min_{w_i} \left(U_{\text{DMVPT}} = 0.5\sigma_p^2 + \delta \sum_{i=1}^{N} w_i^2 \right), \tag{9.2}$$

$$\text{s.t.} \sum_{i=1}^{N} w_i r_i = r_p \tag{9.3}$$

$$\sum_{i=1}^{N} w_i = 1, \tag{9.4}$$

$$w_i \geq 0; \quad i = 1, 2, \ldots, N. \tag{9.5}$$

Namely, when the diversity booster (the second term in U_{DMVPT} (9.2)) completely dominates the minimizing objective function at very high values of the diversity strength δ, it yields equal weights for all portfolio constituents.

EWP is agnostic not only to the returns and volatility of portfolio constituents but also to their asset type. If the latter matters to investors, then the very notion of diversity must be specified. In fact, there is no broadly accepted way of defining and managing portfolio diversity (Meucci, 2009). A case in point is offered by Lee (2011). In the Russell 1000 universe of equities, the consumer discretionary and consumer staples sectors were both weighted at approximately 11% in March 2010. However, EWP based on the constituents of the Russell 1000 puts the weight of the consumer discretionary sector at almost three times the weight of the consumer staples sector due to the difference in the number of publicly traded stocks included in each of these two sectors. Hence, if equal sector weight needed be preserved, portfolio weights should be modified accordingly.

In general, EWPs are overweight in small-cap stocks, have low turnover, and have the CAPM beta close to one.[2] Another feature of EWP is that it coincides with the maximum Sharpe MVP when all portfolio asset returns and volatilities, and correlations between portfolio assets are equal.

9.3 Minimum Variance Portfolio

The *minimum variance portfolio* (MinVP) has the lowest ex ante volatility on the mean–variance frontier. Its constituents are the assets with smallest volatilities and correlations. MinVP can be derived simply by minimizing portfolio variance σ_p^2 (9.1) outside the full quadratic problem (9.1)–(9.5). This implies that MinVP within the MVPT framework is based on the assumption that all portfolio asset returns are equal (to some value r_0). Indeed, in this case, the constraint (9.3) does not depend anymore on portfolio weights:

$$\sum_{i=1}^{N} w_i r_i = r_0 \sum_{i=1}^{N} w_i = r_0 = r_p. \tag{9.6}$$

The weights of a long-short (LS) MinVP can be represented in the following vector form:

$$w_{LS} = \frac{\sum^{-1} l}{l' \sum^{-1} l}, \tag{9.7}$$

where $\sum$ is covariance matrix and l is vector of ones. Clarke *et al.* (2011) have shown that (9.7) can be transformed into

$$w_{LS,i} = \frac{\sigma_{p,LS}^2}{\sigma_i^2} \left(1 - \frac{\beta_i}{\beta_{LS}} \right), \tag{9.8}$$

where $\sigma_{p,LS}^2$ and σ_i^2 are variances of the *LS* MinVP and security i, respectively; β_i is the CAPM market beta of security i, and β_{LS} is

LS threshold beta that can be calculated as

$$\beta_{LS} = \frac{\frac{1}{\sigma_M^2} + \sum \frac{\beta_i^2}{\sigma_i^2}}{\sum \frac{\beta_i^2}{\sigma_i^2}}. \tag{9.9}$$

In (9.9), σ_M^2 is market variance. It follows from (9.8) that the securities in MinVP with $\beta_i < \beta_{LS}$ have negative weights.

While the general MVP optimization problem does not have an analytic solution for long-only (LO) portfolios, Clarke *et al.* (2011) derived the formula for the weights of the LO MinVP

$$w_{LO,i} = \frac{\sigma_{p,LO}^2}{\sigma_i^2} \left(1 - \frac{\beta_i}{\beta_{LO}}\right) \quad \text{if} \quad \beta_i < \beta_{LO}, \tag{9.10a}$$

$$w_{LO,i} = 0 \quad \text{if} \quad \beta_i > \beta_{LO}. \tag{9.10b}$$

In (9.10), $\sigma_{p,LO}^2$ is variance of the long-only MinVP, and the long-only threshold β_{LO} is similar to β_{LS} (9.9) but the summation of the terms $\sum \frac{\beta_i^2}{\sigma_i^2}$ is only over the terms with $\beta_i < \beta_{LO}$

$$\beta_{LO} = \frac{\frac{1}{\sigma_M^2} + \sum_{\beta_i < \beta_{LO}} \frac{\beta_i^2}{\sigma_i^2}}{\sum_{\beta_i < \beta_{LO}} \frac{\beta_i^2}{\sigma_i^2}}. \tag{9.11}$$

It should be noted that (9.11) is not a closed form solution since β_{LO} is present in both the left-hand and the right-hand sides of the equation. Still, the MinVP weights can be found by sorting securities from low to high betas and examining the running sums.

Several studies demonstrated that MinVP may sometimes outperform other risk-based asset allocation schemes not only in terms of lowest risk but also in terms of superior returns, and hence in terms of the Sharpe ratio (Haugen & Baker, 1991; Clarke *et al.*, 2006, 2011; Reigneron, 2019), particularly if a shrinkage constraint[3] is added to the portfolio derivation (Behr *et al.*, 2013).

It follows from (9.8) and (9.10) that MinVP has higher weights for stocks with lower volatility and lower CAPM betas. As a result, MinVP may be highly concentrated. Generally, MinVPs have very low CAPM betas and high turnover.

9.4 Maximum Diversification Portfolio

Choueifaty & Coignard (2008) introduced so-called *diversification ratio, D*, being the ratio between portfolio's undiversified and diversified volatility

$$D = \sum_i^N w_i \sigma_i / \sigma_P. \qquad (9.12)$$

Obviously, $D = 1$ when all portfolio asset returns are uncorrelated. The *maximum diversification portfolio* (MDP) is derived as the solution to the maximization problem

$$\boldsymbol{w}_{MD} = \text{argmax}_{w_i}(D). \qquad (9.13)$$

If all portfolio asset volatilities are equal, MDP coincides with MinVP. Also, if all portfolio assets have the same Sharpe ratio, then MDP is the maximum Sharpe MVP. Similarly to MinVP, MDP is tilted to low-volatility and low-beta stocks, and has high turnover.

Somewhat ironically, MDP may be highly concentrated (Jurczenko *et al.*, 2013). This is the result of that MDP, as it follows from its definition (9.12)–(9.13), is maximum risk-diversified portfolio rather than maximum asset-diversified portfolio. Note that, as I indicated in Section 9.2, the definition of portfolio diversity is a problem *per se*.

9.5 Risk Parity Portfolio

Maillard *et al.* (2010) defined the risk parity portfolio (RPP) using the notion of *marginal risk contribution* $\partial \sigma_p / \partial w_i$, where $i = 1, 2, \ldots, N$ and N is the number of assets in portfolio. The qualifier "marginal" implies that this variable yields the change in portfolio volatility caused by a small increase in the weight of portfolio constituent i. Since volatility σ_p is a homogeneous function[4] of degree 1,

$$\sigma_i = w_i \partial \sigma_p / \partial w_i, \sigma_p = \sum_i \sigma_i. \qquad (9.14)$$

RPP (also called *equal risk contributions portfolio* (ERCP)) is derived by the choice of such weights w_i that satisfy the conditions

$$w_i \partial\sigma_p/\partial w_i = w_j \partial\sigma_p/\partial w_j \quad \text{for all } i \text{ and } j; \; \text{s.t.} \sum_i w_i = 1.$$

$$(9.15)$$

In the simplistic case when all correlations between portfolio constituents are equal, (9.15) is reduced to the condition

$$w_i \sigma_i = w_j \sigma_j, \quad \text{s.t.} \sum_i w_i = 1, \tag{9.16}$$

which yields an analytic solution

$$w_i = \frac{\sigma_i^{-1}}{\sum_j \sigma_j^{-1}}. \tag{9.17}$$

RPP in the form (9.16)–(9.17) is sometimes called *equal risk balance portfolio* (ERBP) (De Carvalho *et al.*, 2012).

Finding the general solution for the ERCP directly from (9.15) represents a computational challenge, particularly in the case of a high number of portfolio constituents. Maillard *et al.* (2010) redefined ERCP in terms of the optimization problem

$$\boldsymbol{w} = \underset{w_i}{\text{argmin}}(f), \; \text{s.t.} \sum_i w_i = 1 \quad \text{and} \quad w_i > 0, \tag{9.18}$$

where

$$f = \sum_i \sum_j (w_i(\boldsymbol{\sigma}_p\boldsymbol{w})_i - w_j(\boldsymbol{\sigma}_p\boldsymbol{w})_j)^2. \tag{9.19}$$

Note that the solution to (9.18)–(9.19) is unique only for LO portfolios.

Maillard *et al.* (2010) have shown that the ERCP volatility is always between the volatilities of EWP and MVP

$$\sigma_{\text{MinVP}} < \sigma_{\text{ERCP}} < \sigma_{\text{EWP}}. \tag{9.20}$$

Another property of the ERCP is that its weights are inversely proportional to the portfolio asset betas in respect to the ERCP (Lee, 2011). Namely,

$$w_i \beta_i = w_j \beta_j = 1/N. \tag{9.21}$$

Hence, the higher the volatility and/or the correlation of an asset with other assets, the lower its weight within the RPP.

New developments for risk parity portfolios are described by Baitinger *et al.* (2017), Benichou *et al.* (2017), and Deguest *et al.* (2013).

Notes

1. Maximum drawdown is formally defined in Section 14.2.
2. The CAPM beta is defined in Section 10.2.
3. Shrinkage is discussed in Section 8.2.
4. Homogeneous function f of order k satisfies the condition: $f(ax) = a^k f(x)$.

Chapter 10

Factor Models

10.1 Introduction

I devote the first section of this chapter to the classical Capital Asset Pricing Model (CAPM) that was developed independently by Sharpe, Lintner, and Mossin in the 1960s (see Elton *et al.*, 2009, for a review). Then, I discuss the Arbitrage Pricing Theory (APT) offered by Ross (1976) in Section 10.3. Further developments within the multi-factor framework including the Fama & French (1993, 2015) models and so-called *smart betas* are described in Section 10.4.

10.2 Capital Asset Pricing Model

The CAPM is based on the portfolio selection approach outlined in Chapter 7. Within the CAPM, entire universe of risky assets (the market) with all their possible returns and volatilities is considered. The SPDR S&P 500 ETF (SPY) that mimics the S&P 500 Index is usually used as a tradable proxy to the equity market. The efficient frontier for market portfolio is called the *capital market line*. In a nutshell, the CAPM describes the asset's price sensitivity to the market return that is treated as *market risk* (also called *systematic risk*), which is *non-diversifiable risk* in the sense that it cannot be compensated by adding securities of the same class (i.e., equities in our case) to portfolio.

It is assumed in the CAPM that all investors have homogenous expectations of asset returns and volatilities, and correlations between the risky assets. Also according to the CAPM, investors behave rationally, i.e., they all hold optimal mean–variance efficient portfolios. This implies that all investors have risky assets in their portfolio in the same proportions as the entire market has. Hence, the CAPM promotes passive investing in the index mutual funds. Among the other CAPM assumptions, all investors are price takers of publicly traded financial assets and have the same single-period investment horizon. Investors' trading costs and taxes are neglected.

Within the CAPM, the optimal investing strategy is simply choosing portfolio on the capital market line with acceptable risk level. Therefore the difference among rational investors is determined only by their risk aversion, i.e., by the proportion of their wealth allocated to the risk-free assets.

The CAPM defines return of a risky asset i with the *security market line* (SML)

$$E[R_i] = R_f + \beta_i(E[R_M] - R_f). \tag{10.1}$$

In (10.1), R_M is the market portfolio return and parameter *beta* β_i equals

$$\beta_i = \mathrm{cov}[R_i, R_M]/\mathrm{var}[\underline{R}_M]. \tag{10.2}$$

In contrast to the capital allocation line (7.3) that measures risk in terms of portfolio volatility, SML measures risk with beta, i.e., with sensitivity of the risky asset i to the excess market returns. Namely, $\beta_i > 1$ means that the asset is more volatile than entire market while $\beta_i < 1$ implies that the asset has lower sensitivity to the market movements.

While Eq. (10.1) can be introduced as an heuristic model, the CAPM can be also derived by considering two-asset portfolio with weights w and $(1 - w)$ for the risky security i and market portfolio M, respectively. We then have

$$E[R_p] = wE[R_i] + (1 - w)E[R_M], \tag{10.3}$$

$$\sigma_p^2 = w^2\sigma_i^2 + (1 - w)^2\sigma_M^2 + 2w(1 - w)\sigma_{iM}, \tag{10.4}$$

where R_p, R_i, R_M are returns of portfolio, risky asset, and market, respectively; σ_p^2, σ_i^2, σ_M^2 are variances of portfolio, risky asset, and market, respectively; covariance $\sigma_{iM} = \rho_{iM}\sigma_i\sigma_M$.

At $w = 0$, the curve (10.3) must be tangent to the capital market line. This implies that the slops of both curves are equal at $w = 0$. It follows from (10.3) and (10.4) that the slope of (10.3) equals

$$\frac{dE(R_P)}{d\sigma_P}\Big|_{w=0} = \frac{dE(R_P)}{dw}\Big/\frac{\sigma_P}{dw}\Big|_{w=0} = \frac{\sigma_M(R_i - R_M)}{\sigma_{iM} - \sigma_M^2}. \quad (10.5)$$

On the contrary, the slope of the capital market line is (see (7.4)):

$$s_M = (E[R_M] - R_f)/\sigma_M. \quad (10.6)$$

Then equating the right-hand sides of (10.5) and (10.6) yields the CAPM equations (10.1) and (10.2).

The CAPM being an equilibrium model has no explicit time dependence. It considers only one time period and treats risk-free interest rate as an exogenous parameter. However in real life, investors make decisions on distribution of their wealth into investing and consumption spanning over many periods. An interesting direction in the portfolio theory (that is beyond the scope of this book) aims at describing the investment and consumption processes within a single framework. Then, risk-free interest rate is determined by the consumption growth and by the investor risk aversion. The most prominent theories in this direction are the intertemporal CAPM (ICAPM) and the consumption CAPM (CCAPM) (see, e.g., Merton, 1990; Campbell *et al.*, 1997).

Time series analysis of returns can be based on the CAPM ideas. It is usually assumed that returns are independently and identically distributed. Then the OLS method can be used for estimating β_i in a single-factor regression equation for the excess return $Z_i = R_i - R_f$ (Grinold & Kahn, 2000)

$$Z_i(t) = \alpha_i + \beta_i Z_M(t) + \varepsilon_i(t). \quad (10.7)$$

There have been several noted criticisms of the CAPM. First, the CAPM implies that investing in risky assets yields average returns higher than the risk-free return. Hence the rationale for investing in risky assets becomes questionable in bear markets. Another problem is that portfolio diversification advocated by the CAPM is helpful if returns of different assets are uncorrelated. Unfortunately, correlations between the asset returns may grow in bear markets

(Silvapulle & Granger, 2001). One more disadvantage of the CAPM is its high sensitivity to a chosen proxy for the market portfolio. In fact, entire market includes not only equities but also other financial assets, land, real estate, art — in fact, any sources of tradable wealth.

In the absence of time dependence, CAPM can be accurate only conditionally, within given time period where the state variables that determine economy are fixed (Campbell *et al.*, 1997). As a result, the CAPM often fails in empirical tests (Roll, 1977; Fama & French, 2004). Then it seems natural to extend CAPM to a multi-factor model, which I describe in the following sections.

10.3   The Arbitrage Pricing Theory

The CAPM equation (10.1) implies that return on a risky asset is determined only by a single non-diversifiable risk, namely by the risk associated with the entire market. The APT (Ross, 1976) represents a generic extension of the CAPM into the multi-factor framework.

The APT is based on two postulates. First, return for asset $i (i = 1, \ldots, N)$ at every time period is a weighed sum of the risk factor contributions $f_j(t)(j = 1, \ldots, K; K < N)$ plus an asset-specific random component $\varepsilon_i(t)$

$$R_i(t) = \alpha_i + \beta_{i1} f_1 + \beta_{i2} f_2 + \cdots + \beta_{iK} f_K + \varepsilon_i(t). \qquad (10.8)$$

In (10.8), β_{ij} are the factor weights (betas).[1] It is assumed that the expectations for all factor values and for the asset-specific innovations are zero

$$E[f_j(t)] = E[\varepsilon_j(t)] = 0, j = 1, \ldots, K. \qquad (10.9)$$

Also, the time variations of the risk factors and of the asset-specific innovations are independent

$$\text{cov}[f_j(t), f_j(t')] = \text{cov}[\varepsilon_j(t), \varepsilon_j(t')] = 0, t \neq t', \quad j = 1, \ldots, K, \qquad (10.10)$$

and uncorrelated

$$\text{cov}[f_j(t), \varepsilon_i(t)] = 0, \quad i = 1, \ldots, N, \quad j = 1, \ldots, K. \qquad (10.11)$$

However, cross-sectional correlations between the risk factors and between the asset-specific innovations may exist, i.e., $\mathrm{cov}[f_j(t), f_k(t)]$ and $\mathrm{cov}[\varepsilon_i(t), \varepsilon_k(t)]$ may differ from zero.

The APT (10.8) is formulated as a linear model, in part because significant random innovations can seriously complicate estimation of the factor weights within a non-linear model. However, technically, one can always introduce a new linear factor that represents a nonlinear term (e.g., $f_{k+1} = f_k^2$).

The second postulate of APT requires that there are no arbitrage opportunities. This implies that any portfolio in which all factor contributions are canceled out must have return equal to that of the risk-free asset. These two postulates lead to the APT theorem. In its simple form, it states that there exist such $K + 1$ constants λ_0, $\lambda_1, \ldots \lambda_K$ (not all of them equal zero) that

$$E[R_i(t)] = \lambda_0 + \beta_{i1}\lambda_1 + \cdots + \beta_{iK}\lambda_K. \qquad (10.12)$$

While λ_0 has the sense of the risk-free asset return, the numbers λ_j are named the *risk premiums* for the jth risk factors.

Now, consider *well-diversified portfolio* that consists of N assets with the weights w_i that satisfy the condition $\sum_{i=1}^{N} w_i = 1$, so that each $w_i < W/N$ where $W \approx 1$ is a constant. The specific of a well-diversified portfolio is that it is not overweighed with any of its constituents. The APT turns out to be more accurate for well-diversified portfolios rather than for individual stocks. The general APT states that if return of a well-diversified portfolio equals

$$R(t) = a + \beta_1 f_1 + \beta_2 f_2 + \cdots + \beta_K f_K + \varepsilon(t), \qquad (10.13)$$

where

$$a = \sum_{i=1}^{N} w_i a_i \quad \text{and} \quad \beta_k = \sum_{i=1}^{N} w_i \beta_{ik}, \qquad (10.14)$$

then the expected portfolio return is

$$E[R(t)] = \lambda_0 + \beta_1 \lambda_1 + \cdots + \beta_K \lambda_K. \qquad (10.15)$$

Note that returns of the assets that constitute a well-diversified portfolio satisfy also the simple APT (10.8).

The proof of the APT theorem can be illustrated using a simple example with two assets and one factor f (recall that the number of factors K must be less than the number of portfolio assets N). The asset returns are equal

$$r_1 = a_1 + \beta_1 f, \quad r_2 = a_2 + \beta_2 f. \tag{10.16}$$

Portfolio with the weights w and $1 - w$ for assets 1 and 2, respectively, has return

$$r_p = wa_1 + (1 - w)a_2 + [w\beta_1 + (1 - w)\beta_2]f. \tag{10.17}$$

This portfolio is risk-free (i.e., $r_p = r_f$) when the term in the square brackets of (10.17) equals zero. In this case,

$$w = w_f = \beta_2/(\beta_2 - \beta_1). \tag{10.18}$$

Then

$$w_f a_1 + (1 - w_f)a_2 = r_f. \tag{10.19}$$

Plugging (10.18) into (10.19) yields

$$(a_2 - a_1)\beta_2/(\beta_2 - \beta_1) = r_f - a_2. \tag{10.20}$$

Also, due to symmetry of subscripts,

$$(a_1 - a_2)\beta_1/(\beta_1 - \beta_2) = r_f - a_1. \tag{10.21}$$

As a result,

$$a_i = r_f + \beta_i \lambda = E[r_i], \tag{10.22}$$

where

$$\lambda = (a_2 - a_1)/(\beta_2 - \beta_1) = (a_1 - a_2)(\beta_1 - \beta_2). \tag{10.23}$$

A similar yet more cumbersome approach can be used for proving the APT theorem for an arbitrary portfolio (see, e.g., Elton *et al.*, 2009).

APT does not specify the risk factors. Chen *et al.* (1986) listed several essential sources of risks. They include both macroeconomic factors, such as inflation risk, interest rate, and the corporate factors, e.g., return on equity[2] (ROE). Since then, multiple multi-factor models have been developed and widely used in active portfolio management (Grinold & Kahn, 2000). An overview of these models is offered in Section 10.4.

10.4 Multi-Factor Models

10.4.1 *Implementation issues*

A multitude of the factors that are used for analysis and forecasting of portfolio returns may need some transformations prior to using them in econometric models. First, it is rescaling that converts the original variables (x) into the dimensionless ones (z). Usually the *standardization* is used for this purpose

$$z = (x - x_m)/\sigma. \tag{10.24}$$

In (10.24), x_m and σ are mean and standard deviation of x, respectively.

Orthogonalization is used for removing relationships between factors (Fabozzi *et al.*, 2007). For example, to orthogonalize the factor x using averages according to relevant industries (or sectors), first, the industry scores S_k for each industry k are calculated

$$S_k = \frac{\sum\limits_{i=1}^{n} x_i w_{i,k}}{\sum\limits_{i=1}^{n} w_{i,k}}. \tag{10.25}$$

In (10.25), x_i is a factor and $w_{i,k}$ represents the weight of stock i in industry k. Then the industry–neutral factor z_i is calculated as

$$z_i = x_i - \sum_k S_k w_{i,k}. \tag{10.26}$$

Transformations of data are sometimes used in financial modeling for obtaining data samples closer to normally distributed or for replacing nonlinear dependencies by linear ones. Log and power-law functions are examples of such transformations.

Dummy variables are used in factor models for accounting for categorical events, e.g., seasonality effects, such as the "January effect."[3] Dummy variables that can have only values of 0 or 1 are called *binary variables*. More details about implementation of dummy variables are provided in Appendix B.2.

Handling data *outliers*. Empirical data samples may contain some extreme values that seem to be inconsistent with others. Outliers may be results of measurement errors, recording typos, or "black swan" events, such as market crashes or a presence of a billionaire in a population sample. Sometimes, depending on expert judgment, extreme values can be simply discarded. So-called *winsorization* is a more sophisticated approach in which extreme values are replaced with more realistic limiting values. For example, any value that is greater than the 97.5 percentile of the entire data range is considered outlier and replaced with the 97.5 percentile value. As for "black swan" events, their contribution to the sample statistics can be reduced by resampling (see Section 14.3).

Sometimes there are data gaps in the data samples of interest. If there is no requirement on homogenous data spacing, these gaps may be dropped from the data sample. Otherwise, gaps must be filled prior to data analysis. For example, one needs to calculate daily returns using market daily closing prices but some daily prices, $p(k)$, are absent in the sample. Then the gap neighbors' averages, $0.5[p(k-1) + p(k+1)]$, or more sophisticated interpolation techniques can be used.

Multicollinearity exists when two or more independent variables are highly correlated. This certainly complicates causal analysis and, hence, forecasting. Since matrices with collinear columns cannot be inverted, numerical solvers used for the OLS estimation may even crash in the case of high correlations. There is no straightforward theory for mitigating multicollinearity. Removing one or more of highly correlated independent variables that is based on the expert analysis may be needed for addressing the multicollinearity problem. It should be noted that multicollinearity may be just a temporary effect and longer time series may decrease or even eliminate it.

Besides the standard OLS method, two other estimation techniques, the LASSO regression and ridge regression (mentioned in Section 7.4), have recently gained popularity in econometric analysis (see, e.g., James *et al.*, 2013, for the general theory, and Gerakos & Gramacy, 2013, and Bryzgalova *et al.*, 2020, for applications). The former adds to the OLS minimizing function a term that penalizes high number of regressors, which hopefully improves the model interpretability. The latter, too, modifies the OLS minimizing function in order to yield a more robust solution in the case of highly correlated factors.

The Fama–MacBeth (1973) regression method may be used for estimation cross-sectional returns in multi-factor models with correlated residuals. It is performed in two steps. Consider for simplicity a one-factor model for n-asset model for a sample of T time periods $(t = 1, 2, \ldots, T)$. On the first step, β_i are estimated from the regression

$$R_{i,t} = \alpha_i + \beta_i f_t + \varepsilon_{i,t}, \quad t = 1, 2, \ldots, T. \quad (10.27)$$

On the first step, β_i are estimated for each asset $i = 1, 2, \ldots, n$. On the second step, T cross-sectional regressions of the returns using estimates of β_i (named $\hat{\beta}_i$ below) from the first step are calculated for each time period $t = 1, 2, \ldots, T$.

$$R_{i,t} = \gamma_{0,t} + \gamma_{1,t} \hat{\beta}_i + \varepsilon_{i,t}, \quad i = 1, 2, \ldots, n. \quad (10.28)$$

Finally, the values of $\gamma_{0,t}$, $\gamma_{1,t}$ and $\varepsilon_{i,t}$ are averaged over T periods

$$\gamma_k = \frac{1}{T} \sum_{t=1}^{T} \gamma_{k,t}, \quad k = 0, 1; \quad \varepsilon_i = \frac{1}{T} \sum_{t=1}^{T} \varepsilon_{i,t}. \quad (10.29)$$

Then expected return of asset i equals

$$E[R_i] = \gamma_0 + \gamma_1 \hat{\beta}_i + \varepsilon_i, \quad i = 1, 2, \ldots, n. \quad (10.30)$$

Estimation of the standard errors for the regression equation (10.30) may be complicated since the innovations ε_i are generally heteroscedastic and auto-correlated. The Newey–West method can be used to address this problem (Petersen, 2005).

10.4.2 *The Fama–French models*

Fama & French (1993) expanded the CAPM to a three-factor model in order to address several *market anomalies*.[4] Namely, the three-factor model states that the excess equity portfolio (or a single stock) return $R_{i,t} - R_{f,t}$ can be explained by its sensitivity to (1) market excess return, (2) the difference between the return on portfolio of small stocks and the return on a portfolio of large stocks (denoted by SMB for "small vs. big"), and (3) the difference between the return on a portfolio of high book-to-market stocks and the return of on a portfolio of low book-to-market stocks (HML, i.e., "high vs. low")[5]

$$R_{i,t} - R_{f,t} = \alpha_i + \beta_i (R_{M,t} - R_{f,t}) + s_{i,t} SMB_t + h_{i,t} HML_t + \varepsilon_{it}. \quad (10.31)$$

In (10.31), the CAPM notations are used; $s_{i,t}$ and $h_{i,t}$ are the weights for SMB and HML, respectively; $R_{f,t}$ is return of one-month Treasury bills. Fama & French (1993) used *portfolio sorts* in order to estimate the factors SMB and HML. Specifically, they partitioned all US firms listed either on the NYSE, or AMEX, or NASDAQ into six portfolios: Small Value, Small Neutral, Small Growth, Large Value, Large Neutral, and Large Growth. SMB is the average return on the three small portfolios minus the average return on the three big portfolios

$$\text{SMB} = 1/3\,(\text{Small Value} + \text{Small Neutral} + \text{Small Growth})$$
$$-1/3\,(\text{Big Value} + \text{Big Neutral} + \text{Big Growth}). \quad (10.32)$$

HML is the average return on the two value portfolios minus the average return on the two growth portfolios

$$\text{HML} = 1/2\,(\text{Small Value} + \text{Big Value})$$
$$-1/2\,(\text{Small Growth} + \text{Big Growth}). \quad (10.33)$$

While the three-factor model turns out to be more accurate than the CAPM, it still neglects much of the variation in average returns related to profitability and investment (see Novy-Marx, 2013, among others). This motivated Fama & French (2015) to add profitability and investment factors to the three-factor model. The resulting five-factor model has the following form:

$$R_{i,t} - R_{f,t} = \alpha_i + \beta_i(R_{M,t} - R_{f,t}) + s_{i,t}\text{SMB}_t + h_{i,t}HML_t$$
$$+r_i RMW_t + c_i CMA_t + \varepsilon_{it}. \quad (10.34)$$

In (10.34), RMW_t is the difference between the returns of diversified portfolios with highly profitable and weakly profitable stocks, and CMA_t is the difference between the returns of diversified portfolios of firms with low (conservative) and high (aggressive) investments that are defined as annual change in total company's assets.

Portfolio sorts for this model include various combinations between all five factors. The five-factor model's performance is not sensitive to the way its factors are defined. With the addition of profitability and investment factors, the value factor of the three-factor model becomes redundant for describing average returns in the samples examined by Fama & French (2015).

The five-factor model performs better than the three-factor model. However, as Fama & French (2015) admit, the model fails to capture low average returns on small stocks whose returns behave like those of firms that invest a lot despite low profitability.

Blitz *et al.* (2018) offer additional criticisms of the Fama–French models. Specifically, they indicate that sometimes the CAPM relation between market beta and return may be flat, or even negative. On the other hand, the Fama–French models neglect well documented momentum effect. Also, Blitz *et al.* (2018) express a number of concerns with regard to robustness of the two new factors.

Carhart (1997) eliminated one of the drawbacks of the Fama–French models, namely lack of accounting for the momentum effects. His four-factor model shows significant improvement over the single market factor CAPM model in explaining equity portfolio performance (see also Chan *et al.*, 2002).

10.4.3 *Smart betas*

In recent years, investment professionals have developed numerous factor models (*smart betas*), as well as factor-based indices, and exchange traded funds (ETFs) based on these models. Size, Value, Quality, Low Volatility (called also Low Risk or Low Beta), High Dividends, Growth, and Momentum are among the most popular factors.

Size is a self-explanatory quantitative factor included in the Fama–French model, though it can be derived with portfolio sorts other than (10.32). In fact, Small/Large Value/Growth portfolios included in the SMB along with their mid-size variations are often treated as independent factor models that are implemented in various ETFs. Low Volatility and High Dividends factors, too, have straightforward quantitative definitions. However, Value and Quality are synthetic factors (Hsu *et al.*, 2018). Specifically, the value factor is generally constructed from stocks that have a high book-to-price ratio, high earnings-to-price ratio, high dividend-to-price ratio, or some combination of these three valuation measures. On the contrary, quality factor portfolios are based on the following attributes: earnings growth, earnings growth stability, low volatility, high profitability, high return on assets (ROA), low debt ratio, and low accounting accruals.

While the growth and momentum stocks may be overlapping at times, they are not always identical. Growth companies are characterized with profits and earnings increasing faster than the economy. However, momentum is a purely technical indicator determined by past stock price dynamics. While the growth nature of a business may last relatively long, momentum can be interrupted by a single negative news.

It should be noted that the weighting schemes and sorting specifics may influence portfolio exposure to different factors (see the recent review by Lesyk *et al.*, 2020).

While various factor models are highly popular in the investment community, they are not free from contradictions. Harvey *et al.* (2016) reviewed 314 factors published in the academic literature and questioned performance robustness of many of them (see also Arnott *et al.*, 2019). Among the problems related to factor-based investing are possible exposure of the factor of interest to other factors (which leads to multicollinearity), neglecting tail behavior of performance distribution, and increased correlations among various factors in bear markets. It is said sometimes that these problems constitute selection bias (Novy-Marx, 2015).

Notes

1. In the machine learning lingo, factor weights are called *loadings*.
2. ROE = E/BV where E and BV are the company's earnings and book value, respectively. In a nutshell, BV equals the company's assets minus its debt.
3. The January effect is an opinion that stock prices fall in December and grow in January. This effect (when it exists) can be explained in that investors tend to sell off under-performing stocks at the end of year for tax purposes.
4. Within the EMH/CAPM worldview, any mispricing that cannot be explained with the CAPM is called market anomaly.
5. Book-to-market is defined as BV/MV. The company's market value (MV) is defined as a product of the company's number of all (outstanding) shares and their current market price.

Part IV

Active Trading Strategies

I use the term *active trading strategies* for describing the trading strategies based on changing market conditions that offer limited prospects either for profiting (opportunistic strategies) or for minimizing trading loss (optimal execution strategies).

Chapter 11

Technical Analysis-Based Strategies

11.1 Introduction

Technical analysis-based strategies (TABSs) employ various methods for forecasting the future direction of price. These methods (sometimes referred as *charting*) are generally based on analysis of past prices but may also rely on other market data, such as trading volume and volatility (see, e.g., Kaufman, 2005, among others).[1] As I indicated in Chapter 4, the very premise of TABSs is in conflict with even the weakest form of the efficient market hypothesis. Therefore, TABSs are discarded by some influential economists.[2] Yet, TABSs continue to enjoy popularity not only among practitioners but also within a distinctive part of the academic community (see for reviews, Park & Irwin, 2007; Menkhoff & Taylor, 2007). What is the reason for the "obstinate passion" to TABSs, as Menkhoff & Taylor (2007) put it?[3] One explanation was offered by Lo *et al.* (2000): TABSs fit very well into the visual mode of human cognition. Indeed, people like discovering patterns. Some, unfortunately, even develop apophenia.[4] As a result, TABSs have become a very popular tool for price forecasting prior to the pervasive electronic computing era.

Obviously, TABSs would not have survived if there were no records of success, though possibly anecdotal and sometimes exaggerated by the TABSs' proponents. There have been a number of reports demonstrating that while some TA strategies could be profitable in the past, their performance has deteriorated in recent years (see, e.g., Kerstner, 2003; Aronson, 2006; Neely *et al.*, 2009). In a nutshell, simple TABSs were profitable in equities and in FX until the

1980s and 1990s, respectively. This conclusion *per se* does not imply the death sentence to TABSs. The very assumption that any particular trading strategy can be profitable for years seems to be overly optimistic. It is hard to imagine a practitioner who keeps putting money into a strategy that has become unprofitable after a certain (and not very long) period of time. Fortunately (for believers), TABSs offer uncountable opportunities for their potential improving, and hence, there is always a chance for success. Generally, TABSs are determined by several input parameters, and there are no hard rules for determining them. Moreover, these parameters may need frequent adjustment for maintaining effectiveness of the chosen strategy.

Another possible venue for increasing profitability of TABSs is diversification across trading strategies and/or trading securities. For example, several trading strategies can be used simultaneously for the same asset. Timmerman (2006) concluded that simple forecasting schemes, such as equal-weighting of various strategies, are difficult to beat. One popular approach is using multiple time frames (Kaufman, 2005). Hsu & Kuan (2005) have shown that trading strategies based on several simple technical rules can be profitable even if the stand-alone rules do not always make money. Namely, Hsu & Kuan (2005) considered three strategies along with several technical rules (such as moving averages and channel breakouts described below). The first strategy, the learning strategy, is based on the periodic switching of investments to the best performing rule within a given class of rules. Then the voting strategy assigns one vote to each rule within a given rule class. There are two choices: long positions and short positions. If most votes pointed at, say, a long position, this position is initiated. Finally, the position-changing strategy expands the voting strategy to fractional long/short allocation according to the ratio of long/short votes.

Another option is either to diversify or replace portfolio assets for a chosen strategy, or to use various TABSs for various assets. While diversification has practical limits in partitioning available investment capital among multiple strategies and instruments, it may provide rich opportunities for implementing profitable TABSs.

Neely *et al.* (2010) suggested combining *trend strategies* with an economic-variable model. This, too, may be a promising approach as the fundamental values improve in the end of recessions when prices are still depressed. On the contrary, trend models are more sensitive to the beginning of recessions since the economic variables are generally updated monthly or quarterly. Hence, TABSs may be useful not only *per se* but also in combination with the fundamental value analysis.

A generic notion of *bar* is widely used in TABSs. Bar is usually defined with the time interval. In classical TABSs, trading-day bar duration is used. Other major bar parameters include opening price, closing price, intraday minimum price, and intraday maximum price. In some strategies, such bar parameters as average price or volume-weighted average price may be involved.

Classical TABSs are described using daily market closing prices and, unless specified otherwise, I imply the bar closing price while referring to price. It should be noted that closing (and opening) of equity markets has an obvious meaning. However, it is less definitive in FX that operates around the clock during the workdays.

With proliferation of HFT in recent years (see Section 1.7), there have been numerous attempts to apply TABSs to intraday price dynamics. Then, shorter-time or equal-volume bars are used. The size of the latter is determined with some trading volume that is typical for a given asset. Equal-volume bars have a shorter time duration within active trading hours (e.g., right after market opening) and a longer time duration during passive hours (e.g., around lunch time). However, little has been published in academic literature about profitability of TABSs on the intraday timescales (Park & Irwin, 2007). One may expect that the noise-to-signal ratio is prohibitively high for the TABSs at sub-minute timescales. Marshall *et al.* (2008) studied intraday TABSs profitability in the US equity market and found that none of the 7846 popular technical trading rules were profitable after data snooping bias was taken into account.

An important rule in the formulation of any trading strategies is avoiding *look-ahead bias*. Namely, trading rules should be expressed only in terms of lagged values. Indeed, while back-testing of trading strategies can be expanded into models defined in terms of present values, there is no practical way for implementing them in practice. For example, if a trading decision based on daily closing prices should be made before or at market closing today, the most recent price used in the trading rule must be yesterday's closing price.[5]

In the following sections, I provide an overview of the major TABSs, including trend strategies, momentum and oscillator strategies, and strategies based on complex geometric patterns.

11.2 Trend Strategies

Trend strategies have a long history that can be traced to the early 20th century (see the review by Antonacci, 2015). Arguably, the first scientific analysis of trend strategies was done by Cowles & Jones (1937). Trend strategies can be defined with a famous motto: *Buy low, sell high.* The question is how low is *low* and how high is *high?* In other words, determining the market entry and exit points is the main challenge for trend strategies. I describe below several prominent approaches to this challenge.

11.2.1 *Filter rules*

According to the simple *filter rule* (sometimes called the *naive trading rule*), one should buy (sell) at the next opening if the last closing price P_k is higher (lower) than the former closing price P_{k-1} by a certain threshold $\delta > 0$ (often chosen higher than the asset daily volatility):

$$\text{Buy} : P_k/P_{k-1} > 1 + \delta, \tag{11.1a}$$

$$\text{Sell} : P_k/P_{k-1} < 1 - \delta. \tag{11.1b}$$

The naïve trading rule is sometimes used as a benchmark for comparative testing of other trading strategies (Dunis *et al.*, 2003). In a more generic approach, the highest (lowest) closing prices for a given past period of length n are used for the trading decision (Taylor, 2005). Namely,

$$\text{Buy} : P_k/M_k > 1 + \delta, \tag{11.2a}$$

$$\text{Sell} : P_k/m_k < 1 - \delta, \tag{11.2b}$$

where

$$M_k = \max(P_{k-1}, \ldots, P_{k-n}), \tag{11.3a}$$

$$m_k = \min(P_{k-1}, \ldots, P_{k-n}). \tag{11.3b}$$

Several studies show that some filter rules with various δ and s might be profitable in FX (but not in equities) until the 1980s, but this is not the case anymore, particularly if realistic transaction costs are accounted for (Park & Irwin, 2007; Menkhoff & Taylor, 2007). Still, filter rules offer great flexibility in formulating new strategies that may be worthy of further exploration. For example, Cooper (1999) suggested using prices *and* trading volumes at two lagged weekly periods for deriving trading signals and demonstrated that the stocks with increasing trading volume have weaker reversals (i.e., more pronounced trends), which leads to returns higher than those obtained from the buy-and-hold strategy.

11.2.2 *Moving-average rules*

Adding lagged periods in determining trends brings us to the moving averages techniques, which were already introduced for forecasting volatility (see Section 5.2). In the moving-average strategy, two moving averages (the short one and the long one) are compared to make a trading decision.

Let's denote the simple moving average (SMA) over n lagged periods at time t with $sma(P_t, n)$ so that

$$sma(P_t, n) = (P_{t-1} + P_{t-2} + \cdots + P_{t-n})/n. \qquad (11.4)$$

Now, consider the relative difference between the short-term (fast) $sma(P_t, S)$ and the long-term (slow) $sma(P_t, L)$:

$$r_t = [sma(P_t, S) - sma(P_t, L)]/sma(P_t, L). \qquad (11.5)$$

The SMA strategy is defined with the following trading signals:

$$\text{Buy}: r_t > \delta, \qquad (11.6a)$$

$$\text{Sell}: r_t < -\delta. \qquad (11.6b)$$

Typical ratios L/S in the known literature vary in the range $4 \div 20$.

Another popular moving average is exponential moving average (EMA)

$$ema(P_t, \beta) = \beta P_t + (1 - \beta)^* ema(P_{t-1}, \beta). \tag{11.7}$$

As was indicated in Section 5.2, the smoothing coefficient β has the following relation to the number of lagged periods in SMA:

$$\beta = 2/(n+1). \tag{11.8}$$

The recurrence formula (11.7) needs the value of P_0, which is usually chosen to be equal to the $sma(P_t, n)$ for a short initial period of length n.

An example of the moving-average strategy (and the challenges it faces) is given for SPY in Fig. 11.1. While the buy signal in April 2009 can be noticed in a rather wide range of δ (i.e., there is a pronounced trend), low δ can generate the sell signal in February 2010, which could probably be ignored. Indeed, exiting the market too early may

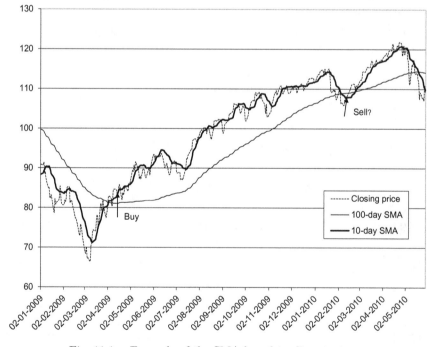

Fig. 11.1.   Example of the SMA-based trading strategy.

cut potential future profits. Still, for risk-averse investors, protection from potential losses is more important.

Several adaptive moving-average strategies have been proposed by practitioners to account for nonstationary nature of price dynamics (Kaufman, 2005). The idea here is to treat the lags S and L as variables that depend on price variations. An example of such an approach is the Chande's Variable Index Dynamic Average (VIDYA), in which an EMA-type exponential smoothing is determined with price volatility:

$$VIDYA_t = \beta k P_t + (1 - \beta k)^* VIDYA_{t-1}. \tag{11.9}$$

In (11.9), β is the smoothing coefficient and $k = \mathrm{stdev}(P_t, S)/\mathrm{stdev}(P_t, L)$ is the relative volatility calculated for short (S) and a long (L) past periods. Thus, the contribution of past prices in the current value of VIDYA decline with increasing market volatility.

11.2.3 *Channel breakouts*

A *channel* (or *band*) is an area that surrounds the price trend line within which price movements do not indicate formation of a new trend. The upper and the bottom channel walls are called *resistance* and *support*. Trading strategies based on the channel breakouts are popular among practitioners and in academy (Park & Irwin, 2007). The trading rules for channel breakouts can be formulated as follows (Taylor, 2005): if a trader has a long position at time t, the sell signal is generated when

$$P_t < (1 - B)m_{t-1}. \tag{11.10}$$

If trader has a short position at time t, the buy signal is generated when

$$P_t > (1 + B)M_{t-1}. \tag{11.11}$$

In (11.10)–(11.11), B is the channel bandwidth and the values of m_t and M_t are defined in (11.3). Finally, if trader is neutral at time t, the conditions (11.10) and (11.11) can be used as the signals for acquiring short and long positions, respectively.

Fig. 11.2. Example of the Bollinger bands based trading strategy.

A more risky strategy may use a buy signal when

$$P_t > (1 + B)m_{t-1} \qquad (11.12)$$

and a sell signal when

$$P_t < (1 - B)M_{t-1}. \qquad (11.13)$$

In the widely used *Bollinger bands*, the price trend line is defined with the price SMA (or EMA) rather than with m_{t-1} and M_{t-1}, and the bandwidth is determined by the asset volatility

$$B_t = k^*\text{stdev}(P_t, L). \qquad (11.14)$$

The parameters k and L in (11.14) are often chosen to be equal to 2 and 20, respectively. An example of the Bollinger bands with these parameters in Fig. 11.2 shows several close sell signals in August 2008 that indicate an impending price drop. On the other hand, current choice of k misses price reversal in March 2009.

11.3 Momentum Strategies

As far as TABSs are concerned, the notion of *momentum* is used for describing the rate of price change. In particular, K-day momentum on day t equals

$$M_t = P_t - P_{t-K}. \tag{11.15}$$

Momentum smoothens price and can be used either for generating trading signals or as a trend indicator. For example, a simple momentum rule may be a buy (sell) signal when momentum switches from a negative (positive) value to a positive (negative) one.

Often, momentum is referred to as the difference between current price and its moving average (e.g., EMA), which leads to further price smoothing

$$m_t = P_t - ema(P_t, K). \tag{11.16}$$

Momentum can also be used as an indicator of trend fading. Indeed, momentum approaching zero after a big price move may point toward possible market reversal.

11.3.1 *Time series momentum*

Moskowitz *et al.* (2012) and Baltas & Kosowski (2013) described the so-called *time series momentum* (TSM), which implies persistent momentum for given security that lasts 12 months and more. TSM has a sense of the *longitudinal momentum* in contrast to the *momentum arbitrage* that has a sense of *cross-sectional momentum* (see Section 12.5).

As Jegadeesh & Titman (2011) indicated, a natural cause of momentum profitability is behavioral effects, namely, investors' delayed reaction to information (Delong *et al.*, 1990; Barberis *et al.*, 1998). Two other effects may also play a role in TSM. First, large investment institutions with high trading volumes must minimize implementation shortfall, i.e., market impact of trading due to limited liquidity (Perold, 1988). This problem is addressed by splitting intended trading volumes into small pieces, so-called child orders (see Chapter 15). These orders are submitted to the market according to various time schedules that may last prolonged periods (Johnson, 2010). Also, one can expect that the new pension contributions and other regularly scheduled money allocations are often invested in recent winners, thus, prolonging TSM.

Cai & Schmidt (2020a) compared performance of TSM and buy-and-hold (B&H) strategy for the S&P 500 Index (^GSPC) during the period starting in January 1950 and ending in April 2019 for two types of monthly returns (see Table 11.1). First, these were returns for the periods beginning and ending on the first days and the last days of the calendar months, respectively. In this case, returns for each given month were added to the list of the TSM returns if the aggregate return for the last 12 months was positive. Otherwise, zero return was added to the list of the TSM returns (i.e., assumed that there was no trading). The B&H list of returns contained all monthly returns starting with the 13th month of the original sample. Hence each sample of monthly TSM returns and of monthly B&H returns had $N_m - 12$ data points, where N_m is the number of calendar months in the data sample.

Second, in order to increase the sample sizes and avoid possible end-of-month bias, 21 trading-day returns were used as a proxy for monthly returns. Also, the 12-month lookback period was replaced with the 252 trading-day period. This lookback period was moved by one day at a time (rather than moving by one month at a time in the case of the calendar monthly returns). Hence, the samples of 21-day returns had $N_d - 252$ data points, where N_d is the number of trading days in the original sample.

Both monthly and 21-day samples yield qualitatively similar results but only the latter demonstrates statistically significant differences due to a much larger size of the data sample. TSM underperformed B&H in terms of returns but outperformed in terms of the Sharpe ratio due to its lower volatility. The reason for that is that TSM misses some price growth opportunities that exist in the case when the 12-month lookback returns are negative. On the other hand, TSM has a lower volatility because it exposes the trading capital to market risk on a smaller number of days than B&H.

An early comparative analysis of TSM and SMA was offered by Ferreira *et al.* (2014) and Marshall *et al.* (2017). Cai & Schmidt (2020a) compared performance of SMA, B&H, and TSM for all 10-year and 20-year periods in January 1950–April 2019 (see Table 11.2). For the entire period of January 1950–April 2019, the SMA with the short/long periods of 63/252 trading days significantly

Table 11.1.   Performance of B&H and TSM in January 1950–April 2019.

| Sample | Data points | | Ann return | | | Ann std. deviation | | Sharpe | | |
	Total	Lookback return > 0	B&H	TSM	p-Value	B&H	TSM	B&H	TSM	p-Value
Monthly	820	604	7.3%	6.5%	0.48	14.4%	11.1%	0.51	0.58	0.37
21-day	17169	12644	7.6%	6.3%	0.00	15.2%	11.4%	0.50	0.55	0.01

Table 11.2.   Performance of B&H, TSM, and SMA in January 1950–April 2019.

			10-year period		
				SMA	
Short/long SMA	B&H	TSM	63/252	30/126	15/63
Ann return	6.7%	5.4%	5.9%	4.5%	4.4%
Ann Sharpe	0.47	0.49	0.56	0.46	0.45
			20-year period		
Ann return	6.8%	5.9%	6.4%	6.2%	4.2%
Ann Sharpe	0.45	0.50	0.57	0.57	0.42

Table 11.3.   Performance of B&H, TSM, and SMA in January 1995–April 2019.

		10-year period	
	B&H	TSM	SMA 63/252
Ann return	6.9%	6.9%	7.0%
Ann Sharpe	0.42	0.55	0.57
		20-year period	
Ann return	8.3%	7.9%	7.8%
Ann Sharpe	0.49	0.60	0.60

outperformed both B&H and TSM in terms of the Sharpe ratio but B&H was superior in terms of returns (all *t*-test *p*-values were less than 0.01). However, the outperformance of B&H lasted only for the time periods that ended before 2004.

For a more recent data sample (for which the ends of the 10-year periods and 20-year periods started in January 1995), the B&H returns outperformed only for the 20-year periods, and performance of TSM and SMA was practically the same both in terms of returns and the Sharpe ratio (see Table 11.3). Thus, comparative performance of various trend-following strategies varies with the trading time period. This may point at a regime change in early 2000s, possibly related to proliferation of high-frequency trading.

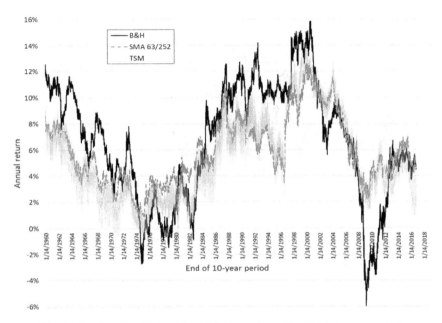

Fig. 11.3. The B&H, TSM, and SMA returns for the 10-year periods.

TSM was much more sensitive to the starting date of trading than B&H and SMA. That is why the charts for the TSM returns look more like bands rather than lines (see Fig. 11.3). Also, the B&H returns and the TSM returns in January 1950–April 2019 were positive for all 20-year periods but not for all 10-year periods. However, the SMA returns were always positive for both the 10-year periods and the 20-year periods.

The profitability of B&H and the trend-following trading strategies, TSM and SMA, at sufficiently long time periods can be explained with that the optimal ARMA model of the monthly ^GSPC returns in January 1950–April 2019 has a positive mean.

11.3.2 *Moving average convergence/divergence*

Moving Average Convergence/Divergence (*MACD*) is a momentum indicator widely popular among practitioners. In MACD, momentum is calculated as the difference between fast EMA and slow EMA. Typical fast and slow periods are 12 and 26 days, respectively.

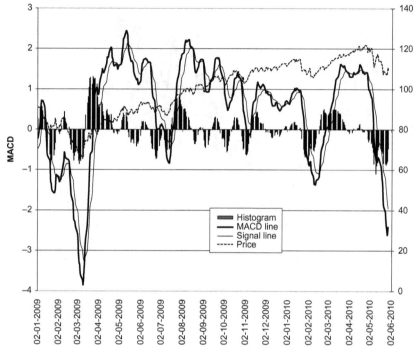

Fig. 11.4. An example of MACD for SPY.

This difference

$$\text{MACD}_t = ema(P_t, 12) - ema(P_t, 26) \qquad (11.17)$$

is called the *MACD line*. Its exponential smoothing (performed usually over nine days) is called the *signal line*:

$$signal\_line = ema(\text{MACD}_t, 9). \qquad (11.18)$$

Since the signal line evolves slower than the MACD line, their crossovers can be interpreted as trading signals. Namely, buying opportunity appears when the MACD line crosses the signal line from below. On the contrary, crossing the signal line by the MACD line from above can be interpreted as a selling signal.

The differences between the MACD and signal line in the form of a histogram often accompanies the MACD charts (see Fig. 11.4). This difference fluctuates around zero and may be perceived as an *oscillator*, another pattern widely used in TABSs.

11.4 Oscillators

11.4.1 *Relative strength index*

Obviously, trends can have reversals and price momentum is often bounded in the range due to competing bullish and bearish market sentiments. Then the oscillator signals can be used for indicating the overbought and oversold assets. One of the most popular oscillators is the *relative strength index* (RSI). This oscillator is determined with directional price moves during a given time period N (usually N is chosen in the range from 5 to 14 days).

$$\text{RSI}_N = 100^* RS/(1 + RS), RS = n_{\text{up}}/n_{\text{down}}. \qquad (11.19)$$

In (11.19), n_{up} and n_{down} are the numbers of upward moves and downward moves of closing price within the chosen time period, respectively. Often, these numbers are exponentially smoothed

$$n_{\text{up}}(t) = (1 - \beta)^* n_{\text{up}}(t - 1) + \beta U(t), \qquad (11.20a)$$

$$n_{\text{down}}(t) = (1 - \beta)^* n_{\text{down}}(t - 1) + \beta D(t), \qquad (11.20b)$$

where

$$U(t) = 1, P_t > P_{t-1}; \quad U(t) = 0, \quad P_t \le P_{t-1}, \qquad (11.21a)$$

$$D(t) = 1, P_t < P_{t-1}; \quad D(t) = 0, \quad P_t \ge P_{t-1}. \qquad (11.21b)$$

Typical RSI values for the overbought/oversold securities are 70/30. For some volatile assets, RSI reaches the overbought/oversold conditions quite frequently. Then, the RSI spread may be widened to 80/20 (Kaufman, 2005).

An example in Fig. 11.5 shows that RSI correctly pointed at impending price reversal when it exceeded the value of 80 in mid-January and mid-April. However, the high RSI value in March was a "false alarm."

11.4.2 *Stochastic oscillators*

Another popular oscillator, the *stochastic oscillator,* is defined as

$$\%K = \frac{P - L(N)}{H(N) - L(N)} * 100. \qquad (11.22)$$

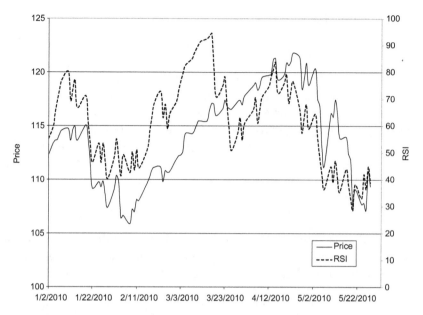

Fig. 11.5.   An example of RSI for SPY.

In (11.22), P is the most recent price, and $H(N)$ and $L(N)$ are the highest and the lowest prices within the N last days, respectively. Usually N is chosen within the range 5–14 days.

Sometimes *slow %K* (denoted with *%D*) equal to the 3-day SMA of *%K* is used. Similarly, *slow %D* is the 3-day SMA of *%D*. While RSI and stochastic indicators yield rather similar estimates for given security, the latter, particularly the slow *%D*, are notably smoother than the former. RSI may be more accurate in flagging overbought and oversold securities. On the other hand, crossings of *%D* and slow *%D* can be used in defining a trading strategy similar to MACD (Kaufman, 2005).

11.5   Complex Geometric Patterns

Trends and oscillators have relatively simple visual forms and straightforward definitions. However, some other TABSs are based on the visual patterns that may be easily recognizable with a human eye but represent a challenge for quantitative description. These include *head-and-shoulder* pattern (*HaSP*), inverse HaSP, broadening tops

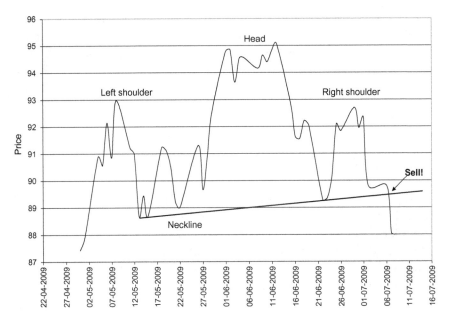

Fig. 11.6.   Example of the head-and-shoulder pattern.

and bottoms, triangle tops and bottoms, double tops and bottoms, and others (Edwards & Magee, 2001; Kaufman, 2005). The main challenge in finding persistent complex geometric patterns in time series is filtering out the noise that may produce false leads. The smoothing technique with a kernel regression was successfully used for analysis of TABSs by Lo *et al.* (2000) in equities, and by Omrane & Van Oppens (2004) in FX.

In this section, I describe HaSP as an example of a complex geometric pattern. Visually, HaSP is determined with five price extremes: three maxima that refer to two shoulders surrounding the head, and two valleys between the shoulders and the head (see Fig. 11.6).

HaSP has a neckline — the support line connecting the shoulder minima. The trading idea based on HaSP is a selling signal when price breaks through the neckline from above. Inverse HaSP is a mirror image of HaSP in respect to the time axis. This pattern generates a buy signal when price breaks through the neckline from below.

There has been a common opinion that the TABSs should not be over-fitted (e.g., Kaufman, 2005; Kerstner, 2003; Lo *et al.*, 2000).

The problem with overly complicated models is that they are highly sensitive to the noise present in training data samples and, as a result, have poor forecasting ability. Lo *et al.* (2000) have a relatively simple definition of HaSP. Namely, HaSP is determined just with five consecutive extremes: E1, E2, E3, E4, and E5, such that

- E1 is a maximum;
- E3 > E1; E3 > E5;
- E1 and E5 are within 1.5 percent of their average;
- E2 and E4 are within 1.5 percent of their average.

However, Omrane & Van Oppens (2004) defined HaSP with nine rules including conditions for the relative heights of the head and shoulders and timings between them. Both accounts by Lo *et al.* (2000) and Omrane & Van Oppens (2004) have demonstrated potential profitability of some complex geometric patterns. However, these profits might be too small for covering transaction costs.

Notes

1. Edwards & Magee (2001) provide the classical introduction to TABSs. The sheer number of books devoted to TABSs is overwhelming: a search on Amazon.com using the key words *technical analysis* for new book releases with at least four-star reader ratings in December 2020 yielded 282 entries.
2. This may be the reason why the classical Fama-French models do not include the momentum factor (see Section 10.4).
3. Menkhoff & Taylor (2007) primarily discuss applications of TABSs in FX and indicate that the FX traders may have an additional rationale for choosing TABSs as a tool for trading decisions. Namely, estimating fair values for the FX rates is more complicated than that for equities. Still, the popularity of TABSs among the equity traders seems to be as strong as in FX.
4. Apophenia refers to propensity to see connections and patterns in random information.
5. On the NYSE, traders must submit market-on-close order by 3:45 P.M. If intraday prices are available, one can possibly assume that price, say at 3:44 P.M., is near the closing price and include its value in a trading decision at this moment.

Chapter 12

Arbitrage Strategies

12.1   Introduction

According to the Law of One Price, equivalent assets (i.e., assets with the same payoff) must have the same price (see, e.g., Bodie & Merton, 1998). In competitive markets, asset price must be the same worldwide provided that it is expressed in the same currency, and the transportation and transaction costs can be neglected. Violation of the Law of One Price leads to the *deterministic arbitrage*, which is risk-free profiteering by buying an asset in a cheaper market and immediately selling it in a more expensive one. Deterministic arbitrage is sometimes called *pure arbitrage* (Bondarenko, 2003).

Arbitrage can exist only for a limited time until mispricing is eliminated due to increased demand and finite supply of a cheaper asset.[1] Deterministic arbitrage should be discerned from *statistical arbitrage*, which is based on statistical deviations of asset prices from their expected (fair) values and may incur losses (Jarrow *et al.*, 2005). Note that some practitioners use the term *statistical arbitrage* for denoting a specific type of trading strategies (see Section 12.2).

In the FX market, a popular example of arbitrage is so-called *triangle arbitrage*. It appears in case of imbalance among three related currency pairs. Namely, exchange rates for three currencies X, Y, and Z must satisfy the condition

$$(X/Y)^*(Z/X)^*(Y/Z) = 1. \tag{12.1}$$

An arbitrage opportunity appears if (12.1) is violated. For example, if the product of two exchange rates, $(EUR/JPY)^*(USD/EUR)$, is smaller than USD/JPY, one can buy JPY with USD, then buy EUR with JPY, and finally, make profits by buying USD for EUR.[2]

Many arbitrage trading strategies are based on hedging the risk of financial losses by combining long and short positions in the same portfolio. An ultimate long/short hedging yields a *market-neutral portfolio*, in which the risks from having long and short positions are supposed to compensate each other. Market-neutral strategy can be described in terms of the CAPM (see Section 10.2). Indeed, since market-neutral strategy should completely eliminate market risk, market-neutral portfolio beta β_i (10.2) is expected to equal zero. The so-called *beta hedge* is based on this idea (see Section 12.4).

As a simple example of market-neutral strategy, consider two companies within the same industry, A and B, one of which, say A, yields higher returns for some time. A simple investing idea might be buying shares A and neglecting shares B. A more risky strategy may involve simultaneously buying shares A and short selling shares B. Obviously, if the entire sector rises, this strategy does not bring as much money as simply buying shares A. However, if the entire market falls, one may expect that shares B will have a higher loss than shares A. Then, profit from short selling shares B would compensate for the loss resulting from buying shares A. One possible problem with the latter strategy is that it is based on the belief in the persistent inferiority of company B in respect to company A. A more sophisticated strategy, named *pair trading*, employs the idea of *mean reversion* (see, e.g., Vidyamurthy, 2004). It is based on the expectation that the divergence in returns of the companies A and B is a temporary effect due to market inefficiency, which will be eliminated over some time. Pair trading strategy is then the opposite of what I just described above. Namely, one should buy shares B and sell shares A. Such a strategy can be profitable only under some conditions described in Section 12.3.

Not all arbitrage trading strategies are market-neutral: The extent of long/short hedging is often determined by the asset fund manager's discretion. The hedge fund industry has been using a classification that includes not only the strategy type but also instruments and geographic investment zones (Stefanini, 2006; Khandani & Lo, 2011). This chapter continues with an overview of the major hedging strategies in Section 12.2. Then, Sections 12.3–12.5 are devoted to various arbitrage types: pair trading, beta hedging, and momentum arbitrage, respectively. Finally, arbitrage risks are discussed in Section 12.6.

12.2 Hedging Strategies

Long/short hedging strategies are widely used by financial institutions, most notably by the hedge funds. Detailed specifics of these trading strategies are not widely advertised for the obvious reason: the more investors target the same market inefficiency, the faster it is wiped out. Still, common ideas for the long/short hedging are well publicized. Stefanini (2006) offered a general review of various arbitrage strategies and their historical performance.

Let's start with *equity hedge*, which itself has several forms. Pair trading and its special case, *ADR arbitrage,* fit into this category. American depositary receipts (ADRs) are securities that represent shares of non-US companies traded in the US markets. Variations in market liquidity, trading volumes, distinct trading hours, and exchange rates may create discrepancies between prices of ADRs and their underlying shares.

Equity hedge may not be exactly the market-neutral one. Moreover, the ratio between long and short equity positions may be chosen depending on the market conditions. In recent years, the so-called *130/30* (or more generally *1X0/X0*, where $X = 2 \div 5$) mutual funds have gained some popularity. These funds have 130% of their capital in long positions, 30% of which is funded by short positions. Sometimes, these portfolios are named long/short funds. On the contrary, portfolios with *dedicated short bias* always have more capital in short positions than in the long ones.

Sometimes, one of long/short positions (e.g., the long one) is stock index futures while the other (short) one consists of all stocks that constitute this index (so-called *index arbitrage*). The idea behind this strategy is that the index futures may not always reflect short-term prices variations of the index constituents.

One should discern *equity market-neutral strategy* and *statistical arbitrage.* According to Khandani & Lo (2011), practitioners use the term *statistical arbitrage* for describing the most challenging trading style, namely, "highly technical short-term mean-reversion strategies involving large numbers of securities (hundreds to thousands, depending on the amount of risk capital), very short holding periods (measured in days to seconds), and substantial computational, trading, and IT infrastructure." Equity market-neutral strategy is a less demanding approach that may involve lower frequency of trading and fewer securities. Economic parameters may also be incorporated into predicting models derived under the umbrella of market-neutral strategies.

Convertible arbitrage involves *convertible bonds* that can be converted into shares of the same company. Convertible bonds often decline less in a falling market than the shares of the same company do. Hence, the idea of the convertible arbitrage is buying convertible bonds and shorting the underlying stocks.

Fixed-income arbitrage implies taking long and short positions in different fixed-income securities. Using analysis of correlations between different securities, one can buy those securities that seem to become underpriced and sell short those that look overpriced.

One type of the fixed-income arbitrage is the *issuance-driven arbitrage*, specifically, arbitraging *on-the-run* vs. *off-the-run* US Treasury bonds. Newly issued (on-the-run) Treasuries usually have yields lower than the older off-the-run Treasuries but both yields are expected to converge with time.

A more generic *yield curve arbitrage* is based on anomalies in dependence of the bond yield on maturity. Generally, the longer is maturity, the higher is yield as investors who lock their capital in bonds for a longer time expect higher return. However, yield curve sometimes becomes inverted, which represents arbitrage opportunities. Note that prolonged inverted yield curve may point at impending recession. Other forms of the fixed income arbitrage can be based on comparison of yields for Treasuries, corporate bonds, and municipal bonds.

Mortgage-backed securities (MBS) arbitrage is a particular form of the fixed income arbitrage. It has its own specifics since MBS have a prepayment option. Namely, mortgage borrowers can prepay their loans fully or partially prior to the mortgage term, which increases the uncertainty of the MBS value. There are so many different MBS that this makes them a separate field of the arbitrage expertise.

The strategies listed above can be referred to as *relative value arbitrage*. Another group of arbitrage strategies is called *event-driven arbitrage*. A typical example here is *merger arbitrage* (also called *risk arbitrage*). This form of arbitrage involves buying shares of a company that is expected to be bought and short selling the shares of the acquirer. The rationale behind this strategy is that businesses are usually acquired at a premium, which sends down the stock prices of acquiring companies. Another event-driven arbitrage strategy focuses on financially distressed companies. Their securities are sometimes sold below their fair values as a result of market overreaction to the news of distress.

Multi-strategy hedge funds use a synthetic approach that utilizes various hedging strategies and different securities. Looking for the arbitrage opportunities across the board is technically more challenging yet potentially more rewarding. Finally, *global macro* hedge funds apply their multiple strategies to various instruments traded worldwide.

12.3 Pair Trading

The general idea behind pair trading was outlined in the introduction to this chapter. APT provides some theoretical background to this trading strategy (see Section 10.3). Indeed, APT states that expected return for an asset i can be expressed in the form

$$E[R_i(t)] = \lambda_0 + \beta_{i1}\lambda_1 + \cdots + \beta_{iK}\lambda_K, \qquad (12.2)$$

where λ_0 has the sense of the risk-free asset return, and λ_j is the risk premium for the jth risk factor betas β_{ij}.

APT implies that similar companies have the same risk factors and any deviation of returns from (12.2) is a mispricing, which yields arbitrage opportunities. Namely, shares of an underpriced company should be bought while shares of a fairly priced (or overpriced) company should be shorted. However, as it was pointed out in Section 10.3, APT itself does not determine the risk factors. Hence defining if security is mispriced in respect to the APT benchmark is hardly possible. Luckily, market-neutral strategies do not need outside benchmarks: they are based on relative mispricing, which can be determined using cointegration analysis.

12.3.1 *Cointegration and causality*

Cointegration is an efficient statistical technique developed by Engle and Granger for an analysis of common trends in multivariate time series (see, e.g., Hamilton, 1994; Alexander, 2001). One might think that the correlation analysis might be used in the selection of trading pairs. However, the correlation analysis can be applied only to stationary variables. Hence, it requires preliminary de-trending of prices or, in other words, can be applied only to returns. Correlations are a measure of a short-term relationship that may be affected by volatility. Therefore, trading strategies based on the correlation analysis need frequent rebalancing. On the contrary, cointegration describes long-term trends that may be stable even when correlations are broken (Alexander, 1999).

It is said that two non-stationary time series are cointegrated if their linear combination is stationary.[3] While the difference between two arbitrary prices series (the spread) may vary unpredictably, it is stationary for cointegrated series. If the spread deviates from its stationary value, it is expected that mean reversion will bring it back, or, in other words, mispricing will be eliminated.

Formally, two time series x, $y \sim I(1)$ are cointegrated if there is such a constant α that

$$z = x - \alpha y \sim I(0). \qquad (12.3)$$

The standard technique offered by Engle & Granger (1987) for finding if two time series are cointegrated is derivation of the linear regression

$$x_t = \alpha y_t + c + \varepsilon_t. \qquad (12.4)$$

Then the residuals ε_t are tested for stationarity. Usually, the augmented Dickey–Fuller (ADF) test is used for unit roots (see, e.g., Hamilton, 1994; Tsay, 2005). If stationarity is not rejected, then the cointegration condition (12.3) holds. In the context of the cointegrated portfolios, the residuals are sometimes called *tracking errors*[4] (Alexander *et al.*, 2001).

The concept of cointegration is closely related to the *Granger causality*, which implies that changes in the direction of one series precede changes of the other one. Consideration of the Granger causality is based on the *error correction model*

$$\Delta x_t = \delta_1 + \sum_{i=1}^{M_1} \beta_{1i} \Delta x_{t-i} + \sum_{i=1}^{M_2} \beta_{2i} \Delta y_{t-i} + \gamma_1 z_{t-1} + \varepsilon_{1t}, \quad (12.5)$$

$$\Delta y_t = \delta_2 + \sum_{i=1}^{M_3} \beta_{3i} \Delta x_{t-i} + \sum_{i=1}^{M_4} \beta_{4i} \Delta y_{t-i} + \gamma_2 z_{t-1} + \varepsilon_{2t}, \quad (12.6)$$

where Δ is the difference operator, and the coefficients δ_i, β_{ij}, and γ_i can be estimated using the linear regression. The *Granger representation theorem* states that cointegration and the error correction model are equivalent. Namely, if x_t and y_t are cointegrated, then $\gamma_1 < 0$ and $\alpha\gamma_2 > 0$. If this is the case, any deviation of z from its stationary value will be corrected in the future.

It is said that x "Granger-causes" y when x and y are cointegrated and lagged terms of time series x are significant in the dynamics of the time series y. It should be noted that the Granger causality is not true causality. It may be simply that both x and y are determined by a common factor but have different lagging dependencies. Moreover, the direction of the Granger causality may change over time; that is, the leader and the follower may change their mutual roles. An example of such a role change was found in the analysis of futures and spot prices (Alexander *et al.*, 2001).

12.3.2 *Pair selection*

Providing that (12.3) holds, the typical pair trading strategy has the following form (Vidyamurthy, 2004): buy a portfolio consisting of long shares A with log price x_t and short shares B with log price y_t when

$$x_t - \alpha y_t = c - \Delta, \quad (12.7)$$

and sell this portfolio when

$$x_t - \alpha y_t = c + \Delta. \quad (12.8)$$

The challenges for implementing this strategy are the selection of stocks A and B for the trading portfolio, and defining the optimal value of Δ. Within the APT framework, it is natural to pick up stocks from the same industry as their prices are expected to be determined with the same risk factors. However, the number of equities within the same industry is often insufficiently high for finding arbitrage opportunities, and the search for cointegrated pairs can be extended into entire equity sectors (such as materials, financials, etc.) or even beyond them (Gatev *et al.*, 2006).

In general, choosing Δ in the strategy (12.7)–(12.8) should be based on an analysis of residuals ε_t. Practitioners sometimes suggest entering the market when prices diverge by more than two historical standard deviations σ (Chan, 2009). Vidyamurthy (2004) advises to calculate Δ by maximizing the trading profits. If the cumulative distribution function of the spread is $\Pr(\Delta)$, then the probability that profits exceed Δ equals $(1 - \Pr(\Delta))$ and the profits W depend on Δ as

$$W \sim \Delta(1 - \Pr(\Delta)). \qquad (12.9)$$

Minimization of the right-hand side of (12.9) yields an optimal Δ. In particular, if the spread follows the normal distribution, the profits have a maximum when $\Delta = 0.75\sigma$.

Another problem with implementation of the cointegration technique is arbitrariness in choosing an independent variable in the linear regression (12.3). In other words, two options exist:

$$p_t^A = \alpha^A p_t^B + c^A + \varepsilon_t^A \quad \text{with} \quad \alpha^A = \text{Cov}(\varepsilon_t^A, \varepsilon_t^B)/\text{Var}(\varepsilon_t^A),$$
$$(12.10)$$

and

$$p_t^B = \alpha^B p_t^A + c^B + \varepsilon_t^B \text{ with } \alpha^B = \text{Cov}(\varepsilon_t^A, \varepsilon_t^B)/\text{Var}(\varepsilon_t^B). \quad (12.11)$$

Vidyamurthy (2004) suggests choosing the variable with lower volatility as the independent one.

Rather than employing the Engle–Granger cointegration framework, Gatev *et al.* (2006) used the concept of weakly dependent stocks. Namely, Gatev *et al.* (2006) have chosen such counterparts in trading pairs that minimize the sum of squared deviations between the two normalized price series (the *distance measure*). More recently,

Huck & Afawubo (2015) studied performance of pair trading for various combinations of constituents of S&P 500 index and found advantages of the cointegration technique over the distance measure.

Another practical criterion in choosing trading pairs is that a successful outcome must be realized within acceptable time frame. Since residuals are expected to fluctuate around zero value due to mean reversion, even visual inspection of the chart for ε_t may give an idea about possible round-trip execution time for a given pair. *The zero-crossing rate* of a mean-reverting process can be used as a quantitative measure of the execution time. For a stationary ARMA process, the zero-crossing rate can be estimated with the Rice's equation (see for a review, Abrahams, 1986).

Elliott *et al.* (2005) used the Ornstein–Uhlenbeck equation for modeling mean reversion of the spread $X(t)$:

$$dX(t) = \rho(\mu - X(t))dt + \sigma dW. \tag{12.12}$$

In (12.12), dW is the standard Brownian motion, and the parameters ρ, μ, and σ are estimated from an empirical time series.

The Ornstein–Uhlenbeck equation (12.12) has the following standard form:

$$dZ(t) = -Z(t)dt + \sqrt{2}dW(t). \tag{12.13}$$

For (12.13), the first passage time to $Z(t) = 0$ for the initial value $Z(0) = s$ has the probability density distribution[5]

$$f_{\text{FPT}}(t) = \sqrt{\frac{2}{\pi}} \frac{|s|e^{-t}}{(1 - e^{-2t})^{3/2}} \exp\left(-\frac{s^2 e^{-2t}}{2(1 - e^{-2t})}\right). \tag{12.14}$$

Elliott *et al.* (2005) suggested that the timing of pair trading can be based on the time that yields the maximum value of $f_{\text{FPT}}(t)$:

$$\hat{t} = 0.5 \ln\left[1 + 0.5(\sqrt{(s^2 - 3)^2 + 4s^2} + s^2 - 3)\right]. \tag{12.15}$$

Namely, Elliott *et al.* (2005) chose the most likely time T when $X(T) = \mu$

$$T = \hat{t}/\rho. \tag{12.16}$$

Then, the trading strategy for a chosen value of s would be entering pair trade when the spread is higher than $\mu + s\sigma/\sqrt{2\rho}$ or lower than $\mu - s\sigma/\sqrt{2\rho}$, and later unwinding this trade at time T.

12.4 Beta Hedging

The CAPM-based single-factor model (10.7) of Chapter 10 offers a natural way for hedging diversifiable market risk of individual securities. Namely, if one invests capital W_i in stock i, beta hedging implies short selling the cash amount $\beta_i W_i$ of the market proxy. While the idea of beta hedging seems to be quite transparent, very little can be found in the literature about its efficiency. An accurate estimation of beta represents a challenge *per se*. A popular protocol for monthly beta forecasts is using monthly returns over the prior 5 years (Fama & MacBeth, 1973). However, Cenesizoglu *et al.* (2016) have recently found that the realized beta estimator from daily returns over the prior year generates the most accurate beta forecast among estimators based on daily returns.

As I indicated in Chapter 7, the estimation errors of expected returns and covariance matrix may lead to a better performance of estimation-free EWPs in respect to MVPs. Since estimation of the CAPM beta has the same accuracy problem, one may ask if market-neutral hedging, i.e., shorting cash amount W_i of the market proxy can compete with beta hedging.

In the known literature, there is no universally accepted performance measure of beta hedging. The Sharpe ratio being risk-adjusted return that is widely used for long portfolios does not provide the complete picture. Indeed, one may expect that investors willing to implement beta hedging are more concerned with their explicit losses rather than with volatility risk. Hence, efficiency of preventing losses should be an intrinsic part of performance measures for beta hedging. Still, one should remember that profits remain the main motivation for investing.

Nadler & Schmidt (2019b) considered several novel performance measures including a synthetic one that accounts for both risk-adjusted return and loss of trading strategy. Namely, Nadler & Schmidt (2019b) used the rebalancing periods of length τ and performed simulations of trading started on each day of the data sample until the rebalancing date was within the sample. Then, portfolio returns $R_{i\tau}$ were used for performance analysis; $i = 1, 2, \ldots, N_\tau$; N_τ is the number of rebalancing periods within given data sample. In these notations, annualized Sharpe ratio equals

$$Sh_\tau = \bar{R}_\tau / \sigma_\tau \sqrt{\frac{252}{\tau}}, \tag{12.17}$$

where $\bar{R}_\tau$ and σ_τ are mean value and standard deviation of returns $R_{i\tau}$, respectively. Another chosen performance measure is the sum of all negative returns for given rebalancing period over the entire data sample

$$S_\tau(R_{i\tau} < 0) = \sum_{i=1}^{N_\tau} R_{i\tau}, R_{i\tau} < 0. \tag{12.18}$$

The third performance measure is profit-to-loss (PtoL) ratio that is equal to

$$PtoL_\tau = -\tilde{r}_i / S_\tau(R_{i\tau} < 0), \tag{12.19}$$

where $\tilde{r}_i$ is the median daily return in basis points (BPS). This choice of units yielded $PtoL_\tau$ within in the range $[0, 1]$. Median return was chosen in (12.19) rather than mean return because the distribution of returns can be significantly skewed. Finally, a new synthetic measure, the performance rank Z_τ being the product of Sh_τ and $PtoL_\tau$ was introduced

$$Z_\tau = Sh_\tau \times PtoL_\tau. \tag{12.20}$$

Z_τ accounts for both mean return and median return, as well as for investor aversion to volatility risk and to explicit losses. Nadler & Schmidt (2019) found that the Sharpe ratio and $PtoL_\tau$ do not necessarily have maximums simultaneously for the same trading strategy. Hence, Z_τ may serve as an arbiter in this case. It should be noted that the return-based performance measures including $PtoL_\tau$, Sh_τ, and Z_τ are not applicable in bear markets.

Nadler & Schmidt (2019b) also explored rebalancing effects for momentum-based weighting of long portfolios on efficiency of beta hedging. Namely, they examined whether momentum weighting of portfolio's long assets in terms of past returns, or Sharpe ratios, or informational ratios[6] in respect to SPY has advantages over equal weighting. Two long portfolios beta-hedged with SPY were considered. The first portfolio consisted of nine major US equity sector SPDR ETFs in 2003–2017. The second portfolio contained five high-growth technology stocks in 2006–2017. For these portfolios, beta hedging always outperformed market-neutral hedging. In particular, beta hedging cut the losses of the ETF-based portfolio in the bear market of 2008 by about 25–30 times (depending on the rebalancing period).

Momentum-based weighting of long assets was found to be preferable for high-growth stocks at short rebalancing periods. In most cases, though, beta hedging with equal weighting of long assets had a better performance. For the high-growth portfolio, beta hedging decreased maximum losses by about 8–9 times. But in contrast to the ETF portfolio, the highest high-growth portfolio losses were in 2008.

12.5 Momentum Arbitrage

I introduced momentum strategies in Section 11.3. One of them, TSM, represents longitudinal momentum that is determined by price dynamics for a given security. In this section, I describe *cross-sectional momentum* (CSM) that has received significant attention both in academia (see Jegadeesh & Titman, 2011, for a review) and from practitioners (Asness *et al.*, 2014; Gray & Vogel, 2016). In a nutshell, the conventional CSM pattern implies that the winners in past short-term periods (less than 3 months) underperform past losers in the next 1–3 months, i.e., exhibit mean reversion of returns. On the contrary, the winners in longer past periods (about a year) outperform past losers in the next 1–3 months, which implies persistent momentum. Hence, the CSM arbitrage can be based on implementing a market-neutral portfolio with the former winners and former losers on the long and short portfolio sides, respectively.

It was suggested that the CSM profitability may be determined by positive serial correlations in risk factor returns. However, Fama & French (1996), Grundy & Martin (2001), and Jegadeesh & Titman (2001) found that this correlation is very small, and the Fama–French three-factor model does not explain performance of the CSM strategies. It is generally believed that profitability of momentum strategies is mostly caused by investor behavioral effects (see discussion in Section 11.3). It should be noted, though, that the CSM-based strategies may dramatically underperform during the bear markets (Grundy & Martin, 2001; Barroso & Santa-Clara, 2015; Daniel & Moskowitz, 2016).

Nadler & Schmidt (2019a) tested the conventional CSM pattern for several portfolios in 2007–2017 and 2011–2017 that consist of proxies[7] to

(I) An equity portfolio consisting of 28 major equity US ETFs.

(II) A multi-asset portfolio consisting of portfolio I plus a gold ETF, five international equity ETFs, and five bond ETFs.

(III) The constituents of several US equity sector ETFs.

Nadler & Schmidt (2019a) also compared performance of the CSM strategies with that of equal-weight benchmark portfolios (EWBPs). The reason for that is that most of the market indexes and ETFs have market cap weighting. However, since the CSM-based winner/loser baskets are equally weighted, the relevant benchmarks should be equally weighted, too.

Nadler & Schmidt (2019a) found that performance of the CSM strategies depends on portfolio holdings and whether the bear market of 2008 is included in the data sample. The conventional CSM pattern was statistically significant only for a multi-asset ETF portfolio in both 2007–2017 and 2011–2017, and for the proxies of the SPDR S&P 500 ETF and the Industrials Select Sector SPDR ETF in 2011–2017. As the examples in Tables 12.1 and 12.2 for the SPY proxy demonstrate, the losers beat the winners for all lookback periods during the interval 2007–2017 that includes the bear market of 2008. However, the CSM performance in 2011–2017 has the conventional pattern in which winners outperform losers at the lookback periods greater than 6 months.

Nadler & Schmidt (2019a) found also other, unconventional CSM patterns that can be explored for arbitraging past winners and past losers of the equity sector ETF constituents between themselves and/or with their EWBPs.

12.6 Arbitrage Risks

Arbitrageurs face multiple risks. Liu & Longstaff (2004) emphasize the arbitrage riskiness by quoting a bond trader: "So there's an

Table 12.1. CSM performance statistics for the SPY proxy in 2007–2017.

| Basket size | Lookback, days | Basket returns | | p-Values | | Benchmark returns | p-Values | | | |
| | | Winners | Losers | Winners vs. losers | | | Winners vs. benchmark | | Losers vs. benchmark | |
				Unpaired	Paired		Unpaired	Paired	Unpaired	Paired
50	21	1.18%	1.49%	0.12	0.01	1.23%	0.73	0.29	0.19	0.00
50	63	1.49%	1.73%	0.24	0.07	1.23%	0.09	0.00	0.02	0.00
50	126	1.41%	1.96%	0.01	0.00	1.23%	0.24	0.00	0.00	0.00
50	252	1.25%	1.71%	0.04	0.01	1.23%	0.91	0.80	0.03	0.00
50	252[a]	1.26%	1.62%	0.09	0.02	1.23%	0.88	0.70	0.07	0.00

[a]The last month of the 1-year lookback period is skipped to address 1-month reversal in stock returns described by Lo & MacKinlay (1990), and Boudoukh *et al.* (1994).

Table 12.2. CSM performance statistics for the SPY proxy in 2011–2017.

Basket size	Lookback, days	Basket returns		p-Values			p-Values			
		Winners	Losers	Winners vs. losers		Benchmark returns	Winners vs. benchmark		Losers vs. benchmark	
				Unpaired	Paired		Unpaired	Paired	Unpaired	Paired
50	21	1.23%	1.36%	0.38	0.09	1.36%	0.32	0.00	0.97	0.91
50	63	1.49%	1.42%	0.66	0.46	1.36%	0.31	0.00	0.70	0.36
50	126	1.57%	1.51%	0.71	0.57	1.36%	0.10	0.00	0.36	0.04
50	252	1.56%	1.28%	0.10	0.01	1.36%	0.12	0.00	0.66	0.35
50	252[a]	1.56%	1.20%	0.03	0.00	1.36%	0.12	0.00	0.32	0.03

[a]The last month of the 1-year lookback period is skipped to address 1-month reversal in stock returns described by Lo & MacKinlay (1990), and Boudoukh et al. (1994).

arbitrage. So what? This desk has lost a lot of money on arbitrages."
Indeed, an event-driven arbitrage may go wrong simply because an
event does not happen (a merger may be annulled). Or, the market
perceives this event in an unconventional way: for example, investors
decide that an acquirer did not overpay for the purchase of an
acquiree, and both stocks go up right after the acquisition announcement. A distressed business may never recover, and the list goes on.

As for the relative-value arbitrage, past mean reversion pattern
may be broken in the future. Moreover, it is usually implied that
investors have unlimited patience and resources for living through
times of widening spread until mean reversion brings the spread back
to its average value. In real life, market-neutral portfolio is not self-
funded as brokers who lend shares for short selling require collateral.
Moreover, brokers have a right to request the borrowed shares any
time. If the spread keeps widening after the market-neutral portfolio
was set up, an investor may receive a margin call from the broker.
In the case of investor's limited capital, this may force partial liquidation of the portfolio at a loss. For highly leveraged hedge funds,
such a loss may become quite dramatic. A classic example here is
the demise of a very large (and initially very successful) Long-Term
Capital Management (Lowenstein, 2000). This hedge fund (that had
two Nobel laureates in economics on its advisory board) used various
arbitrage strategies with a huge margin (debt-to-equity ratio of over
25 to 1) that stopped working, in part due to the Russian financial
crisis of 1998.

Another case in point is unprecedented losses that long/short
hedge funds had in August of 2007 (Khandani & Lo, 2011). These
losses were caused by forced liquidations of significant portfolio volumes, possibly due to margin calls. Initial liquidation might happen
even outside the pure long/short group of hedge funds. However,
it had put a pressure on entire equity market and caused stop-loss
trading and de-leveraging processes.

Several accounts address the risks of widening spread and limited trading horizon in the market-neutral arbitrage (Jurek & Yang,
2007; Liu & Timmermann, 2009). Here, I focus on a stylized and
instructive model offered by Liu & Longstaff (2004). In this model,
the investment capital is split into a riskless asset R_t and an arbitrage
opportunity A_t. The dynamics of a riskless asset has the following

form:

$$dR = rRdt, \qquad (12.21)$$

where r is an interest rate. Providing that the initial value R_0 is 1,

$$R_t = \exp(rt). \qquad (12.22)$$

It is assumed in the Liu–Longstaff model that A_t is described with the *Brownian bridge* process that converges to zero at time T:

$$dA = -\frac{\alpha A}{T - t}dt + \sigma dZ. \qquad (12.23)$$

In (12.23), $\alpha > 0$ determines the rate with which A_t converges to zero, $\sigma > 0$ is volatility, and dZ is the standard Brownian motion. The value of A_t corresponds to a portfolio with a long notional amount invested in underpriced security and the same but short amount invested into overpriced security. The solution to (12.23) for $t \leq s \leq T$ is

$$A_t = \left(\frac{T - s}{T - t}\right)^{\alpha} A_t + \sigma \int_t^s \left(\frac{T - s}{T - \tau}\right)^{\alpha} dZ_\tau. \qquad (12.24)$$

Within the Liu–Longstaff model, the investor's total wealth at time t equals

$$W_t = N_t A_t + P_t R_t, \qquad (12.25)$$

where N_t and P_t are the numbers of the arbitrage and riskless units held in the portfolio. Assuming that there are no additional capital flows, the wealth dynamics have the following form:

$$dW = NdA + rPRdt = NdA + r(W - NA)dt$$
$$= \left[rW - \left(r + \frac{\alpha}{T - t}\right)NA\right]dt + \sigma N dZ. \qquad (12.26)$$

It follows from (12.26) that

$$W_T = W_t \exp\left(\int_t^{eT} \left(r - \left(r + \frac{\alpha}{T-s} \right) \frac{NA}{W} - \frac{\sigma^2 N^2}{2W^2} \right) ds \right.$$

$$\left. + \sigma \int_t^T \frac{N}{W} dZ \right). \tag{12.27}$$

If the margin requirement per unit of the given arbitrage is $\lambda > 0$, then the collateral constraint on the portfolio is

$$W_t \geq \lambda |N_t|. \tag{12.28}$$

Liu & Longstaff (2004) maximize the expected utility function $E[\ln(W_T)]$ in terms of the variable N_t that satisfies the constraint (12.28). The optimal values of N_t depend on the following conditions:

$$N_t = W_t/\lambda \text{ if } A_t < -\sigma^2/[r + \alpha/(T-t)], \tag{12.29a}$$

$$N_t = \frac{r + \frac{\alpha}{T-t}}{\sigma^2} A_t W \text{ if } |A_t| < \sigma^2/[r + \alpha/(T-t)], \tag{12.29b}$$

$$N_t = -W_t/\lambda \text{ if } A_t > \sigma^2/[r + \alpha/(T-t)]. \tag{12.29c}$$

This result implies that due to the collateral constraints, investors should use only a finite capital in arbitrage. This capital coincides with the maximum defined with (12.28) in the cases (12.29a) and (12.29c). However, a lower value is optimal in the case (12.29b). Liu & Longstaff (2004) show also that when their optimal strategy is used, the arbitrage portfolio can experience losses prior to convergence at time T.

The drawback of the Liu–Longstaff model is that it implies that the time of mean reversion, T, is known. Jurek & Yang (2007) replaced the Brownian bridge process in the Liu–Longstaff model with the Ornstein–Uhlenbeck equation, which implies uncertainty of T. Jurek & Yang (2007) also assumed that investors optimize the CRRA utility function for a given horizon T. They found that risk-averse investors are expected to be more aggressive in pursuing arbitrage opportunities if they have a longer T. This implies that portfolio managers who are required to report their performance less frequently may display a riskier behavior. The Jurek–Yang model points also at some critical mispricing level, beyond which the amount of investment into the arbitrage should be reduced.

While the arbitrage strategies discussed in this section are market neutral, Liu & Timmermann (2009) showed that a truly optimal strategy for investors with the CRRA risk aversion may yield unbalanced long and short positions. Hence, risk-averse investors may prefer to optimize their portfolios without imposing the constraint of market neutrality.

Popularity of arbitrage strategies in asset management may have become its own curse since arbitrage opportunities do not last long. Khandani & Lo (2011) and Avellaneda & Lee (2010) found that performance of statistical arbitrage has generally degraded since 2002.

Lopez de Prado (2018b) lists several challenges that should be overcome for deriving new profitable trading strategies. They include (but are not limited to):

- "Sisyphus paradigm" (as Lopez de Prado put it) implies the lack of team work and intense competition among portfolio managers working in the same firm. As a result, many of them choose to use similar strategies described in the academic literature that quickly fail.
- Simplistic back-testing.
- Ignoring non-stationarity of time series.
- High correlations between the independent variables included in the factor models.

Hopefully, this book may help the readers to address some of these problems.

Notes

1. Market regulations may sometimes maintain arbitrage opportunities for an indefinite time: an example is the difference in pricing of drugs in the United States and Canada.
2. An accurate evaluation of the triangle arbitrage should account for the bid/ask spreads and liquidity.
3. Here it is assumed that price follows the random walk, that is, price dynamics is an integrated process I(1). See more about integrated processes in Appendix B.

4. This definition of the tracking error should not be confused with the one that is used in portfolio management and refers to the variance of residuals between returns of the tracking equity index and portfolio of interest (see (7.29) in Chapter 7).

5. Cf. with the first passage time for the Brownian motion (3.2) in Chapter 3.

6. See Section 14.2 for the definition of the informational ratio.

7. To avoid survival bias, Nadler & Schmidt (2019b) used the ETF proxies that included in the winner/loser baskets only those ETF constituents that were traded during the entire lookback periods for which past performance was estimated.

Chapter 13

News and Sentiment-Based Strategies

13.1 Introduction

Traditional active investing strategies, such as TABSs and statistical arbitrage, are based on analysis of price dynamics. In recent years, investors' attention turned to unconventional information that is sometimes called *alternative data* (Denev & Amen, 2020). This trend has been amplified by advances in natural language processing that helps to digitize unstructured data and new machine learning techniques promising, on par with traditional econometric methods, to improve investment decisions (Lopez de Prado, 2018a; Dixon *et al.*, 2020).

Alternative data include (but are not limited to)

- Corporate news including public companies' quarterly reports;
- Macroeconomic announcements released by the government agencies;
- Commentaries in press and on the websites of news providers (such as Bloomberg, CNBC, and *Wall Street Journal*, among others);
- Opinions on social networks (tweets and comments on various message boards);
- Web searches.

More exotic alternative data, such as

- Customer data (credit card transactions, loan applications, consumer comments on retail web sites);
- Aerial images of agricultural fields, mall parking lots, etc.;

- Geopolitical events;
- Seasonal effects;

among others (see, e.g., Novy-Marx, 2014) are outside the scope of this book.

Here I offer the following classification for structuring the material I intend to discuss. In a nutshell, I partition alternative data into two groups, namely, *hard news*, i.e., macroeconomic and financial data, and *soft news* that represents the textual information related to expert and investor opinions, and to consumer interests.

Hard news is (or can be easily) quantified and hence can be directly incorporated into the price forecasting models. Hard news is also used for constructing *market sentiment indicators* (or *indexes*). Therefore, when I use the term "market sentiment" in conjunction with the terms "index" or "indicator," it is based on hard news. In our days, hard news is either obtained using the electronic data feeds from news providers or scraped from the web. Soft news, too, is extracted from the web and interpreted using the practices that are called *opinion mining* or sentiment analysis (see for a review, Kearney & Liu, 2014; Liu, 2020). While soft news usually lags hard news, it may keep investor attention and consequently prolong the effects of the latter. Finally, I use the term *textual news sentiment* (that can be based on both hard news and soft news) to emphasize its source.

Of course, there is nothing surprising that the news, whether it represents quantitative information or only contains influential opinions (which are usually based on interpretation of quantitative data), can affect market prices. The problem is to figure out which news and opinions have statistically significant market impact and whether they have long-lasting or transient effects.

I devote Section 13.2 to the text news sentiment. Then, I proceed with describing market impact of hard news in Section 13.3. First, I offer two examples of how corporate earnings reports and macroeconomic announcements may affect stock prices. Further, I provide an overview of the market sentiment indexes. Finally, in Section 13.4, I discuss recent advances in opinion mining including analysis of tweets and Google searches.

13.2 Textual News Sentiment

In general, textual news sentiment is based on extraction of relevant information from various economic and financial news sources, such as Dow Jones, Thomson Reuters, Bloomberg, *Wall Street Journal*, and *New York Times*. This information may be collected on the aggregated market level, sector level, or for individual companies (Das & Chen, 2007). Then the informational contents of individual news and, sometimes, their expert analysis are assigned sentiments in terms of their optimistic/pessimistic or positive/neutral/negative connotations using either psychosocial (Tetlock *et al.*, 2008), or financial (Loughran & McDonald, 2011) dictionaries, or the Thomson–Reuters neural network dictionaries (Heston & Sinha, 2017). Early academic research demonstrated that textual news sentiments can predict returns within 2 days after news release (see Tetlock, 2007; Garcia, 2013; Boudoukh *et al.*, 2013; Chen *et al.*, 2014; Sinha, 2016).

Heston & Sinha (2017) found that the specialized financial dictionary (Loughran & McDonald, 2011) is superior to the general psychosocial dictionary for predicting stock returns. Specifically, the specialized dictionary predicts larger returns that last longer and have less reversal than the general dictionary. Yet, the Thomson–Reuters neural network produces a better predictability than either dictionary approach. When the news is aggregated over 1 day, the sentiment may predict returns over 1 or 2 days that are largely reversed later. However, aggregating news over 1 week produces dramatic increase in predictability. Stocks with news over the past week may have predictable return for up to 13 weeks.

Bommes *et al.* (2018) offers a detailed description of a machine learning protocol for analysis of textual information. Their results demonstrate high sensitivity of returns to news sentiment on the sector level. In particular, Consumer Staples, Health Care and Materials sectors strongly react to negative news.

13.3 Impact of Financial and Macroeconomic News

It is generally believed that stock prices rise on average around the earnings announcements days even though some of these reports may be disappointing (see Beaver, 1968; Chari *et al.*, 1988; Ball & Kothari, 1991; Livnat & Mendenhall, 2006; Frazzini & Lamont, 2007; Savor & Wilson, 2016; Williams, 2015; Heitz *et al.*, 2019, and references therein).

Some macroeconomic announcements, such as the ISM Manufacturing Reports, Non-Farm Payrolls, and Housing Starts, among others, have a similar effect: equity prices rise on average around the announcement days (Balduzzi *et al.*, 2001; Andersen *et al.*, 2003; Evans, 2011; Savor & Wilson, 2013; Nadler & Schmidt, 2016b). Both these anomalies are explained by that the investors demand additional premiums for holding assets during uncertainty prior to releases of new, economically sensitive information. I discuss these effects below.

13.3.1 *Impact of corporate earnings on stock prices*

For accurate estimation of the earnings uncertainty premium, one should filter out persistent price momentum and the contributions of all other events happening around the announcements days. Schmidt (2020c) expanded various approaches used in the current research of both macroeconomic announcements and earnings announcements into a generic regression model. First, in the spirit of the CAPM, stock returns are regressed on the equity market return modeled with the S&P 500 Index (^GSPC) return. This may filter out implicitly the price shocks caused by macroeconomic and geopolitical news. Price dynamics of equity sectors may notably differ from that of the entire market (see analysis of corrections in various US equity sectors by Schmidt, 2020a). Therefore, stock returns are also regressed on the returns of their equity sectors (modelled by the SPDR equity sector ETF returns).

Finally, the model takes into consideration that while the macro-economic and financial news may affect the direction of price momentum, they alone do not determine its strength and duration (Nadler & Schmidt, 2014b). Therefore, the regression model is augmented with the auto-regressive and moving average (ARMA) terms (Tsay, 2005) and with the GJR-GARCH stochastic volatility that accounts for asymmetric distributions of negative and positive returns (Glosten *et al.*, 1993).

Impact of earnings announcements (I) is described with three terms

$$I = \delta_D D + \delta_+ SUE_+ + \delta_- SUE_-. \tag{13.1}$$

The first term in (13.1) accounts for the shock of announcements using a binary variable (D) that is equal to one on the days of announcements, and zero on all other days. The other two terms describe the effect of earnings surprises and are proportional to the *standardized unexpected earnings* (SUE), separately for positive (SUE_+) and negative (SUE_-) surprises. SUE is sometimes scaled by the earnings consensus (see, e.g., the NASDAQ website, *www.nasdaq.com*, and the Zacks Investment Research website, *www.zacks.com*)

$$\text{SUE}_1 = \text{dEPS}/\text{EPS}_c, \text{dEPS} = \text{EPS}_a - \text{EPS}_c. \qquad (13.2)$$

In (13.2), EPS_a is the announced earnings per share and EPS_c is consensus of the earnings per share prior to the announcement. SUE_1 has a drawback in that it becomes unusable when EPS_c is equal to zero.

Latane & Jones (1977) suggested scaling of earnings surprises with their standard deviation

$$\text{SUE}_2 = \text{dEPS}/\text{sd}(\text{dEPS}). \qquad (13.3)$$

A similar approach was introduced by (Balduzzi *et al.*, 2001) for analysis of the impact of the macroeconomic announcements.

Livnat & Mendenhall (2006) and Heitz *et al.* (2019) used scaling by the stock price P of either the earnings surprise

$$\text{SUE}_3 = \text{dEPS}/P \qquad (13.4)$$

or the difference between current earnings and earnings four quarters ago

$$\text{SUE}_4 = (\text{EPS}_q - \text{EPS}_{q-4})/P. \qquad (13.5)$$

Schmidt (2020c) has chosen SUE in the form (13.3) since it can be used for analysis of impact of both macroeconomic surprises and earnings surprises. To discern possible asymmetry of positive and negative earnings surprises, SUE is set as

$$SUE_+ = SUE_2, SUE_- = 0 \quad \text{if} \quad \text{dEPS} > 0, \qquad (13.6a)$$

$$SUE_- = SUE_2, SUE_+ = 0 \quad \text{if} \quad \text{dEPS} < 0. \qquad (13.6b)$$

On all days without announcements, $SUE_+ = SUE_- = 0$.

The regression model for analysis of the earnings impact on daily stock return $r(t)$ has the following form:

$$r(t) = \mu + \beta_M r_M(t) + \beta_S r_S(t) + \sum_{k=1}^{p} a_k r(t-k)$$

$$+ \sum_{k=1}^{q} b_k \varepsilon(t-k) + I(t) + \varepsilon(t). \tag{13.7}$$

In (13.7), r_M and r_S are the total market and equity sector returns, respectively, and I is defined with Eqs. (13.1), (13.3), and (13.6). White noise, $\varepsilon(t)$, is assumed to have the GJR-GARCH(1, 1) form

$$\varepsilon(t) = z(t)\sigma(t), \sigma^2(t) = \omega + \alpha_1 \varepsilon^2(t-1) + \beta_\sigma \sigma^2(t-1)$$

$$+ \gamma J(t-1)\varepsilon^2(t-1) \tag{13.8}$$

where $z(t)$ is IID process with zero mean and unit variance, $\sigma(t)$ is conditional variance, and

$$J(t-1) = \begin{cases} 1, & \varepsilon(t-1) < 0 \\ 0, & \varepsilon(t-1) \geq 0 \end{cases}. \tag{13.9}$$

Schmidt (2020c) analyzed the effects of earnings announcements in January 1999–September 2019 on an equal-weight portfolio of stocks that constituted the Dow Jones Index (DJI) in October 2019. Specifically, an equal-weight portfolio of 29 stocks that constituted DJI in October 2019 was considered. One DJI constituent, Dow Chemical, for which prices prior to its merger with DuPont in 2015 were not available, was excluded from the list.

The average daily returns for the equal-weight portfolio of the DJI constituents within the holding periods *around* the earnings announcements (r_A) and *outside* these holding periods (r_O) are listed in Table 13.1. The holding period around an earnings announcement is defined with two indexes (k, l) related to the buying day k and the selling day l in respect to the announcement day. Since market closing prices were used, the index of zero was assigned to the announcement day or to its prior day, depending on whether the earnings were announced after or before closing of the NYSE. For example, the holding period denoted by (0, 2) implies that the portfolio is

Table 13.1. Summary statistics for the equal-weight portfolio of the DJI constituents.

# of stocks	Holding period	(0,3)	(0,2)	(0,1)	(−1,1)	(−2,1)	(−3,1)	(−5,1)	(−10,1)	(−15,1)	(−30,1)	(−40,1)	(−45,1)	(−50,1)
29	r_A around earnings	0.08%	0.10%	0.17%	0.16%	0.14%	0.13%	0.12%	0.09%	0.08%	0.06%	0.05%	0.05%	0.05%
	r_O outside earnings	0.04%	0.03%	0.03%	0.03%	0.03%	0.03%	0.03%	0.03%	0.03%	0.04%	0.03%	0.05%	0.05%
	p-Value	0.29	0.33	0.18	0.04	0.01	0.00	0.00	0.00	0.00	0.01	0.01	0.68	0.41
	# of negative r_{Ai}	48.3%	44.8%	44.8%	31.0%	27.6%	20.7%	20.7%	13.8%	6.9%	10.3%	3.4%	3.4%	3.4%
26	r_A around earnings	0.03%	0.03%	0.05%	0.10%	0.09%	0.10%	0.10%	0.07%	0.07%	0.06%	0.04%	0.04%	0.04%
	r_O outside earnings	0.04%	0.04%	0.03%	0.03%	0.03%	0.03%	0.03%	0.03%	0.03%	0.04%	0.03%	0.06%	0.06%
	p-Value	0.98	0.88	0.85	0.23	0.10	0.02	0.01	0.02	0.00	0.04	0.04	0.06	0.02
	# of negative r_{Ai}	53.8%	50.0%	53.8%	34.6%	30.8%	23.1%	23.1%	15.4%	7.7%	11.5%	3.8%	3.8%	3.8%

bought on the announcement day (or on its prior day) and sold two trading days later.

The p-values provided in Table 13.1 indicate whether the differences between r_A and r_O are statistically significant. The table also lists the percentage of the portfolio constituents with negative average daily returns around the earnings announcements, r_{Ai} where $i = 1, 2, \ldots, N, N = 29$ (the number of the DJI constituents) and 26 (when the portfolio top 10% performers are dropped).

The first conclusion that can be drawn from the summary statistics is that outperformance around the earnings announcements is the highest when the portfolio is liquidated on the next day after announcements, (i.e., $l = 1$). Short holding periods (with $k > -3$) have the highest average returns r_A. In this case, however, the differences between r_A and r_O become statistically insignificant when the top 10% performers are dropped from the portfolio.

Also, short holding periods have a high percentage of portfolio constituents with negative returns r_{Ai}. Hence, while it may be tempting to use short holding periods for higher profits, these profits may be unsustainable in future or for other portfolios. On the contrary, r_A significantly outperform r_O (with or without top 10% portfolio performers) during longer holding periods ($-40 \leq k \leq -3$). Note that since an average calendar month has 21 trading days, 40 trading days correspond to about 2 months.

Schmidt (2020c) found that with the exception of the JP Morgan stock, all DJI constituents in 1999–2019 had statistically significant positive SUE, which points out at analysts' overly conservative earnings estimates. This, however, does not necessarily translate into stock outperformance around earnings announcements. While r_A are usually much higher than r_O for the holding period of $(0, 1)$, the p-values for the null hypothesis ($r_A = r_O$) for most of the stocks are higher than 0.10. This can be explained by high volatility of returns around announcements. In a nutshell, these results imply that trading around the earnings announcement days has a much better chance to be profitable for portfolios than for individual stocks.

13.3.2 *Market impact of macroeconomic news*

Effects of macroeconomic announcements on asset prices have been a popular topic in economic literature. Indeed, macroeconomic developments being undiversified risk factors yield additional risk premiums in multifactor asset models with risk aversion (Ross, 1976). Studies of these effects are complicated since, as Chen *et al.* (1986) indicated, the economic theory does not determine which economic variables are responsible for excess returns. Since then various authors addressed this problem. In particular, Balduzzi *et al.* (2001) studied effects of 17 public news releases on the US bond market. Flannery & Protopapadakis (2002) employed a GARCH model to identify which macroeconomic surprises (out of 17 candidates) influence realized equity returns or their conditional volatility. Andersen *et al.* (2003) analyzed effects of multiple US and German economic news on intra-day FX rates using an ARMA model with GARCH volatility. Hautsch & Hess (2007) used a Bayesian learning model and showed that the price impact at the time of an announcement is proportional to both the unexpected portion of the announcement and precision of new information (relative to the precision of information available before an announcement). Gilbert *et al.* (2010) expanded the Bayesian framework to forecast FOMC decisions, to *nowcast*[1] GDP growth and inflation, and investigate how the specifics of macroeconomic announcements may explain the differential impact of news on asset prices. Goeij *et al.* (2010) found that the differences in the risk premiums attributed to macroeconomic announcements depend on the state of the economy. Evans (2011) studied intra-day price jumps associated with macroeconomic announcements. Gilbert (2011) showed that there is an empirical relation between stock returns on macroeconomic news announcement days and the future revisions of the released data.

Savor & Wilson (2013) described excess asset returns on the days of macroeconomic announcements for multi-year time periods prior to 2009. This effect is explained with that investors demand additional premium for holding assets during uncertainty prior to releases of economic reports.

Nadler & Schmidt (2016b) extended findings made by Savor & Wilson (2013) to a more recent period. Specifically, they analyzed an impact of 18 macroeconomic announcements on prices of several US equity ETFs during the period from January 2009 to August 2013. The macroeconomic announcements suggested by Andersen *et al.* (2003) and used by Nadler & Schmidt (2016b) are listed for the SPY returns in Table 13.2.

Table 13.2. US macroeconomic news announcements and summary statistics for SPY.

| Economic Indicators | | SPY (mean return = 0.0006) | | | | | | |
| | # in the sample | Return | corr[a] | p-Value[b] | Return/surprise, %[c] | | Model p25 | Model p5 |
Announcements					+/+	+/−		
Real Activity								
Non-farm payroll	54	0.0001	0.39	0.75	76.0	44.8	1	1
Retail sales	55	0.0017	0.38	0.46	74.2	45.8		
Industrial Production & Utilization	55	0.0009	−0.13	0.84	46.2	62.1		
Personal Income & Outlays	55	−0.0019	−0.06	0.19	50.0	52.2		
Consumer Credit	54	0.0002	0.02	0.72	50.0	66.7		
GDP	55	0.0029	−0.11	0.14	60.0	60.0		
Consumption								
New Home Sales	55	0.0027	0.13	0.16	59.3	60.7	1	
Investment								
Durable Goods Orders	55	0.0004	0.12	0.88	61.5	51.7		
Factory Orders	56	−0.0005	−0.20	0.48	57.7	46.7	1	
Government Purchases								
Treasury budget	52	0.0022	−0.14	0.30	59.4	63.2		

Net Exports								
Trade Balance	55	0.0031	0.24	0.12	75.0	51.9	1	1
Prices								
Producer Price Index	55	0.0011	0.16	0.71	67.7	50.0		
Consumer Price Index	55	0.0001	−0.16	0.76	52.9	57.1		
Forward-Looking								
Consumer Confidence Index	55	0.0009	0.04	0.84	65.4	56.7		
ISM manufacturing report	55	0.0022	0.24	0.47	72.7	50.0	1	1
Housing Starts	55	0.0012	0.29	0.69	64.0	43.3	1	1
Index of Leading Indicators	55	−0.0036	−0.09	0.03	48.5	59.1	1	1
Jobless claims	239	0.0010	−0.09	0.56	55.9	63.6	1	1

[a]Correlation between returns and announcement surprises. [b]p-Value for the difference between returns on the announcement days and for entire sample. [c] $+/+$ $(+/-)$ is the percentage of positive returns on the days with positive (negative) announcement surprises.

An ARMA(p, q)+GARCH(m, n) model with linear external terms that accounts for possible effects of macroeconomic announcements was used in this work. This model had the first minimum of Akaike information criterion at $m = 2$ and $n = p = q = 1$:

$$r_i(t) = \mu_i + a_{i,1}r_i(t-1) + b_{i,1}\varepsilon_i(t-1)$$

$$+ \sum_{k=1}^{N} d_{ik}D_k(t) + \sum_{k=1}^{N} s_{ik}S_k(t) + \varepsilon_i(t), \tag{13.10}$$

$$\varepsilon_i(t) = z(t)\sigma_i(t), \sigma_i^2(t) = \omega_i + \alpha_{i,1}\varepsilon_i^2(t-1) + \alpha_{i,2}\varepsilon_i^2(t-2)$$

$$+ \beta_{i,1}\sigma_i^2(t-1). \tag{13.11}$$

In Eq. (13.10), $k = 1, 2, \ldots, N = 18$ are the announcements indices included in the model; D_k are the dummy variables equal to unity on the days of announcements k and zero otherwise; the surprise values S_k are defined according to Balduzzi *et al.* (2001)

$$S_k(t) = [A_k(t) - E_k(t)]/\Sigma_k, \tag{13.12}$$

where $A_k(t)$ and $E_k(t)$ are actual and expected (consensus) values of macroeconomic indicator k at time t; Σ_{Sk} is standard deviation of S_k. In Eq. (13.11), $z(t)$ is IID process with zero mean and unit variance.

According to the model (13.10)–(13.12), there are several macroeconomic announcements with high statistical significance. First, these are ISM Manufacturing Index and Non-Farm Payrolls (Andersen & Bollerslev (1998) and Gilbert *et al.* (2010) call them the "kings" of announcements). The other significant announcements are International Trade Balance, Index of Leading Indicators, Housing Starts, Jobless Claims, and, to a lesser extent, Factory Orders, New Home Sales, GDP, and Retail Sales. Some of these indicators (e.g., those for Non-Farm Payrolls and ISM Manufacturing Reports) have statistically significant positive coefficients for the event variables D_k regardless of surprises, which may compensate, at least partially, negative news. This implies that securities may be oversold at the times of uncertainty prior to announcements. Another possibility is contrarian expectations of the market. For example, poor economic reports might encourage Federal Reserve to continue its activist policies during the economic slowdown following the bear market of 2008.

Nadler & Schmidt (2016b) compared performance of the B&H strategy with three strategies that realize returns on the announcement days. Specifically, they choose:

- Realized returns on the announcement days of all 18 macroeconomic indicators listed in Table 13.2 (Model #18).
- Realized returns on the days of announcements of those macroeconomic indicators whose regression coefficients have statistical significance of p-value < 0.05 (Model p5).
- Realized returns on the days of announcements of those indicators whose regression coefficients have statistical significance with p-value < 0.25 (Model p25). The reason for including this model was that smaller thresholds, e.g., p-value < 0.15, yielded practically the same macroeconomic indicators as the Model p5.

The macroeconomic indicators included in Model p5 and Model p25 are marked in Table 13.2 and the results of comparison for SPY are listed in Table 13.3.

The B&H mean daily returns are lower than those for the other strategies considered here. For example, mean daily returns of Model #18 are at least 30% higher than those of B&H; yet their differences are not statistically significant (p-value > 0.6). Mean daily returns for Model p5 are dramatically higher than that of Model #18 and have better statistical significance than that of B&H. However, compound

Table 13.3. Performance of announcement-based trading strategies for SPY.

		Days with Announcements		
	B&H	Model #18	Model p25	Model p5
T[a]	1153	766	495	214
Mean daily return	0.0006	0.0008	0.0013	0.0017
p-Value[b]	na	0.71	0.09	0.16
Sigma[c]	0.013	0.012	0.012	0.013
Compound return	0.69	0.86	0.92	0.44
Sharpe ratio	1.63	2.59	3.33	2.37

[a]Number of days in the market. [b]p-Value for the difference between the B&H and model strategies. [c]Standard deviation of mean returns on the announcement days.

returns for Model p5 may be lower than those of Model #18, and even lower than those of B&H. The reason for inferior compound returns of Model p5 is a relatively low number of trading days in respect to the number of days in B&H during the bull market of 2009–2013. The low number of trading days, however, improves the effective Sharpe ratio since the trading strategy has a shorter exposure to the market risk. Model p25 has the highest compound return and the highest Sharpe ratio. These results point at a possibility for profitable trading around the macroeconomic announcements.

Nadler & Schmidt (2014b) used a similar approach for implementing forecasting models that are based exclusively on market impact of macroeconomic announcements. At first, macroeconomic surprises were defined as in (13.12): $S(t) \sim A(t) - E(t)$, where $A(t)$ and $E(t)$ are actual and expected (consensus) values of macroeconomic indicators at time t, respectively. Nadler & Schmidt (2014b) found that regressing returns on *actual change*, $AC(t) \sim A(t) - A(t-1)$, and *expected change*, $EC(t) \sim E(t) - A(t-1)$, yields statistically significant indicators similar to those for surprises $S(t)$. The advantage of $AC(t)$ vs. $S(t)$ is that the former is not based on the subjective nature of consensus. As for $EC(t)$, it does not have a look-ahead bias pertinent to $S(t)$ since $E(t)$ is usually known prior to publishing $A(t)$. Hence $EC(t)$ can be used for short-term forecasting. Seven macroeconomic indicators including ISM Manufacturing Reports, Non-Farm Payrolls, International Trade Balance, Index of Leading Indicators, Housing Starts, Jobless Claims, and Consumer Credit were highly significant (with p-value less than 0.1) for all three regression models. With proper fitting, AC-, EC-, and S-based indexes based on the shocks caused by macroeconomic announcements can be used for qualitative modeling the price dynamics. A similar idea was discussed by Scotti (2013) and implemented in the Citigroup Economic Surprise Index. An example in Fig. 13.1 shows that the indexes based on seven most significant macroeconomic announcements resemble the SPY price dynamics in 2009–2014. However, the effects of macroeconomic announcements alone do not describe the strength of the bull market during this period (cf. the scales on vertical axis for price and indicators in Fig. 13.1).

Nadler & Schmidt (2015) studied impact of macroeconomic announcements on the ETF trading volumes. They found that the ISM Manufacturing Reports, Non-Farm Payrolls, Housing Starts,

Fig. 13.1. SPY price and its fits based on seven macroeconomic indicators.

and to a lesser extent, Jobless Claims, Leading Indicators, and CPI significantly increase daily trading volumes. However in contrast to prices, trading volumes were not sensitive to the announcements surprises.

13.3.3 Market sentiment indexes

The term "sentiment analysis" can mean several things as far as financial applications are concerned (Algaba *et al.*, 2020). Kearney & Liu (2014) discern two types of sentiments: investor sentiment, which includes only the subjective judgments of investors, and textual sentiment, which may also contain a more objective reflection of the state of economy and/or of the conditions in a certain firm. Kräussl & Mirgorodskaya (2017) suggest that media sentiment may translate into investor sentiment. Here I focus only on quantitative sentiment indicators that are based on the conventional financial market data (hard news). These indicators reflect investor expectations of a future market (or individual stock) direction.

Arguably the most famous market sentiment indicator is the Chicago Board Options Exchange's (CBOE) Volatility Index (VIX) based on the concept of implied volatility introduced in Section 5.2. Specifically, VIX represents expectation of volatility over the next 30 days that is estimated using the S&P 500 Index options. VIX is sometimes called the "fear index": increasing VIX implies falling market ahead. Other implied volatility-based indices are described by Moran & Liu (2020).

Another popular market sentiment indicator is the put-call ratio.[2] Increasing number of call options suggests growing market ahead. In fact, all technical indicators described in Chapter 11 can be treated as quantitative sentiment indexes as they reflect investors' opinions based on historical patterns rather than follow from some fundamental theory.

A noted direction in the economic literature describes how sentiment-driven investors can cause prices to depart from fundamental values. Within this framework, investors' market-wide sentiment may cause mispricing of "the shares of certain firms — newer, smaller, more volatile, unprofitable, non-dividend paying, distressed or with extreme growth potential... One possible definition of investor sentiment is the propensity to speculate" (Baker & Wurgler, 2006). Market-wide sentiment in this field is quantified with indexes based on several macroeconomic proxies. Baker & Wurgler (2006) list six such proxies: the closed-end fund discount, NYSE share turnover, the number and average first-day returns on IPOs, the equity share in new issues, and the dividend premium. Stambaugh *et al.* (2012) explored the role of investor sentiment in a broad set of anomalies in cross-sectional stock returns. Assuming that overpricing should be more prevalent than underpricing due to short-sale constraints, they found that each anomaly is stronger (its long-short strategy is more profitable) following high levels of sentiment. Also, the short leg of each strategy is more profitable following high sentiment. However, sentiment exhibits no relation to returns on the long legs of the strategies. Ho & Hung (2012) tested the predictive ability of investor sentiment on the return and volatility at the aggregate market level in the US, four largest European countries and three Asia-Pacific countries. They found that in the US, as well as in France and Italy, periods of high consumer confidence levels are followed by low market returns. In Japan, both the level and the change in consumer confidence boost the market return in the next month. Also, shifts in sentiment significantly moved conditional volatility in most of the countries.

Huang *et al.* (2015) modified the Baker–Wurgler sentiment index by eliminating a common noise component in sentiment proxies and showed that the new index has much greater predictive power.

13.4 Opinion Mining

13.4.1 *Blogging platforms*

In recent years, multiple web blogging platforms have been used for discussing investment decisions. Twitter, a microblogging platform that allows for posting messages (tweets) of not more than 140 characters, is an extremely popular web network (there were more than 300 millions of users worldwide in 2020). Tweets have become a noted source for sentiment analysis and opinion mining (Pak & Paroubek, 2010). Hence, it is not surprising that there have been multiple attempts to use tweets for forecasting future market moves. Here is a short overview of recent work in this field.

In a noted publication, Bollen *et al.* (2011) analyzed the contents of daily tweets by two mood tracking tools, OpinionFinder that measures positive vs. negative mood, and Google-Profile of Mood States. It was found that predicting the daily up and down changes in the closing values of the Dow Jones Industrial Average (DJIA) had an accuracy of 87.6%. However, Lachanski & Pav (2017) found several drawbacks in this methodology, which illustrates the challenges in implementing and interpreting the soft news sentiment.

Vincent & Armstrong (2010) suggested using tweets for identifying breaking points at which profitable strategies stop working. They used a simple genetic algorithm with FX data as the reference benchmark. This algorithm made a decision every two minutes whether to hold US dollars or Euro and compared its performance to a hybrid algorithm, which stopped trading and went through a relearning phase after each Twitter alert. In the tests over a 5-month period, the hybrid algorithm performed significantly better than the benchmark algorithm.

Tafti *et al.* (2016) examined if unusual twitter volume about a firm indicates an oncoming surge of trading of its stock within the hour, over and above what would normally be expected for the stock for that time of day and day of week. Tafti *et al.* (2016) expressed reservations on whether this information may yield a profitable trading strategy.

Hartmann *et al.* (2018) compared the impact of changes in Google search volume and in tweets number on financial markets. It was found that tweets had a much higher impact on the number of traders entering the market and on price volatility.

Oliveira *et al.* (2017) described a robust methodology for assessing the value of microblogging data (including tweets) to forecast various stock market variables: returns, volatility and trading volume for diverse indices and portfolios.

Several other blogging platforms, including the Reddit group WallStreetBets and Stocktwits, have drawn significant investor attention at the time of writing this book. In January of 2021, the WallStreetBets community spotted a number of stocks, most prominently GameStop, that were severely shorted by some hedge funds (recall short selling described in Section 1.2). Then, these stocks were chosen for so-called *short-squeeze*, namely, aggressive buying of shorted stocks, which increased their price and forced short sellers to buy these stocks to cover their margin positions and, thus, further increasing their price. As a result, the GameStop price at some point shot up more than 1500% before falling down and continued to be extremely volatile for several months. This example demonstrates ability of the modern social networks to affect financial markets, at least, temporarily. In principle, such effects can be described using agent-based modeling (see Section 6.4).

Not surprisingly, a new ETF, VanEck Vectors Social Sentiment, was launched within 2 months after the GameStop sensation. This ETF follows the BUZZ NextGen AI US Sentiment Leaders Index, whose criteria for inclusion include the company's minimum market capitalization and significant positive interest on the social networks. It should be noted that a similar ETF based on the same sentiment index was launched in 2016 but closed in 2019.

13.4.2 *Google searches*

There has been growing interest in using web search data in economics and finance. In particular, Preis *et al.* (2010) and Bordino *et al.* (2012) found that the web query volumes are correlated with

Table 13.4. Performance of persistent interest portfolios and the benchmarks in 2009–2015.

	Persistent interest portfolio, 6-week window			
	Top10	Top25	Top50	Top100
Average Return	0.00325	0.00419	NA	NA
Std. Deviation	0.01220	0.0112	NA	NA
Sharpe ratio	4.22	5.94	NA	NA
Max drawdown	0.140	0.098	NA	NA
	Persistent interest portfolio, 12-week window			
	Top10	Top25	Top50	Top100
Average Return	0.00257	0.00313	0.00367	NA
Std. Deviation	0.0124	0.0116	0.0112	NA
Sharpe ratio	3.27	4.45	5.73	NA
Max drawdown	0.216	0.216	0.098	NA
	Persistent interest portfolio, 24-week window			
	Top10	Top25	Top50	Top100
Average Return	0.00167	0.00241	0.00263	0.00322
Std. Deviation	0.0115	0.0104	0.0102	0.0109
Sharpe ratio	2.30	3.69	4.08	4.70
Max drawdown	0.162	0.097	0.097	0.096
	Benchmarks			
	SPY	IYC	XLP	XLY
Average Return	0.00064	0.00084	0.00060	0.00087
Std. Deviation	0.0099	0.0100	0.0073	0.0110
Sharpe ratio	1.03	1.33	1.30	1.25
Max drawdown	0.110	0.108	0.068	0.116

stock trading volumes. Choi & Varian (2012) examined web search data from Google Trends (https://www.google.com/trends/) for short-term forecasting of various macroeconomic indicators including automobile sales, unemployment claims, and consumer confidence. Scott & Varian (2013) have expanded this approach with Bayesian analysis. Preis *et al.* (2013) found patterns in Google searches that can be interpreted as early signs of stock market moves.

Nadler & Schmidt (2016a) concluded that some companies among the S&P 500 constituents in 2009–2015 had persistently high web search scores. Many of these companies provide consumer products and/or services. Equal-weight and market cap-based portfolios with the most 25–100 searched companies (so-called *persistent interest portfolios*) did not outperform such ETFs as S&P 500 SPDR (SPY), Consumer Staples Select Sector SPDR ETF (XLP), Consumer Discretionary Select Sector SPDR (XLY), and iShares US Consumer Services (IYC). However, mean–variance portfolios of companies with high web search scores significantly outperformed the benchmarks in terms of average returns and Sharpe ratios (see Table 13.4). Shorter rebalancing windows and longer company lists yielded better performance. Mean–variance portfolios were more volatile than the benchmark returns but did not necessarily have higher maximum drawdowns.

It should be noted that the number of weights in a mean–variance portfolio cannot exceed the rank of covariance matrix that in turn cannot be higher than the number of observations (i.e., number of returns for each portfolio constituent) in the sample. Therefore, mean–variance portfolios for short rebalancing windows cannot be based on long lists of companies (e.g., 6-week window that has at most 30 trading days cannot be used for deriving portfolio weights based on the "Top 50" list).

Notes

1. Nowcast is updating a low-frequency (e.g., quarterly) forecast with higher-frequency (e.g., weekly) news.
2. Put option is a financial instrument that gives a right to sell an asset at a predetermined price. Call option is a right to buy an asset at a predetermined price.

Chapter 14

Back-Testing of Trading Strategies

14.1 Introduction

"It is difficult to make predictions, particularly about the future," a famous quip goes. Asset management institutions transform this wisdom into the standard disclaimer, "Past investment performance does not guarantee future returns." Yet, forecasting has been widely used in economics, finance, and natural sciences (e.g., climate modeling) — arguably in every field in which time series analysis is involved. The term *back-testing* implies that the forecasting models are fitted and tested using past empirical data. A simple approach consists of splitting the entire available data sample into two parts, one of which (with earlier data) is used for *in-sample* calibration of the predicting model, while the other one is reserved for *out-of-sample* testing of the accuracy of the model. It is usually assumed that the entire testing sample is variance-stationary, that is, sample mean and volatility are constant.

If it is expected that the optimal model parameters may evolve in time, *walk-forward validation* can be used. In this case, moving-window sampling is implemented. For example, if a 10-year data sample is available, the first 5-year data are used for in-sample calibration and the sixth-year data are used for out-of-sample testing. Then, the data from the second to the sixth year are used for in-sample calibration and the seventh year is tested out-of-sample, and so on.

In general, the choice of the data sample is not always determined by the rule "more is better" since long time series may be nonstationary. Moreover, long samples may include *regime shifts* caused by macroeconomic events or changes in market regulation policies. Markov-switching models are sometimes used for a unified description of data samples with regime shifts (see, e.g., Tsay, 2005). However, that technique is beyond the scope of this overview.

There is always a danger of model *overfitting*, i.e., implementing a model with unreasonably many parameters. The result of overfitting may have a deceptively high in-sample accuracy — and disastrously poor out-of-sample forecast. In this case, the model is fitted to the in-sample noise rather than to the deterministic relationship. The LASSO regression mentioned in Section 10.4 may be useful for addressing overfitting.

Two maximum likelihood-based criteria, *Akaike information criterion* (AIC) and the *Bayesian information criterion* (BIC), are often used for choosing an optimal number of model parameters n. In the general case,

$$\text{AIC} = 2n - 2\ln[L_{\max}(n, N)], \tag{14.1}$$

$$\text{BIC} = n\ln(N) - 2\ln[L_{\max}(n, N)]. \tag{14.2}$$

In (14.1) and (14.2), $L_{\max}(n, N)$ is the maximum likelihood for the chosen model and N is the number of observations. In particular, for the ARMA(p, q) models with Gaussian noise,

$$\text{AIC}(p, q, N) = \ln(\sigma_{p,q}^2) + 2(p + q), \tag{14.3}$$

$$\text{BIC}(p, q, N) = N\ln(\sigma_{p,q}^2) + (p + q)\ln(N), \tag{14.4}$$

where $\sigma_{p,q}^2$ is the maximum likelihood estimator of the sample error variance. The combination of model parameters that yields the minimal values of AIC and BIC is considered optimal. BIC has a stronger penalty for higher number of model parameters. Therefore, AIC and BIC may point at different combinations of the ARMA parameters p and q for the same data sample (see, e.g., Schmidt, 2020a). It should be noted that the models optimized in-sample using AIC or BIC may be inferior out-of-sample. Hence, the ultimate choice between the AIC-fitted and BIC-fitted models should be based on their forecasting accuracy.

Then, there is a problem of *data snooping*[1] bias, namely, uncovering dependencies between variables that are statistically significant for a given data sample but turn out irrelevant out of sample (see, e.g., Lo & MacKinlay, 1990; Hsu & Kuan, 2005; Hsu *et al.*, 2010). A well-publicized example of data snooping is described by Sullivan *et al.* (1999) who quoted Leinweber's finding that the best predictor in the United Nations database for the S&P 500 index is production of butter in Bangladesh.

Data snooping bias can appear also during testing of different strategies on a same historical data sample. Namely, some strategies may work better than others on a given data sample simply due to luck.

A general solution to the data snooping bias is *resampling*. *Bootstrap* is arguably the most popular resampling technique. The idea of bootstrap was introduced by Efron (see for details, Davidson & Hinkley, 1997). In a nutshell, bootstrap implies creating multiple data sets by randomly drawing the elements of a given data sample. Other resampling techniques include *jackknife* (creating data subsets by randomly dropping sample elements), and *permutation tests*, in which the order of elements of a given sample is randomly changed (Aronson, 2006).

Markov chain Monte Carlo (MCMC) simulations comprise another popular resampling method (Davidson & Hinkley, 1997). Within the MCMC protocol that is based on the Bayesian technique, the original sample is used to estimate probabilities of new returns conditioned on current and past returns. These probabilities are then used for generating new samples.

Finally, one may note the *random entry protocol* being a simple resampling procedure that addresses a possible problem of entry point bias, which is particularly important for coupled time series (Schmidt, 2009a).

This chapter continues with an overview of performance measures that are usually used in analysis of trading strategies. Then, the details of various resampling techniques are discussed. Finally, I outline the White's (2000) protocol for comparing the performance of different trading strategies and its extensions by Hansen (2005), Romano & Wolf (2005), and Hsu *et al.* (2010).

14.2 Performance Measures

Performance of trading strategies is usually tested on rather long time intervals (several years), during which given strategy is used multiple times. Total return (or P&L) is often used as the ultimate performance benchmark on par with the Sharpe ratio (recall Section 5.5). P&L is calculated in the end of the trading period after all long and short positions in the trading portfolio are closed. In other words, it is *realized return* that matters. Note that compound returns that are usually listed in asset management statements are not completely realized and may include dividends and reinvestment. We, however, are interested in "pure" trading strategy performance. Hence the same notional amount is used in every *round-trip trade* (i.e., selling security after it was bought or buying security to cover after it was sold short). The length of round-trip trades is determined either by buy/sell trading signals or by chosen holding period.

Market imperfections, such as finite asset liquidity and bid/ask spread are often neglected in back-testing of trading strategies due to their uncertainty though they may have notable contributions to performance. Also, transaction fees associated with frequent trading may become a matter of concern. Hence, practical performance of trading strategies should be evaluated after the fees.

Sometimes, positive P&L is a result of a few extremely lucky strikes accompanied with multiple losses. Therefore, percentage of winning round-trip trades, q, is another important performance measure. If this percentage and the ratio of the average winning amount to average losing amount, r, is assumed to be stable, one can use the *Kelly's criterion* for estimating the optimal fraction of trading capital, f, that should be used in each trade:

$$f = (qr - 1 + q)/r. \qquad (14.5)$$

It can be shown that the Kelly's criterion is equivalent to choosing the trading size that maximizes the geometric mean of outcomes. The derivation of the Kelly's criterion is described in detail by Thorp (2006).[2] Note that the Kelly's formula yields an estimate that is valid only asymptotically. Therefore, risk-averse practitioners are advised to use a value of f lower than the Kelly's criterion suggests.

The total number of trades for given time period is also important. Indeed, frequent trading may lead to more volatile outcomes and higher transaction fees. On the other hand, multiple trades using given strategy generate probability distribution of round-trip returns that can (and should) be used for hypothesis testing, in particular for comparing different strategies. Hence, mean return, μ, and its variance, σ, too, are important performance measures. Note that a positive mean return being accompanied with a high variance does not guarantee the strategy's quality. Providing that distribution of round-trip returns is normal, one can use the t-statistic for hypothesis testing. Namely, for a given number of round-trip trades N, one calculates the t-value:

$$t = \frac{\mu}{(\sigma^2/N)^{1/2}}. \tag{14.6}$$

Then, the t-value can be used for finding *statistical significance* (or *p-value*) of the null hypothesis from the Student's distribution. Note that this distribution is the function of degrees of freedom, which in case of a single security equals $(N - 1)$. Usually, the null hypothesis in analysis of trading strategies is that mean return is zero. For example, if p-value is less than 0.05, the hypothesis of zero return can be rejected in more than 95% of cases.

Obviously, if two strategies have the same average return, the one with lower variance is more attractive. Providing that the return distributions are normal, two trading strategies A and B can be compared using the following t-statistic:

$$t = \frac{\mu_A - \mu_B}{(\sigma_A^2/N_A + \sigma_B^2/N_B)^{1/2}}. \tag{14.7}$$

In this case, the degrees of freedom equal $N_A + N_B - 2$. The t-statistic (14.7) can also be used for analysis of profitability of a single strategy if indexes A and B refer to buy and sell signals, respectively (Brock *et al.*, 1992).

Distributions of returns often are not normal. Then the nonparametric Wilcoxon–Mann–Whitney (WMW) test can be used. Note that the WMW test compares sample medians rather than means. When the distributions of returns are skewed, the t-test and the WMW test may yield opposite conclusions. Accepting the WMW rejection of the null hypothesis when the t-test does not reject it can lead to false positives (Sawilowsky, 2005). Yet for the risk-averse investors, false positives may be even less attractive than false negatives as far as choosing investment strategy is concerned.

The Sharpe ratio (5.28) is a very important performance measure. Generally its annualized value is used. For the B&H strategy, the annual Sharpe ratio can be expressed via asset mean daily return r_d

and volatility σ_d

$$SR_{\text{ann}} = \frac{(r_d - r_{fd})\sqrt{T}}{\sigma_d}. \tag{14.8}$$

In (14.8), r_{fd} is a daily risk-free rate and T is the number of annual trading days assumed to be equal to 252. Note that $r_{\text{ann}} = r_d T$. For derivation of (14.8), it is assumed that returns follow random walk; hence $\sigma_{\text{ann}} = \sigma_d \sqrt{T}$ (see (4.11)).

For active trading strategies, when the trading capital may be in and out of the market, Nadler & Schmidt (2016b) used the following formula:

$$SR_{\text{ann}} = \frac{(r_{\text{annt}} - r_f)}{\sigma_d \sqrt{T}}, \tag{14.9}$$

where T is the number of days when the trading capital was invested in the market and r_{annt} is the annual *trading* return that may differ from the annual asset return r_{ann} since the trading capital was not invested each day of the year. This implies that the trading capital is subjected to the market risk only when it is invested in the market.

Another way to calculate the annual Sharpe ratio for active trading strategy is to use the modified formula (14.8)

$$SR_{\text{ann}} = \frac{(r_{dt} - r_{fd})\sqrt{T}}{\sigma_{dt}}. \tag{14.10}$$

In (14.10), r_{dt} is mean daily trading return, and σ_{dt} is volatility of r_{dt}. Note that the daily trading return equals zero on the days when the capital is not invested in the market.

Sometimes, the *Sortino ratio* is chosen instead of the Sharpe ratio. In the former, only negative returns are included in calculating the standard deviation σ. If a trading strategy (or portfolio) performance is compared with performance of an index (or B&H strategy), the *information ratio* that looks similar to the Sharpe ratio can be used:

$$IR = (E[r_i] - E[r_0])/\sigma_{i0}. \tag{14.11}$$

In (14.11), r_i is given return, r_0 is return of an index, and σ_{i0} is the tracking error (standard deviation between returns of the strategy and returns of the index[3]).

The *maximum drawdown* (MDD) is another important risk measure, particularly for leveraged trades. For a process $X(t)$ on the interval $[0, T]$,

$$MDD = \max[\max(X(s) - X(t)], \quad t \in [0, T] \quad s \in [0, t].$$

$$(14.12)$$

In other words, MDD is the largest drop of price after its peak. An example of MDD can be found in Fig. 4.1 of Chapter 4. In this case, $MDD = P_A - P_D$.

For the random walk with drift, analytical estimation of MDD is quite cumbersome. However, if drift can be neglected, expectation of MDD has a simple formula (Magdon-Ismail & Atiya, 2004):

$$E[MDD] = 1.2533\sigma\sqrt{T}.$$

$$(14.13)$$

In another performance measure, the *Calmar ratio*, the Sharpe ratio is modified by replacing the standard deviation of returns with MDD.

Finally, no trading strategy works forever. A possible signal for dropping a strategy that used to be profitable in the past is a growing number of *consecutive losing trades*. Hence, this number, too, can be handy for tracking the strategy performance.

14.3 Resampling Techniques

14.3.1 *Bootstrap*

Here is an idea behind the bootstrap resampling technique. Let's estimate average wealth of the US residents. It seems not too complicated: take a poll of a large number N of individuals and calculate an average of their wealth. But what if there is a billionaire in our sample? Clearly, the average will look too optimistic.[4] We can treat the billionaire as an outlier and delete him from the sample. Sometimes dropping outliers makes sense, particularly if there are reasons to believe that the sample may have erroneous data due to some measurement errors or recording mistakes. But we know that there are very rich people in US. So, let's leave the billionaire in the sample but do the bootstrap resampling instead. This implies choosing at random the individuals from the original sample with replacement, i.e., all individuals remain in the sample after they were chosen. We have to keep drawing individuals from the original sample until the new sample has the same number of individuals N. When we do this multiple times, most new samples won't have the billionaire in them, and their averages will better reflect true average wealth. Then the final estimate of the average wealth is the average of the averages for all new bootstrap samples. As a result, the billionaire wealth contributes to the bootstrap average wealth with a weight smaller than that of in the original sample.

Sometimes, blocks of several sequential elements of given sample are picked at once (*block bootstrap*). Usually, the block bootstrap is implemented with replacement and blocks are not overlapping. Such an approach may preserve short-range autocorrelations present in the original sample. While a simple estimate of the block size $L \sim N^{1/3}$ can be used, the choice of L in the general case is not trivial. Politis & Romano (1994) offered an expansion of the block bootstrap. This method ensures stationarity of samples that are bootstrapped from a stationary sample — and is called accordingly: *stationary bootstrap*. The block size L in the stationary bootstrap is randomly drawn from the geometric distribution[5] that describes probability that the first occurrence of success requires k independent trials when each success has probability p. The average block size for the stationary bootstrap case equals $1/p$, which can serve as a bridge between simple block bootstrap and stationary bootstrap.

A more sophisticated approach implies estimating a mathematical model that fits given data sample and bootstrapping the model's residuals (Brock *et al.*, 1992). Typical models used for stock prices are the random walk with drift, the ARMA models, and the GARCH models. Note that residuals within this approach are assumed to be IID.

Consider an example with the AR(1) model for logarithmic returns $r_t(4.3)$

$$r_t = \alpha + \beta r_{t-1} + \varepsilon_t, \varepsilon_t = IID(0, \sigma^2). \qquad (14.14)$$

First, the coefficients α and β in (14.14) are estimated using the OLS method. Then, the model residuals are calculated as

$$e_t = r_t - \alpha - \beta r_{t-1}. \qquad (14.15)$$

Further, a new sample of residuals, $\check{e}_t$, is generated using the bootstrap protocol and used for constructing a new sample of returns:

$$\check{r}_t = \alpha + \beta \check{r}_{t-1} + \check{e}_t. \qquad (14.16)$$

Finally, a new price sample is calculated via sampled returns

$$\check{P}_t = \check{P}_{t-1} \exp(\check{r}_t). \qquad (14.17)$$

This sample can be used for another round of testing the trading strategy.

The number of bootstrapped samples needed for good accuracy may reach from several hundred (Brock *et al.*, 1992) to several thousand (Schmidt, 2009a). The fraction of bootstrapped samples for which given strategy yields return that is equal or higher than that of for the original sample can be interpreted as the *p*-value. If this fraction is small (a few percentage points), then either the model chosen for simulations of returns is inadequate or profitability of the chosen strategy for the original sample is a result of data snooping.

14.3.2 *Markov chain Monte Carlo*

Let's introduce the *Markov process*, which is a generic stochastic process determined with relationships between its future, present, and past values. Here I focus on the discrete Markov processes called *Markov chains*. In a nutshell, future value for the Markov chain of the first order is determined by its present value; future value for the Markov chain of the second order is determined by its present value and the most recent past value, and so on. The Markov processes of the first-order cover a very wide class of dynamic short-memory phenomena including diffusional transfer. In fact, the equation for Brownian motion can be derived directly from the definition of the Markov process.[6]

By definition, the Markov chain of the kth order is a sequence of random variables X_i that satisfies the following equation:

$$\Pr(X_n = x | X_{n-1} = x_{n-1}, X_{n-2} = x_{n-2}, \ldots, X_1 = x_1)$$
$$= \Pr(X_n = x | X_{n-1} = x_{n-1}, X_{n-2} = x_{n-2}, \ldots, X_{n-k} = x_{n-k}). \qquad (14.18)$$

In other words, only k past values (sometimes called the initial conditions) determine the present value. In particular, for $k = 1$, only one initial condition is needed:

$$\Pr(X_n = x | X_{n-1} = x_{n-1},\ X_{n-2} = x_{n-2}, \ldots, X_1 = x_1)$$
$$= \Pr(X_n = x | X_{n-1} = x_{n-1}). \tag{14.19}$$

The Markov chain is stationary (or time-homogeneous) if probability in the left-hand side of (14.18) does not depend on index n.

Generally, Markov variables can assume only a finite number of values (*states*). Stationary Markov chains of the first order with N states are determined with N^2 probabilities $\Pr(X_n = x_k | X_{n-1} = x_i) = p_{ik}$, $i,\ k = 1, 2, \ldots, N$. These probabilities are called the *transition kernel*, and the complete set of values p_{ik} is called the *transition matrix*. Note that for each k

$$\sum_{i=1}^{N} p_{ik} = 1. \tag{14.20}$$

Similarly, stationary Markov chains of the second order are determined with N^3 probabilities $\Pr(X_n = x_k | X_{n-1} = x_i,\ X_{n-2} = x_j) = p_{ijk}$, $i,\ j,\ k = 1, 2, \ldots, N$, where

$$\sum_{i,j=1}^{N} p_{jik} = 1. \tag{14.21}$$

In the MCMC-based resampling, the transition matrix is assumed stationary and is calculated using the original sample. Then, drawings from the uniform distribution are mapped onto transition probabilities for generating new samples. For example, consider a two-state Markov chain with $p_{11} = p$, $p_{22} = q$ (which implies that $p_{12} = 1 - p$ and $p_{21} = 1 - q$). Say the current state is 1. If a drawing from the uniform distribution is less than or equal p, then the next state is 1; otherwise, it is 2. If the current state is 2 and a drawing from the uniform distribution is less than or equal q, then the next state is 2; otherwise, it is 1.

Since the transition matrix size grows with the Markov chain's order as the power law, the use of higher orders for multi-state models can become computationally intense. Also, the original sample may be not long enough for reliable estimates of all transition probabilities. Luckily, financial returns do not have a long memory. Hence, low-order Markov chains should suffice for their resampling. In particular, Schmidt (2009a) found that MCMC with Markov chains of the first and second order used in resampling of FX returns on the one-second time grid yielded practically the same results. Still, the usage of MCMC for simulations of returns remains a serious computational challenge since the number of states N (i.e., the number of various price changes) depends on volatility and can be rather high.

14.3.3 *Random entry protocol*

So far, I discussed resampling of a single time series (i.e., returns, as far as trading strategies are concerned). In the general case, trading strategies can be determined not only by price dynamics but also by some liquidity measures, such as trading volume, the bid/ask spread, and the asset inventory available at best price, which also vary with time. Depending on the problem addressed with resampling, one may either want to preserve or destroy correlations between coupled time series. If correlations between two samples are weak, MCMC can be implemented for both coupled samples independently, and bootstrap for coupled samples can be reduced to picking up pairs of variables at the same time. However, if both samples have autocorrelations of varying strength, choosing the bootstrap block size becomes tricky.

On the contrary, it may not be desirable to preserve all autocorrelations in some models. A case in point is the simulation of execution costs of pegged orders where both best prices and aggregated order size at best price determine the trading strategy (Schmidt, 2009a). In this strategy, a bid order is submitted at the best bid price. If this order (or its part) is not filled before the best bid increased, the order (or its unfilled part) is cancelled and resubmitted at the new best bid. Pegging to the best bid continues until the order is completely filled. At first, analysis of this strategy was done with *sequential trading protocol*, which is routinely used in back-testing of trading strategies. In sequential trading,[7] filling an order may lead to immediate submitting of another order. Namely, a signal of exiting long position can be also the signal for entering short position and vice versa. It turns out that negative autocorrelations present in returns yield a systematic bias to the expected execution costs for large orders that are filled in several transactions. Indeed, after filling the rest of the current bid order, a new bid will probably be resubmitted at a higher price due to negative autocorrelations in returns.

While analysis of this execution strategy may benefit from destroying some autocorrelations in returns, it is not clear whether persistent positive autocorrelations of the aggregated order size at best price can be neglected. A simple solution to minimize undesirable correlational effects was offered by Schmidt (2009a). Namely, it was suggested to use the *random entry protocol* rather than sequential trading. The random entry protocol implies choosing a random moment within the given sample for each new submitted order. This certainly helps to avoid the bias due to autocorrelations in returns but preserves autocorrelations in the limit order book. The random entry protocol is similar to the block bootstrap. The difference between the two approaches is that the block size in the former is determined with the time intervals during which orders are filled rather than from the geometric distribution. A natural constraint of the random entry protocol is that in contrast to the bootstrap and MCMC, it can yield only a limited number of distinct trade simulations m.[8] Namely, if the sample size is N and typical number of time intervals needed for filling a large order is n, then $m \approx N - n$.

The random entry protocol may also help in filtering out those trading strategies that are the result of data snooping caused by the *entry point bias*.[9] Indeed, multiple reports of trading performance use data samples starting in the beginning of the year. Yet, investors may start trading on any day of the year. For trading strategies based on daily returns, the walk forward protocol with shifting in-sample by one day at a time can be used for avoiding this bias. However, in the HFT environment based on huge volumes of tick data, the random entry protocol is an appropriate choice.

14.4 Comparing Trading Strategies

14.4.1 *Bootstrap reality check*

The resampling techniques described above can help to decide whether a given trading strategy has a positive return within a given time interval. However, this approach still does not prevent the danger of data snooping in comparative testing of multiple trading strategies on the same data sample. As Brock *et al.* (1992) put it, "There is always the possibility that any satisfactory results obtained may simply be due to chance rather than to any merit inherent in the method yielding the results." One reason for data snooping is that the many strategies that were unsuccessful in the past are eliminated from current comparative testing, so that only a small set of strategies is considered in the end, and the best of them is assumed to be the best among all.

White (2000) illustrates this problem with a newsletter scam. A scammer sends his free forecast to a large group of potential clients, suggesting that the market will go up in one half of letters and that the market will go down in another half. The following week, the scammer sends his newsletter only to those people who got the right forecast. Again, half of them are informed that the market will go up, and the rest that the market will go down. After several such iterations, the scammer gets a group of people who received only correct forecasts and may agree to pay for future advice.

White (2000) has offered the *Bootstrap Reality Check* (BRC) for avoiding data snooping in comparison of trading strategies. It is based on the $l \times 1$ statistic

$$\bar{f} = \frac{1}{n} \sum_{t=R}^{T} f_{t+1}(\hat{\beta}_t), \qquad (14.22)$$

where l is the number of trading strategies, n is the number of prediction periods indexed from R to $T = R + n + 1$, β_t is a vector of parameters that determine the trading strategies. Performance is defined via excess returns in respect to some benchmark model defined with β_0

$$f_{k,t+1}(\beta) = \ln[1 + y_{t+1}S_k(\chi_t, \beta_k)] - \ln[1 + y_{t+1}S_0)(\chi_t, \beta_0)],$$
$$k = 1, \ldots, l. \qquad (14.23)$$

In (14.23), X_t is the original price series, $y_{t+1} = (X_{t+1} - X_t)/X_t$; $S_k(\chi_t, \beta_k)$ and $S_0(\chi_t, \beta_0)$ are the trading signal functions that translate the price sequence $\chi_t = \{X_{t-R}, X_{t-R+1}, \ldots, X_T\}$ into the market positions. The trading signal functions can assume values of 0 (cash), 1 (long position), and –1 (short position). Buy-and-hold strategy or cash position are usually chosen as the benchmark models. In the latter case, β_0 is the risk-free interest rate.

The null hypothesis in BRC is that the performance of the best technical trading rule is no better than the performance of the benchmark. In terms of the average returns for each strategy k, $\bar{f}_k = E(f_k)$, this hypothesis states that

$$H_0 : \max\{\bar{f}_k\} \le 0, k = 1, \ldots, l. \tag{14.24}$$

Rejection of the null hypothesis implies that performance of the best technical trading is superior to the benchmark. The stationary bootstrap is used in BRC for resampling the observed values of $f_{k,t}$. This yields the average bootstrapped values $\bar{f}_{k,i}^*$ for each strategy k where $i = 1, \ldots, N$ are indexes of the bootstrap samples. Then, the following statistics are calculated:

$$\overline{V}_i^* = \max\{\sqrt{n}(\bar{f}_{k,i}^* - \bar{f}_k)\}, i = 1, \ldots, N \quad k = 1, \ldots, l, \tag{14.25}$$

$$\overline{V} = \max\{\sqrt{n}(\bar{f}_k)\}, \quad k = 1, \ldots, l. \tag{14.26}$$

Finally, the percentile of $\overline{V}_i^*$ is compared with $\overline{V}$ for estimating p-value of BRC.

Sullivan *et al.* (1999) have investigated a wide range of technical trading strategies using BRC on the 100-year (1897–1996) daily data sample for the Dow Jones Industrial Average. They have shown that the strategy that was the best (according to BRC) for the given sample outperformed holding cash. However, the best in-sample strategy was not superior to the benchmark when it was tested out of sample.

14.4.2 *New developments*

The ideas used in BRC for avoiding data snooping were expanded further in several directions. First, Hansen (2005) has shown that BRC may have a lower power due to the possible presence of poorly performing strategies in the test. Note that the power of the statistical test relates to the ability of rejecting false null hypotheses. Hansen (2005) enhanced BRC with two contributions. The first one is studentizing the performance statistics, that is, dividing $\bar{f}_k$ by an estimator of their standard deviation σ_k. Also, Hansen (2005) suggested including in the test only promising strategies with performance that satisfy the condition

$$\sqrt{n}(\bar{f}_{k,i}^* - \bar{f}_k)/\sigma_k \leq -[2\ln(\ln n)]^{1/2}. \qquad (14.27)$$

Romano & Wolf (2005), and Hsu *et al.* (2010) suggested using a stepwise protocol for enhancing the data snooping technique. This approach is focused on the family-wide error rate that is defined as the probability of rejecting at least one correct null hypothesis. Namely, the stepwise protocol identifies the strategies that violate the null hypothesis at a predefined significance level. In a nutshell, this protocol starts with calculating a critical value, q, for all bootstrapped strategy performances using a chosen significance level. Next, all $\bar{f}_k$ are rearranged in descending order. The top model k is rejected if its performance exceeds q. If no rejection occurs, the process stops. Otherwise, the model is eliminated and the critical value is recalculated. The process continues until no model is rejected.

An interesting result that Hsu *et al.* (2010) obtained with the stepwise bootstrap is that technical trading strategies that used to be profitable for some emerging market indices in the past have deteriorated after exchange-traded funds replicating these indexes were introduced.

It should be noted that while I discuss here an application of the bootstrap for comparing trading strategies in terms of returns, a similar approach can be used in terms of the Sharpe ratios (Ledoit & Wolf, 2008).

Notes

1. Data snooping is sometimes called data dredging or data phishing.
2. Poundstone (2006) offers a lively description of the history and controversies surrounding Kelly's criterion.
3. Note that the notion of *tracking error* here has the same sense as in (7.29) of Chapter 7 but differs from the one used in Section 12.3.
4. Median value may be preferable to mean value as the former is less sensitive to outliers than the latter.
5. Geometric distribution is described in Appendix A.

6. See, e.g., Schmidt (2004), where two other derivations of the Brownian motion equation are described.
7. The term *sequential trading* is used also for denoting *one trade at a time* in the Glosten–Milgrom market microstructure model (see Section 2.5.2).
8. In practical implementations, simulations that start too close to the end of the given sample, and hence unable to fill the order (or complete a round-trip trade), should be ignored.
9. In my experience with back-testing of HFT strategies in the FX market, beginning trading several minutes earlier/later in the morning might completely ruin (or make up) daily P&L.

Chapter 15

Execution Strategies

15.1 Introduction

The active trading strategies discussed in Chapters 11–13 are derived for producing profits in round-trip trades. These strategies are aimed to offer the signals indicating *what* and *when* to buy and sell. Sometimes, the term *opportunistic algorithms* is used for denoting them (Johnson, 2010).

An important problem that investors face is reducing the losses associated with the trading process. Some of these losses, such as the brokerage fees, commissions, and taxes, are fixed. But others depend on the order placement strategy and therefore may be minimized. *Algorithmic trading* addresses this problem by making automated decisions *where* and *how* to trade. Note that the notion of algorithmic trading is sometimes perceived as equivalent to *black-box trading* (or *automated trading*, or *quantitative trading*). However, the professional trading community attributes algorithmic trading primarily to the optimal execution strategies (Johnson, 2010; Kissell, 2020). Hence, the question of *whether* to trade is beyond the scope of this chapter. It is assumed that the decision to trade given security within a chosen time horizon has been made and we are concerned only with its implementation.

Market impact caused by order execution in conditions of limited liquidity is the main culprit of trading loss. Indeed, submission of a large order can wipe out the top of the order book and possibly several price levels behind it (see Chapter 3). Hence, large orders can move price in the adverse direction. The general solution for reducing trading loss is splitting large orders into multiple *child orders* and spanning their submission over the chosen time interval (so-called *scheduling*).

Perold (1988) introduced the notion of *implementation shortfall* (IS) as a measure of the total transaction costs. IS represents the difference between the actual portfolio return and the paper estimate of this return at the beginning of trading.[1] If trading of an order with size X started at price p_0 (so-called *arrival price*) and ended at price p_N, and the order was split into N child orders of size x_k that were filled at price p_k, then

$$\text{IS} = [\Sigma x_k p_k - p_0 \Sigma x_k] + [(p_N - p_0)(X - \Sigma x_k)] + C.$$

$$\quad\text{[execution cost]} \qquad \text{[opportunity cost]} \qquad (15.1)$$

In (15.1), C is the fixed cost. Sometimes, not all N child orders are executed during the trading day. For example, submission of child orders may be conditioned on specific price behavior. The unfilled order amount, $X - \Sigma x_k$, determines the *opportunity cost*.

The decision *where* to trade is an important choice for institutional trading. As was indicated in Chapter 1, contemporary financial markets consist of multiple liquidity providers including exchanges and ATS. Modern institutional trading systems often have *liquidity aggregators* that facilitate connections to various liquidity sources. These trading systems may use *smart routing processes* for automatic splitting of large orders into child orders and submitting them to the markets with better price and deeper liquidity.

Here, I discuss only the theoretical basics for making decisions on *how* to trade. While the general terminology in this field is still evolving, two major families of execution algorithms are discerned: *benchmark-driven algorithms* (also called *impact-driven algorithms*) and *cost-driven algorithms* (Johnson, 2010; Kissell, 2020). Obviously, any execution algorithm addresses the problem of minimizing execution costs. However, benchmark-driven algorithms are based on some fitting to various market benchmarks rather than on explicit optimization protocols. More sophisticated benchmark-driven algorithms (*price inline algorithms*) adapt dynamically to price changes. Cost-driven algorithms minimize IS explicitly and are often called *implementation shortfall algorithms*.

In Sections 15.2 and 15.3, I review several popular benchmark-driven algorithms and the cost-driven algorithms, including risk-neutral and risk-averse frameworks. Note that the child orders in these two sections are assumed to be market orders that are instantly filled at current best prices. The problem of choice between limit orders and market orders (the taker's dilemma; see Chapter 3) in optimal execution is discussed in Section 15.3.

15.2   Benchmark-Driven Algorithms

15.2.1   *Time-weighted average price*

In the *time-weighted average price* (TWAP) schedule, child orders are spread uniformly over the chosen time interval. Such a simple protocol has a risk of exposure of trader's intentions to other market participants. Some *scalpers* profiting from short-term price moves may realize that a large order is being traded and start trading the same instrument in expectation that the large trading volume will inevitably drive the price. Indeed, market makers adjust their prices to benefit from large trades. To prevent the information leak, the TWAP schedule may be randomized in terms of size and submission time of child orders. Then, periodic execution benchmarks are implemented for following the average schedule. For example, if the trading interval is four hours, 25% of the trading volume must be executed each hour. Then, the child-order sizes may be adjusted on an hourly basis. In more sophisticated TWAP schedules, some adaptive algorithms based on short-term price forecast may be implemented. For example, if price is expected to increase, the buy order schedule may be sped up to decrease the opportunity cost.

15.2.2   *Volume-weighted average price*

Financial markets often have pronounced intraday trading volume patterns (see Section 3.3.1). Therefore, the *volume-weighted average price* (VWAP) schedule may be more appropriate than the TWAP schedule. If an asset during some time interval has N trades with price p_k and volume v_k, its VWAP equals

$$\text{VWAP} = \sum_{k=1}^{N} v_k p_k \bigg/ \sum_{k=1}^{N} v_k. \qquad (15.2)$$

Practical implementation of the VWAP algorithm involves calculation of the percentage of daily trading volume u_k for each trading period k using historical market data:

$$u_k = v_k \Big/ \sum_{i=1}^{N} v_i. \tag{15.3}$$

Then, the size of child order k for the order of total size X equals

$$x_k = X u_k. \tag{15.4}$$

Historical estimates of u_k may have significant variation. Therefore, sophisticated VWAP algorithms have adaptive mechanisms accounting for short-term price trends and the dynamics of u_k. It should be noted that while the VWAP algorithm helps in minimizing the market impact cost, it does not necessarily yield possible price appreciation, which is, in fact, a form of opportunity cost. This becomes apparent when price has a pronounced intraday trend. Indeed, if price grows (falls) on a high volume during a day, the trader might get more price appreciation if the entire buy (sell) order is placed in the morning rather than it is spread over the entire day. On average, however, such an opportunity cost is compensated for buy (sell) orders on days when the price falls (grows).

The VWAP benchmark has become very popular in post-trade analysis. Many buy-side firms use vendor software that provides VWAP trading functionality. How well this software performs can be checked by comparing the realized trading cost with the true VWAP, which is calculated using available transaction data.

15.2.3   *Percent of volume*

In the *percent of volume* (POV) schedule, child orders are submitted with sizes equal to a certain percentage of the total trading volume, γ. This implies that child orders have acceptable market impact (if any), and execution time is not strictly defined. In estimating the size of child order x_k, one should take into account that the child order k must be included in the total trading volume X_k. Hence,

$$\gamma = x_k/(X_k + x_k). \tag{15.5}$$

As a result,

$$x_k = \gamma X_k / (1 - \gamma). \tag{15.6}$$

15.2.4 *Participation weighted price*

Participation weighted price (PWP) benchmark is a combination of VWAP and POV. Namely, if the desirable participation rate is γ and the order volume is N, PWP for this order is VWAP calculated over N/γ shares traded after the order was submitted.

15.3 Cost-Driven Algorithms

Choosing the size of child orders poses the following problem for risk-averse traders: fast execution implies larger child orders, which leads to higher market impact and higher IS. On the contrary, submitting smaller child orders consumes more time and exposes traders to the price volatility risk (market risk). For example, some bad news comes in the middle of execution of a sell order. Obviously, the rest of the order will be sold at a price notably lower than the desired one. Nevertheless, volatility risk is sometimes neglected in the derivation of execution algorithms. Therefore, cost-driven schedules can be partitioned into risk-neutral algorithms and risk-averse algorithms. In the former case, the schedule is derived by minimizing market impact. In the latter case, the schedule is derived by minimizing utility function that has two components: market impact and volatility risk. An overview of both approaches is given below.

15.3.1 *Risk-neutral framework*

Bertsimas & Lo (1998) introduced the following model for optimal execution. In terms of the notations used in the previous section, the objective to minimize the execution cost is

$$\text{Min E} \left[\sum_{k=1}^{N} x_k p_k \right], \{x_k\} \tag{15.7}$$

subject to the constraint

$$\sum_{k=1}^{N} x_k = X. \tag{15.8}$$

It is assumed that price follows the arithmetic random walk in the absence of market impact, and market impact is permanent and linear upon the trading volume.

$$p_k = p_{k-1} + \theta x_k + \varepsilon_k. \tag{15.9}$$

In (15.9), $\theta > 0$ for buy orders and ε_k is an IID process that is uncorrelated with trading volume and has zero mean. Bertsimas & Lo (1998) formulate the dynamic programming problem in terms of the trading volume remaining to be bought, w_k,

$$w_k = w_{k-1} - x_k, \quad w_1 = X, \quad w_{N+1} = 0. \tag{15.10}$$

The dynamic programming protocol is based on the condition that the solution optimal for the entire sequence $\{x_1^*, \ldots, x_N^*\}$ must be optimal for the subset $\{x_k^*, \ldots, x_N^*\}$, $k > 1$. This property is formulated using the Bellman equation that relates the optimal values of the objective function at times k and $k + 1$:

$$V_k(p_{k-1}, w_k) = \text{Min} \, \mathrm{E}[p_k x_k + V_{k+1}(p_k, w_{k+1})], \{x_k\}. \tag{15.11}$$

It follows from the boundary condition $w_{N+1} = 0$ that $x_{T^*} = w_T$. Then, the Bellman equation can be solved recursively: first by going backward and retrieving the relationship between x_k^* and w_k, and then by going forward, beginning with the initial condition $w_1 = X$. It turns out that the model defined above yields a trivial solution:

$$x_1^* = \ldots = x_N^*. \tag{15.12}$$

In other words, the original order should be split into equal pieces. This result is determined by the model assumption that the permanent impact does not depend on either price or the size of the unexecuted order.

More complicated models generally do not have an analytical solution. Yet, they can be analyzed using numerical implementation of the dynamic programming technique offered by Bertsimas & Lo (1998). Obizhaeva & Wang (2013) expanded this approach to account for exponential decay of market impact. Gatheral (2010) described the relationship between the shape of the market impact function and decay of market impact. In particular, Gatheral (2010) has shown that the widely assumed exponential decay of market impact is compatible only with linear market impact.

15.3.2 *Risk-averse framework*

The risk-averse framework for optimal execution was introduced by Grinold & Kahn (2000). Almgren & Chriss (2000) expanded this approach by constructing the *efficient trading frontier*[2] in the space of possible execution strategies.

Here I describe the Almgren–Chriss model for the selling process (the buying process is assumed to be symmetrical). The goal is to sell X units within the time interval T. Let's divide T into N periods with length $\tau = T/N$ and define discrete times $t_k = k^*\tau$ where $k = 0, 1, \ldots, N$. Further, let's introduce a list $n = \{n_0, \ldots, n_N\}$, where n_i is the number of units sold during the interval $t_{i-1} < t \leq t_i$. Another list will also be used: $x = \{x_0, \ldots, x_N\}$, where x_k is the remaining number of units at time t_k to be sold; $x_0 = X$; $x_N = n_0 = 0$. Obviously,

$$x_k = X - \sum_{i=1}^{i=k} n_i = \sum_{i=k+1}^{i=N} n_i. \tag{15.13}$$

It is assumed that price S follows the arithmetic random walk with no drift. Another assumption is that market impact can be partitioned into the permanent part that lasts the entire trading time T, and the temporary part that affects price only during one time interval τ. Then,

$$S_k = S_{k-1} + \sigma\tau^{1/2}d\xi_1 - \tau g(n_k/\tau). \tag{15.14}$$

In (15.14), the function $g(n_k/\tau)$ describes the permanent market impact. The temporary market impact contributes only to the sale price of the order k

$$\hat{S}_k = S_{k-1} + \sigma\tau^{1/2}d\xi_1 - \tau h(n_k/\tau), \tag{15.15}$$

but does not affect S_k. As a result, the total trading cost equals

$$IS = XS_0 - \sum_{k=1}^{N} n_k \hat{S}_k = -\sum_{k=1}^{N} x_k(\sigma\tau^{1/2}d\zeta_k - \tau g(n_k/\tau))$$

$$+ \sum_{k=1}^{N} n_k h(n_k/\tau). \qquad (15.16)$$

Within these assumptions, the expected IS (denoted here by $E(x)$), and its variance, $V(x)$, equal

$$E(x) = \sum_{k=1}^{N} \tau x_k g(n_k/\tau)) + \sum_{k=1}^{N} n_k h(n_k/\tau), \qquad (15.17)$$

$$V(x) = \sigma^2 \tau \sum_{k=1}^{N} x_k^2. \qquad (15.18)$$

The Almgren–Chriss framework is based on minimization of the utility function

$$U = E(x) + \lambda V(x), \qquad (15.19)$$

where λ is risk aversion.[3] Both permanent and temporary market impacts are assumed to be linear upon order size:

$$g(n_k/\tau) = \gamma\, n_k/\tau, \qquad (15.20)$$

$$h(n_k/\tau) = \varepsilon \operatorname{sgn}(n_k) + \eta n_k/\tau. \qquad (15.21)$$

In (15.20)–(15.21), γ and η are constant coefficients, ε is fixed cost (fees, etc.), and *sgn* is the sign function. Then,

$$E(x) = \frac{1}{2}\gamma X^2 + \varepsilon X + \frac{\tilde{\eta}}{\tau}\sum_{k=1}^{N} n_k^2, \quad \tilde{\eta} = \eta - \gamma\tau/2. \qquad (15.22)$$

Minimization of the utility function (15.19) is reduced to equating $\delta U/\delta x_k$ to zero, which yields

$$x_{k-1} - 2x_k + x_{k+1} = \tilde{\kappa}^2\tau^2 x_k \qquad (15.23)$$

with

$$\tilde{\kappa}^2 = \lambda\sigma^2/\tilde{\eta}. \qquad (15.24)$$

The solution to (15.23) is

$$x_k = X \frac{\sinh(\kappa(T - t_k))}{\sinh(\kappa T)}, \quad k = 0, 1, \ldots, N. \tag{15.25}$$

Then, it follows from the definition $n_k = x_k - x_{k-1}$ that

$$n_k = \frac{2X \sinh(\kappa \tau/2)}{\cosh(\kappa T)} \cosh(\kappa(T - t_{k-1/2})), \quad k = 1, 2, \ldots, N, \tag{15.26}$$

where $t_{k-1/2} = (k - 1/2)\tau$ and κ satisfies the relation

$$2(\cosh(\kappa \tau) - 1) = \tilde{\kappa}^2 \tau^2. \tag{15.27}$$

When τ approaches zero, $\tilde{\eta} \to \eta$ and $\tilde{\kappa}^2 \to \kappa^2$. Note that κ is independent of T and characterizes exponential decay of the size of sequential child orders. Namely, κ^{-1} units of time (order's half-life) decrease the child order size by the factor of e. Hence, the higher is risk aversion λ, the shorter is the order's half-life. In fact, if $\kappa^{-1} << T$, then the order can be executed faster than the chosen execution time T implies. An example in Fig. 15.1 illustrates dependence of the child order size on risk aversion.

Almgren & Chriss (2000) define the efficient trading frontier as the family of strategies that have minimal trading cost for a given cost variance, that is, a curve in the space E–V that is determined with (15.17), (15.18), and (15.25). The properties of this frontier are described in detail by Kissell & Glantz (2003).

Several expansions of the Almgren–Chriss framework by Huberman & Stahl (2005), Almgren & Lorenz (2007), and Schied & Schöneborn (2008) have led to models that account for time-dependent volatility and liquidity, sometimes within the continuum-time framework. All these models generally share the assumption that market impact can be represented as a combination of the permanent and short-lived transitory components. However, the findings by Bouchaud *et al.* (2004) in equity markets and by Schmidt (2010a) in FX exhibit the power-law decay of market impact.

In general, market impact of the ith trade at time t_k is some function $F(n_i, t_k - t_i)$. Let's define the *initial market impact* of a child order n_k as $s_k = -F(n_k, 0)$. Note that market impact is negative in

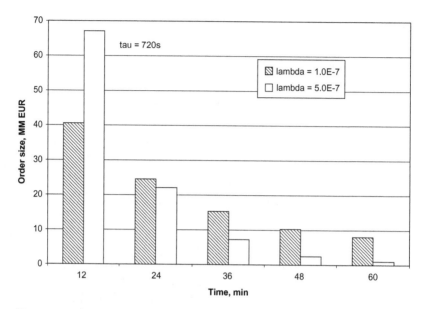

Fig. 15.1. An example of the child order size dependence on risk aversion.

the case of selling; hence, $s_k > 0$. Then, the total market impact after k trades equals to

$$MI(t_k) = \sum_{i=1}^{k} F(n_i, \, t_k - t_i).$$ (15.28)

As a result, price dynamics is more complicated than the one described with (15.14):

$$S_k = S_0 + \sum_{i=1}^{k} [\sigma \tau^{1/2} d\xi_i + F(n_i, (k-i)\tau)].$$ (15.29)

Another drawback of the Almgren–Chriss model and its extensions in the known literature is that that the kth child order may be executed not exactly at price S_k but at the VWAP, $S_{\mathrm{vwap}\,k}$, which for a sell order is within the interval $S_k < S_{\mathrm{vwap}\,k} \leq S_{k-1}$. Let's denote the VWAP increment in respect to S_{k-1} with $c_k(n_k)$. For selling,

$$c_k(n_k) = S_{k-1} - S_{\mathrm{VWAP}k}.$$ (15.30)

Then, the cost of trading has the form

$$IS = \sum_{k=1}^{N} n_k c_k - n_1 \sigma \tau^{1/2} d\xi_1$$

$$- \sum_{k=2}^{N} n_k \sum_{i=1}^{k-1} [\sigma \tau^{1/2} d\xi_i + F(n_i, (k-i)\tau)]. \qquad (15.31)$$

The power-law decay of market impact can be approximated in the following form:

$$c_k(n_k) = \alpha n_k, \qquad (15.32)$$

$$s_k(n_k) = \beta n_k, \qquad (15.33)$$

$$F(n_k, t) = \gamma s_k(n_k)/(t - t_k)^m, \quad t > t_k, \qquad (15.34)$$

where the positive coefficients α, β, γ, and m can be estimated using empirical data.

The presence of long-range memory in the market impact dramatically complicates obtaining a tractable solution for the problem of minimizing the utility function (15.19). However, if one accounts only for the market impact of the most recent $(k-1)$th child order, $F(n_{k-1}, t)$, in (15.31), then the utility function is significantly simplified (Schmidt, 2010a):

$$U(x) = \sum_{k=1}^{N} (\alpha n_k^2 + \beta \gamma n_{k-1} n_k / \tau^m + \sigma^2 \tau x_k^2). \qquad (15.35)$$

Minimization of the utility function (15.35) reduces the optimization problem to solving the equation similar to (15.23):

$$x_{k-1} - 2x_k + x_{k+1} = \kappa_0^2 \tau^2 x_k, \qquad (15.36)$$

with

$$\kappa_0^2 = \lambda \sigma^2 / (\alpha + \beta \gamma \tau^{-m}). \qquad (15.37)$$

Obviously, the slower is decay (the smaller is m), the higher is the order half-time.

Estimation of market impact from empirical data is another nontrivial problem. Usually, trading volume is used as a predictor for market impact (Almgren *et al.*, 2005). However, as was indicated in Section 3.3, the expected market impact may be notably higher than the realized market impact. The reason for this is that those informed traders[4] who do not have strict constraints on execution time may submit large orders only at times with higher liquidity. Therefore, the expected market impact is more appropriate for calibrating the execution models with time constraints.

15.4 The Taker's Dilemma in Optimal Execution

15.4.1 *Introductory comments*

As I pointed out in Chapter 3, taker order has an advantage of immediate execution but has a loss in respect to the corresponding maker order. For example, if a taker buy order is filled at the current best ask price and a maker buy order is filled at the best bid price, the taker loss equals the bid/ask spread per unit of trading asset. Hence, the taker's dilemma is in determining which order type to use. Analysis of this problem in an experimental market by Bloomfield *et al.* (2004) shows that informed traders are inclined to submit limit (i.e., maker) orders while liquidity traders use market (taker) orders more often.

The taker's dilemma can be formulated in terms of minimization of the utility function similar to (15.19) (Schmidt, 2010b). Let P, BB, and BO be order price, best bid, and best ask, respectively. The bid-side distance from best price is defined as $D = BB - P$, and the offer-side distance is defined as $D = P - BO$. Let's introduce the loss function for an order of size V placed at distance D from the best price:

$$L_1(V, D, \lambda) = aV[\lambda\sigma\sqrt{T(V, D)} - D]. \qquad (15.38)$$

In (15.38), V is trading volume and the scaling parameter, a, transforms the units of the right-hand side to cash amount. The first term within the brackets is an estimate of potential loss due to volatility σ; $T(V, D)$ is the expected order execution time and λ is the risk-aversion coefficient. The second term in the brackets is the order P/L in respect to the current market best price.

Schmidt (2010b) found that the loss function might have minimum, which points at optimal placement of the limit order.[5] This approach can be expanded for the optimal slicing of large orders. Consider a large order of size N partitioned into n child orders of amount V ($N = nV$) and assume that each kth child order is placed immediately after the $(k-1)$ th one is filled. Within this strategy, the nth order is on hold during the time it takes to execute $(n - 1)$ previous orders as well as the nth order itself. Therefore, the potential loss, L_n, for the nth order is

$$L_n(V, D, \lambda) = aV \left[\lambda \sigma \sqrt{nT(V,D)} - D \right]. \tag{15.39}$$

Then, the loss function for the entire order is the sum of the individual loss functions from L_1 through L_n:

$$L_{(N=nV)}(V, D, \lambda) = aV \left[\lambda \sigma \cdot \sum_{k=1}^{n} \sqrt{kT(V,D)} - nD \right]. \tag{15.40}$$

Searching the global minimum of (15.40) on the $V - D$ plane for a given risk aversion and total order size N can define the optimal size of child orders and their price. For example, if N is 100, the minimum of (15.40) may answer the question whether to trade 10,000 units using, for example, 100 child orders of size 100 at the best price, or using five child units with size of 2,000 units at a price one penny behind the best price.

The critical element in calculations of optimal child order size and price using the relation (15.38) is an accurate estimation of the expected execution time $T(V, D)$. This is a complicated task. First, the values of $T(V, D)$ depend on the market volatility. This problem is aggravated with the necessity of accounting for those orders that are cancelled prior to their execution or after they are partially filled. Order cancellation can occur for various reasons. In particular, when price moves in an adverse direction, traders (or automated trading algorithms) may decide that price will not revert within an acceptable time horizon and therefore resubmit an order at a new price (see discussion of a relevant strategy below). Cancelled orders constitute a significant percentage of submitted orders and ignoring them can notably skew the results towards shorter execution times (Lo *et al.*, 2002; Eisler *et al.*, 2009).

15.4.2 *The random walk model*

An interesting approach to estimation of limit-order execution time was given by Lo *et al.* (2002). In this work, price dynamics was modeled using the geometric Brownian motion with drift

$$dP(t) = \alpha P(t)dt + \sigma P(t)dW. \tag{15.41}$$

In (15.41), α and σ are constant and dW is the standard Brownian process. Let's denote the current time and price with t_0 and P_0, respectively. Consider the time interval $[t_0; t_0+t]$, where $P_{\min}$ denotes the lowest price observed in this interval. A buy limit order with price P_l will be filled within given time interval $[t_0; t_0 + t]$ if and only if $P_{\min}$ is less than or equal to P_l. This probability can be formulated in terms of the first-passage time (FPT).[6] Namely,

$$P_{\text{FPT}} = \Pr(P_{\min} \le P_l | P(t_0) = P_0) = 1 - \Phi\left(\frac{\log(P_0/P_l) + \mu t}{\sigma\sqrt{t}}\right)$$

$$+ \left(\frac{P_l}{P_0}\right)^{2\mu/\sigma^2} \Phi\left(\frac{\log(P_l/P_0) + \mu t}{\sigma\sqrt{t}}\right), P_l \le P_0. \tag{15.42}$$

In (15.42), $\mu = \alpha - \sigma^2/2$, $\Phi()$ is the standard normal cumulative distribution function. If T is the limit order execution time, the cumulative distribution function $F(t)$ for T equals

$$F(t) = \Pr(T \le t | P(t_0) = P_0) = \Pr(P_{\min} \le P_l). \tag{15.43}$$

The theoretical distribution $F(t)$ (15.42) can be calibrated with empirical data for the limit-order execution time. Namely, the values μ and σ that define $F(t)$ can be estimated from a given sample of returns using the maximum likelihood estimator. Then, the histogram of the empirical limit-order execution times can be computed.

Lo *et al.* (2002) employed the methods of survival analysis to estimate the probability that limit orders will not be cancelled by the time t. They chose a parametric survival distribution in the form of the generalized gamma distribution and estimated it using empirical data on order cancellations for the 100 largest stocks in the S&P 500 for 1994–1995. Then, this survival distribution was used for *censoring* the empirical distribution of the limit-order execution times. Namely, if the order cancellation and execution are independent stochastic processes, the probability that the *time to fill* (TTF) for the limit order is t equals (Eisler *et al.*, 2009):

$$P_{\text{TTF}}(t) = \frac{P_{\text{FPT}}(t)P_{\text{LT}}(> t)}{\int_0^\infty P_{\text{FPT}}(\tau)P_{\text{LT}}(> \tau)d\tau}. \tag{15.44}$$

In (15.44), $P_{\text{LT}}(> t)$ is the probability that the limit order will not be cancelled by the time t.

Unfortunately for practical applications, Lo *et al.* (2002) found that the FPT based on the random walk model does not describe accurately the empirical limit-order execution times. This conclusion was confirmed by Eisler *et al.* (2009) with further analysis of empirical FPT, order cancellation times, and limit-order execution times. In particular, Eisler *et al.* (2009) have shown that the statistical distributions for all three variables (TTF, PTF, and LT) follow the power law with varying scaling exponents, and the FPT distribution decays notably slower than the execution time distribution.

Engle *et al.* (2012) developed empirical measures of the risk and return of order execution and estimated risk–return frontiers for a set of trading strategies. They also examined the choice of trading strategy for investors with different risk tolerances and found that traders appear to select trading strategies that imply extreme risk aversion.

15.4.3 *Modeling execution of pegged orders*

In general, the problem of estimating the limit-order execution time cannot be reduced to estimation of the FPT since limit orders are placed in the order book in price/time priority and hence must reside at the top of the order book prior to their execution. Therefore, the model of limit-order execution should describe the order book depletion that depends on both filling and cancellation of orders. One such model was offered by Schmidt (2009a) for describing a maker strategy based on pegged orders in the institutional FX market. This strategy is much more aggressive than the one described with the utility function (15.39). Namely, rather than submitting a passive bid order at the BB price and waiting until it is filled, the order is canceled and resubmitted each time BB moves in an adverse direction prior to filling entire order.[7]

Schmidt (2009a) used historical data for BB and aggregated order volumes at BB in simulations. The order book depletion rate was estimated using the gamma distribution fitted with empirical data on transactions and order cancellations. In the beginning of each simulation, a *virtual order* was placed at the end of the order queue present at BB. If the new BB was higher than the current one, the virtual order (or its unfilled part) was cancelled and resubmitted at the new BB. If the new BB was the same, the limit order book (LOB) was depleted using the simulated depletion rate. Depending on whether the virtual order was or was not on top of LOB, the depletion rate was determined by the order filling rate or by both the order filling and cancellation rates. Finally, if the new BB was lower than the current one, two scenarios were considered. Namely, if the virtual order was *not* on top of LOB, it was placed on top of LOB. If the virtual order was already on top of LOB, it was depleted with a simulated depletion rate. The simulation process for a given virtual order continued until it was completely filled. The flow chart of this simulation process is given in Fig. 15.2.

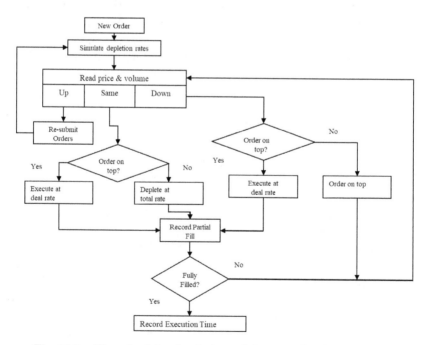

Fig. 15.2.   Flow chart for simulations of the pegged order execution.

The simulations were repeated for several thousand times using various resampling techniques (see Chapter 14). Finally, the averaged execution time and loss were estimated. The main conclusion from these simulations is that the maker strategy described above has an average loss per unit of order size (i.e., the cost in respect to the initial BB) lower than the average bid/ask spread. Hence, pegged orders have some advantage over the taker strategy. However, order execution time remains an important risk factor for pegged orders.

Notes

1. Sometimes, the cost of delay between the time when the decision to trade was made and the beginning of trading is included in IS (Kissell & Glantz, 2003).
2. Almgren & Chriss (2000) used the term *efficient frontier*, which can be confused with the same term used in the portfolio management theory. I use the term *efficient trading frontier* proposed by Kissell & Glantz (2003).
3. Note that the linear relation (15.19) differs from typical exponential utility functions used in economics (see Section 2.3). The advantage of (15.19) is that it simplifies analytical derivation of the efficient trading frontier.
4. In this context, the qualifier "informed" relates to those traders who receive updates of the LOB structure in real time.
5. Schmidt (2010b) studied the taker's dilemma in the FX market but his approach is also valid for equities.
6. FPT was introduced in Section 3.1.
7. Here, only the bid side is considered as the ask side is assumed to be symmetric.

Appendix A

Probability Distributions

While many classical theories in finance are based on the normal (Gaussian) distribution, it has been well documented that empirical financial time series often follow other distributions, too. Here, I provide an overview of probability distributions discussed in this book. For a more detailed description of the material, readers can consult the comprehensive probability courses (e.g., Ross, 2007).

A.1 Basic Notions

Consider a random variable (or *variate*) X. Its *probability distribution*, or *the probability density function* (PDF) $f(x)$, determines probability to find X between the values a and b:

$$\Pr(a \leq X \leq b) = \int_a^b f(x)dx. \tag{A.1}$$

PDF must satisfy the normalization condition

$$\int_{X_{\min}}^{X_{\max}} f(x)dx = 1, \tag{A.2}$$

where the interval $[X_{\min}, X_{\max}]$ is the range of all possible values of X. I shall omit the integration limits when they cover the entire range of possible values. Several distributions widely used in finance are listed in Section A.2.

Another way of describing random variables is to use *the cumulative distribution function*:

$$Pr(X \leq b) = \int_{-\infty}^{b} f(x)dx. \tag{A.3}$$

Obviously,

$$\Pr(X > b) = 1 - \Pr(X \leq b). \tag{A.4}$$

Two characteristics are used to describe the most probable values of random variables: (1) *mean* (or *expectation*), and (2) *median*. Mean of X is the average of all possible values of X that are weighed with PDF $f(x)$:

$$m = E[X] = \int xf(x)dx. \tag{A.5}$$

Median of X is the value M for which

$$\Pr(X > M) = \Pr(X < M) = 0.5. \tag{A.6}$$

Expectation of a random variable calculated using some available information I_t (that may change with time t) is named *conditional expectation*. The conditional probability density is denoted by $f(x|I_t)$. Conditional expectation equals

$$E[X_t|I_t] = \int xf(x|I_t)dx. \tag{A.7}$$

Variance, var, and *the standard deviation, σ,* are the conventional estimates of the deviations from mean values of X:

$$var[X] \equiv \sigma^2 = \int (x - m)^2 f(x)\,dx. \tag{A.8}$$

In the financial literature, the standard deviation of price is used to characterize volatility (see Chapter 5). Higher-order moments of the probability distributions are defined as

$$m_n = E[X^n] = \int x^n f(x)dx. \tag{A.9}$$

According to this definition, mean is the first moment ($m \equiv m_1$), and variance can be expressed via the first two moments, $\sigma^2 = m_2 - m^2$.

Two other important parameters, *skewness* S and *kurtosis* K, are related to the third and fourth moments, respectively,

$$S = E[(x - m)^3]/\sigma^3, \tag{A.10}$$

$$K = E[(x - m)^4]/\sigma^4. \tag{A.11}$$

Both parameters S and K are dimensionless. Zero skewness implies that the distribution is symmetrical around its mean value. The positive and negative values of skewness indicate long positive tails and long negative tails, respectively. Kurtosis characterizes the distribution *peakedness*. Kurtosis of the normal distribution (defined in Section A.3) equals three. The *excess kurtosis*, $K_e = K - 3$, is often used as a measure of deviation from the normal distribution. In particular, positive excess kurtosis (or *leptokurtosis*) indicates more frequent large deviations from the mean value than it is typical for the normal distribution. Leptokurtosis leads to the flatter central part as well as to the so-called fat tails in the distribution. Negative excess kurtosis indicates frequent small deviations from the mean value. In this case, the distribution sharpens around its mean value while the distribution tails decay faster than the tails of the normal distribution.

The *joint distribution* of two random variables X and Y is the generalization of the cumulative distribution (A.3):

$$\Pr(X \le b, Y \le c) = \int_{-\infty}^{b} \int_{-\infty}^{c} h(x, y) dx dy. \tag{A.12}$$

In (A.12), $h(x, y)$ is the joint density that satisfies the normalization condition

$$\int_{-\infty}^{\infty} \int_{-\infty}^{\infty} h(x, y) dx dy = 1. \tag{A.13}$$

Two random variables are *independent* if their joint density function is simply the product of the univariate density functions: $h(x, y) = f(x)g(y)$.

Covariance between two variates provides a measure of their simultaneous change. Consider two variates X and Y that have the means m_X and m_Y, respectively. Their covariance equals

$$\mathrm{cov}(X, Y) = \sigma_{XY} = E[(X - m_X)(Y - m_Y)] = E[XY] - m_X m_Y. \tag{A.14}$$

Clearly, covariance reduces to variance if $X = Y$: $\sigma_{XX} = \sigma_X^2$. Positive covariance between two variates implies that these variates tend to change simultaneously in the same direction rather than in opposite directions. Conversely, negative covariance between two variates implies that when one variate grows, the other one tends to fall and vice versa. Another popular measure of simultaneous change is *the correlation coefficient*:

$$\text{corr}(X, Y) = \text{cov}(X, Y)/(\sigma_X \sigma_Y). \tag{A.15}$$

The values of the correlation coefficient are within the range $[-1, 1]$. In the general case with N variates $X_1, \ldots, X_N$ (where $N > 2$), correlations among variates are described with the *covariance matrix*, which has the following elements:

$$\text{cov}(X_i, Y_j) = \sigma_{ij} = E[(x_i - m_i)(x_j - m_j)]. \tag{A.16}$$

Partial correlation coefficient, $\rho_{ij|k}$, between variables X_i and X_j that is conditioned on variable X_k measures co-movement between the residuals of linear regressions of X_i on X_k, and X_j on X_k (Johnston & DiNardo, 1997). It can be introduced via partial covariance (Whittaker, 1990)

$$\sigma_{ij|k} \equiv \text{cov}(X_i, X_j | X_k) = \text{cov}(X_i, X_j) - \text{cov}(X_i, X_k)$$
$$\times \text{cov}(X_j, X_k)/\text{var}(X_k)$$
$$= \rho_{ij|k} \sigma_{i|k} \sigma_{j|k}. \tag{A.17}$$

In (A.17), partial variance $\sigma_{i|k}^2 \equiv \text{cov}(X_i, X_i | X_k)$ equals

$$\sigma_{i|k}^2 = \sigma_i^2 - \sigma_{ik}^4/\sigma_k^2. \tag{A.18}$$

The partial correlation coefficient can be calculated using Pearson's correlations:

$$\rho_{ij|k} = \frac{\rho_{ij} - \rho_{ik}\rho_{jk}}{\sqrt{1 - \rho_{ik}^2} \sqrt{1 - \rho_{jk}^2}}. \tag{A.19}$$

A time series X is *strictly stationary* if the multivariate cumulative distributions $(x_i, x_{i+1}, \ldots, x_{i+k})$ and $(x_{i+\tau}, x_{i+\tau+1}, \ldots, x_{i+\tau+k})$ are identical for all i, k, and τ. All moments of strictly stationary distributions do not depend on time. In a *weakly stationary* (or *covariance-stationary*) time series, the first two moments, mean and variance, are finite and time-invariant. In this case, autocovariance, $\text{cov}(x_i, x_{i-\tau})$, depends only on the lag τ.

A time series is named *ergodic* if sampling average

$$m_T = (1/T) \sum_{t=1}^{T} x_t, \qquad (A.20)$$

converges to the expectation (A.5) as $T \to \infty$. Ergodicity of a time series implies that its autocovariance decays quickly, In other words, ergodic processes have a short memory.

A.2 Commonly Used Distributions

Here are important probability distributions that are frequently used in quantitative finance.

A.2.1 The uniform distribution

The *uniform distribution* has a constant value within the given interval $[a, b]$ and equals zero outside this interval:

$$f_U = 0, x < a \quad \text{and} \quad x > b; \; f_U = 1/(b-a), \; a \le x \le b. \quad (A.21)$$

The uniform distribution has the following mean, skewness, and excess kurtosis:

$$m_U = 0, \; \sigma_U^2 = (b-a)^2/12, \; S_U = 0, K_{eU} = -6/5. \quad (A.22)$$

The distribution with $a = 0$ and $b = 1$ is called the *standard uniform distribution*.

A.2.2 The binomial distribution

The binomial distribution is a discrete distribution for n successes out of N trials, where the result of each trial is true with probability p and is false with probability $q = 1 - p$ (so-called *Bernoulli trials*):

$$f_B(n; N, p) = C_{Nn} p^n q^{N-n} = C_{Nn} p^n (1-p)^{N-n}, C_{Nn} = \frac{N!}{n!(N-n)!}$$
$$(A.23)$$

The factor C_{Nn} is called the binomial coefficient. Mean and higher-order moments for the binomial distribution are equal, respectively,

$$m_B = Np, \sigma_B^2 = Np(1-p), \quad S_B = (q-p)/\sigma_B, \quad K_{eB}$$
$$= (1 - 6pq)/\sigma_B^2.$$
$$(A.24)$$

In the case of large N and large $(N - n)$, the binomial distribution approaches the *normal* (or *Gaussian*) distribution (see below).

A.2.3 *The Poisson distribution*

The Poisson distribution can be considered as the limiting case of the binomial distribution in the case with $p \ll 1$. The former describes the probability of n successes in N trials assuming that the fraction of successes ν is proportional to the number of trials (i.e., $\nu = pN$)

$$f_P(n, N) = \frac{N!}{n!(N-n)!} \left(\frac{\nu}{N}\right)^n \left(1 - \frac{\nu}{N}\right)^{N-n}.$$
$$(A.25)$$

When the number of trials N becomes very large ($N \to \infty$), the Poisson distribution approaches the limit

$$f_P(n) = \nu^n e^{-\nu}/n!.$$
$$(A.26)$$

Mean, variance, skewness, and excess kurtosis of the Poisson distribution are equal, respectively,

$$m_P = \sigma_P^2 = \nu, \quad S_P = \nu^{-1/2}, K_{eP} = \nu^{-1}.$$
$$(A.27)$$

A.2.4 *The normal distribution*

The *normal* (*Gaussian*) *distribution* has the form

$$f_N(x) = \frac{1}{\sqrt{2\pi}\sigma} \exp[-(x-m)^2/2\sigma^2].$$
$$(A.28)$$

It is often denoted as $N(m, \sigma)$. Skewness and excess kurtosis of the normal distribution equal zero. The standardization transform $z = (x - m)/\sigma$ converts the normal distribution into the *standard normal distribution*

$$f_{SN}(x) = \frac{1}{\sqrt{2\pi}} \exp[-z^2/2]. \tag{A.29}$$

The integral over the standard normal distribution within the interval $[0, z]$ is used as the definition of the *error function* $\mathrm{erf}(z)$:

$$\frac{1}{\sqrt{2\pi}} \int_0^Z \exp(-x^2/2)dx = 0.5 \, \mathrm{erf}(z/\sqrt{2}). \tag{A.30}$$

Then, the cumulative distribution function for the standard normal distribution equals

$$\mathrm{Pr}_{SN}(z) = 0.5[1 + \mathrm{erf}(z/\sqrt{2})]. \tag{A.31}$$

According to the *central limit theorem*, the probability density distribution for a sum of N independent and identically distributed random variables with finite variances and finite means approaches the normal distribution as N grows to infinity. The Box–Miller method is often used for modeling the normal distribution. It is based on drawings from the uniform distribution that is available for simulations in many computer languages. Namely, if two numbers x_1 and x_2 are drawn from the standard uniform distribution, then y_1 and y_2 are the standard normal variates:

$$y_1 = [-2\mathrm{ln}x_1]^{1/2} \cos(2\pi x_2), \; y_2 = [-2\mathrm{ln}x_1]^{1/2} \sin(2\pi x_2). \tag{A.32}$$

A.2.5 *The lognormal distribution*

In the lognormal distribution, the logarithm of a variate has the normal form

$$f_{LN}(x) = \frac{1}{xs\sqrt{2\pi}} \exp[-(\ln x - \mu)^2/2s^2]. \tag{A.33}$$

Mean, variance, skewness, and excess kurtosis of the lognormal distribution can be expressed in terms of the parameters s and μ:

$$m_{LN} = \exp(\mu + 0.5s^2), \tag{A.34a}$$

$$\sigma_{LN}^2 = [\exp(s^2) - 1]\exp(2\mu + s^2), \tag{A.34b}$$

$$S_{LN} = [\exp(s^2) - 1]^{1/2}[\exp(s^2) + 2], \tag{A.34c}$$

$$K_{eLN} = \exp(4s^2) + 2\exp(3s^2) + 3\exp(2s^2) - 6. \tag{A.34d}$$

A.2.6 *The Cauchy distribution*

The *Cauchy (Lorentzian) distribution* is an example of the *stable distribution* with fat tails (see Section A.3). It has the form

$$f_C(x) = \frac{b}{[b^2 + (x - m)^2]}. \tag{A.35}$$

The specific of the Cauchy distribution is that all its moments are infinite. When $b = 1$ and $m = 0$, the distribution is called the *standard Cauchy distribution*:

$$f_C(x) = \frac{1}{1 + x^2}. \tag{A.36}$$

A.2.7 *The gamma distribution*

The *gamma distribution* is characterized with shape α and scale β

$$f_G(x) = x^{\alpha-1} \cdot \frac{\exp(-x/\beta)}{\Gamma(\alpha)\beta^\alpha}. \tag{A.37}$$

Its mean, variance, skewness, and excess kurtosis equal

$$m_G = \alpha\beta, \ \sigma_G^2 = \alpha\beta^2, \ S_G = 2/\alpha^{1/2}, \ K_{eG} = 6/\alpha. \tag{A.38}$$

A.2.8 *The geometric distribution*

The geometric distribution describes the probability that the first occurrence of success requires k independent trials when each success has probability p

$$F_{\text{Geo}}(x) = (1-p)^{k-1}p, \tag{A.39}$$

$$m_{\text{Geo}} = 1/p, \sigma^2_{Geo} = (1-p)/p^2, \; S_{\text{Geo}} = (2-p)/\sqrt{1-p},$$

$$K_{e\text{Geo}} = 6 + \frac{p^2}{1-p}. \tag{A.40}$$

A.3 Stable Distributions and Scale Invariance

The principal property of the *stable distribution* (also known as *Levy distribution*) is that the sum of its variates has the same distribution shape as that of addends (see, e.g., Mantegna & Stanley, 2000; Bouchaud & Potters, 2000). Both the Cauchy distribution and the normal distribution are stable. This means, in particular, that the sum of two normal distributions with the same mean and variance is also the normal distribution.

Consider the Fourier transform $F(q)$ of the probability distribution function $f(x)$:

$$F(q) = \int f(x)e^{iqx}dx. \tag{A.41}$$

The function $F(q)$ is also called the *characteristic function* of stochastic process. It can be shown that the logarithm of the characteristic function for the Levy distribution has the following form:

$$\ln F_L(q) = i\mu q - \gamma|q|^\alpha[1 - i\beta\delta\tan(\pi\alpha/2)], \quad \text{if} \quad \alpha \neq 1, \tag{A.42a}$$

$$\ln F_L(q) = i\mu q - \gamma|q|[1 + 2i\beta\delta ln(|q|)/\pi)], \quad \text{if} \quad \alpha = 1. \tag{A.42b}$$

In (A.42), $\delta = q/|q|$, and the distribution parameters α, β, and γ must satisfy the following conditions:

$$0 < \alpha \leq 2, -1 \leq \beta \leq 1, \gamma > 0. \tag{A.43}$$

The parameter μ relates to the mean of the stable distribution and can be any real number. The parameter α characterizes the distribution peakedness. If $\alpha = 2$, the distribution is normal. The parameter β characterizes skewness of the distribution. Note that skewness of the normal distribution equals zero, and the parameter β does not affect the characteristic function with $\alpha = 2$. For the normal distribution,

$$\ln F_N(q) = i\mu q - \gamma q^2. \tag{A.44}$$

The non-negative parameter γ is the scale factor that characterizes the spread of the distribution. In the case of the normal distribution, $\gamma = \sigma^2/2$ (where σ^2 is variance). The Cauchy distribution is defined with the parameters $\alpha = 1$ and $\beta = 0$. Its characteristic function equals

$$\ln F_C(q) = i\mu q - \gamma|q|. \tag{A.45}$$

The important feature of the stable distributions with $\alpha < 2$ is that they exhibit the power-law decay at large absolute values of the argument x:

$$f_L(|x|) \sim |x|^{-(1+\alpha)}. \tag{A.46}$$

The distributions with the power-law asymptotes are also called the *Pareto distributions*.

Unfortunately, the moments of stable processes $E[x^n]$ with the power-law asymptotes (i.e., when $\alpha < 2$) diverge for $n \geq \alpha$. As a result, mean of a stable process is infinite when $\alpha \leq 1$ and variance of a stable process is infinite when $\alpha < 2$. Therefore, the normal distribution is the only stable distribution with finite mean and finite variance. The stable distributions have an advantage of the flexible description of peakedness and skewness. However, their infinite variance at $\alpha < 2$ restricts their usage in financial applications. The compromise that retains the flexibility of the Levy distribution yet yields finite variance is known as *truncated Levy flight*. This distribution can be defined as

$$f_{TL}(x) = 0, |x| > l, \tag{A.47a}$$

$$f_{TL}(x) = Cf_L(x), -l \leq x \leq l. \tag{A.47b}$$

In (A.47), $f_L(x)$ is the Levy distribution with index α and scale factor γ, l is the cutoff length, and C is the normalization constant.

Sometimes, the exponential cut-off is used at large distances:

$$f_{TL}(x) \sim exp(-\lambda|x|), \lambda > 0, |x| > l. \tag{A.48}$$

Since $f_{TL}(x)$ has finite variance, it converges to the normal distribution according to the central limit theorem.

Appendix B

Elements of Time Series Analysis

Time series analysis is widely used for describing and forecasting price dynamics, and implementing back-testing trading strategies. Here, I present an overview of its main concepts. For more details, readers can consult Alexander (2001), Hamilton (1994), Taylor (2005), and Tsay (2005).

B.1 The ARMA Model

B.1.1 *The autoregressive model*

Let's start with a univariate time series $y(t)$ that is observed at moments $t = 0, 1, \ldots, T$. A time series in which the observation at moment t depends linearly on several lagged observations at moments $t - 1, t - 2, \ldots, t - p$ is called the *autoregressive process* of order p, or $AR(p)$

$$y(t) = a_1 y(t - 1) + a_2 y(t - 2) + \cdots + a_p y(t - p) + \varepsilon(t), t > p.$$
$$(B.1)$$

White noise $\varepsilon(t)$ in (B.1) that is called *residual*, satisfies the following conditions:

$$E[\varepsilon(t)] = 0; \quad E[\varepsilon^2(t)] = \sigma^2; \quad E[\varepsilon(t)\varepsilon(s)] = 0, \quad \text{if} \quad t \neq s. \quad (B.2)$$

The *lag operator* $L^p = y(t - p)$ is often used in describing time series. Note that $L^0 = y(t)$. Equation (B.1) in terms of the lag operator,

$$A_p(L) = 1 - a_1 L - a_2 L^2 - \cdots - a_p L^p, \quad (B.3)$$

has the form

$$A_p(L)y(t) = \varepsilon(t). \tag{B.4}$$

It is easy to show for AR(1) that

$$y(t) = \sum_{i=0}^{t} a_1^i \varepsilon(t - i). \tag{B.5}$$

Obviously, contributions of old noise converge with time to zero when $|a_1| < 1$. In this case, AR(1) does not drift too far from its mean. Hence, AR(1) with $|a_1| < 1$ is a mean-reverting process. Mean and variance of AR(1) are equal, respectively,

$$E[y(t)] = 0, \tag{B.6a}$$
$$\mathrm{var}[y(t)] = \sigma^2/(1 - a_1^2). \tag{B.6b}$$

The process AR(1) with $a_1 = 1$ coincides with the random walk

$$y(t) = y(t - 1) + \varepsilon(t). \tag{B.7}$$

In this case, (B.5) reduces to a sum of past noise shocks that do not weaken with time

$$y(t) = \sum_{i=0}^{t} \varepsilon(t - i). \tag{B.8}$$

Therefore, the random walk does not exhibit mean reversion.

Now, consider the process that represents the first difference of the random walk:

$$x(t) = y(t) - y(t - 1) = \varepsilon(t). \tag{B.9}$$

Obviously, past noise has only transitory character for $x(t)$. Therefore $x(t)$ is mean-reverting. Some processes must be differenced several times (say d times) in order to exclude non-transitory noise shocks. These processes are named *integrated of order d* and denoted with $I(d)$.

The *unit root* is another notion widely used for discerning permanent and transitory effects of random shocks. It is based on the roots of the characteristic polynomial for the $AR(p)$ model. For example, $AR(1)$ has the characteristic polynomial

$$1 - a_1 z = 0. \tag{B.10}$$

If $a_1 = 1$, then $z = 1$ and it is said that the $AR(1)$ characteristic polynomial has the unit root. In the general case, the characteristic polynomial roots can have complex values. It is said that the solution to (B.10) is *outside the unit circle* (i.e., $z > 1$) when $a_1 < 1$. It can be shown that $AR(p)$ is stationary (i.e., mean-reverting) when the absolute values of all solutions to the characteristic equation

$$1 - a_1 z - a_2 z^2 - \cdots - a_p z^p = 0 \tag{B.11}$$

are outside the unit circle.

It is important to remember that only stationary $AR(p)$ processes can be predictable. Therefore, available data samples should be tested for unit roots prior to their usage for deriving and back-testing trading strategies. Rather than solving the (often intractable) characteristic equation (B.11) for analyzing the unit roots, one can use the Dickey-Fuller method (see, e.g., Tsay, 2005) that is implemented in the modern statistical software packages.

If a process $y(t)$ has a non-zero mean value m, then the $AR(1)$ model can be presented in the following form:

$$y(t) = m + a_1[y(t-1) - m] + \varepsilon(t) = c + a_1 y(t-1) + \varepsilon(t). \tag{B.12}$$

In (B.12), the intercept c equals

$$c = m(1 - a_1). \tag{B.13}$$

The general $AR(p)$ model with a non-zero mean can be expressed in terms of the lag operator.

$$A_p(L)y(t) = c + \varepsilon(t), \ c = m(1 - a_1 - \cdots a_p). \tag{B.14}$$

B.1.2   *The moving average model*

Another popular time series process is the *moving average model* MA(q):

$$y(t) = \varepsilon(t) + b_1\varepsilon(t-1) + b_2\varepsilon(t-2) + \cdots + b_q\varepsilon(t-q). \quad \text{(B.15)}$$

Similarly to AR(p), MA(q) can be presented in terms of the polynomial lag operator

$$y(t) = B_q(L)\varepsilon(t), \quad \text{(B.16)}$$

$$B_q(L) = 1 + b_1 L + b_2 L^2 + \cdots + b_q L^q. \quad \text{(B.17)}$$

The moving average model does not depend explicitly on the lagged values of $y(t)$. Yet, it is easy to show that this model implicitly incorporates the past. Consider, for example, the MA(1) model

$$y(t) = \varepsilon(t) + b_1\varepsilon(t-1), \quad \text{(B.18)}$$

with $\varepsilon(0) = 0$. This model can be represented as

$$y(t)(1 - b_1 L + b_1 L^2 - b_1 L^3 + \cdots) = \varepsilon(t). \quad \text{(B.19)}$$

Equation (B.19) describes the AR(∞) process, which illustrates that the MA(1) model does depend on the past. It is said that the MA(q) model is *invertible* if it can be transformed into an AR(∞) model. It is possible only if all solutions to the characteristic equation

$$1 + b_1 z + b_2 z^2 + \cdots + b_q z^q = 0, \quad \text{(B.20)}$$

are outside the unit circle. In particular, MA(1) is invertible if $|b_1| < 1$.

If a MA(q) process has a non-zero mean m, its intercept c coincides with m since the mean of white noise is zero

$$y(t) = c + B_p(L)\varepsilon(t), c = m. \quad \text{(B.21)}$$

B.1.3   *The ARMA model*

The model that contains both lagged observations and lagged noise is named an *autoregressive moving average model* of order (p, q), or

ARMA(p, q):

$$y(t) = a_1 y(t-1) + a_2 y(t-2) + \cdots + a_p y(t-p) + \varepsilon(t)$$
$$+ b_1 \varepsilon(t-1) + b_2 \varepsilon(t-2) + \cdots + b_q \varepsilon(t-q). \tag{B.22}$$

Sometimes, modeling of empirical data requires AR(p) with a rather high number p. Then, ARMA(p, q) may be more efficient in that the total number of its terms $(p + q)$ needed for given accuracy is lower than the number p in the corresponding AR(p).

The *autocorrelation function* (ACF) is a measure of correlation between the current time series value and its own lagged values. ACF for a process $y(t)$ equals

$$\rho(k) = \gamma(k)/\gamma(0), \tag{B.23}$$

where $\gamma(k)$ is autocovariance of order k (see Appendix A):

$$\gamma(k) = E[y(t) - m)(y(t-k) - m)]. \tag{B.24}$$

The obvious properties of ACF are

$$\rho(0) = 1; \; -1 < \rho(k) < 1 \quad \text{for} \quad k \neq 0. \tag{B.25}$$

ACF is closely related to the ARMA parameters. In particular, for AR(1),

$$\rho(1) = a_1. \tag{B.26}$$

ACF for MA(1) equals

$$\rho(1) = b_1/(b_1^2 + 1). \tag{B.27}$$

Note that the right-hand side of (B.27) has the same value for the inverse transformation $b_1 \to 1/b_1$. For example, two processes,

$$x(t) = \varepsilon(t) + 2\varepsilon(t-1), \tag{B.28a}$$
$$y(t) = \varepsilon(t) + 0.5\varepsilon(t-1), \tag{B.28b}$$

have the same $\rho(1)$ even though $y(t)$ is an invertible process while $x(t)$ is not.

ACFs have typical patterns for various processes, which can be used for identification of empirical time series (Hamilton, 1994).

ACF for SPY prices in 2012 - 2015

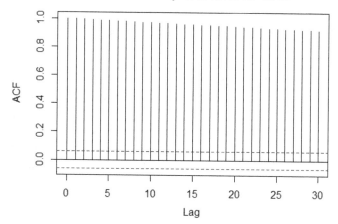

Fig. B.1.   An example for ACF of price.

ACF for SPY returns in 2012 - 2015

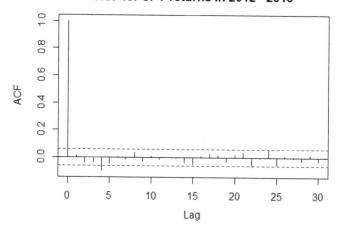

Fig. B.2.   An example for ACF of return.

It should be noted that ACFs of prices decay rather slowly while the ACFs of returns decay fast (cf. Figs. B.1 and B.2).

ARMA modeling is widely used for forecasting. Consider a forecast of a variable $y(t + 1)$ based on a set of n variables $x(t)$ known at moment t. This set can be just past the values of y, that is: $y(t)$, $y(t - 1), \ldots, y(t - n + 1)$. We denote the forecast with $\hat{y}(t + 1|t)$. The quality of forecast is usually defined with some loss function.

The *mean squared error* (MSE) is the conventional loss function in many applications:

$$\text{MSE}(\hat{y}(t+1|t)) = E[(y(t+1) - \hat{y}(t+1|t)^2]. \qquad \text{(B.29)}$$

The forecast that yields the minimum of MSE turns out to be the expectation of $y(t+1)$ conditioned on $x(t)$:

$$\hat{y}(t+1|t) = E[y(t+1)|\boldsymbol{x}(t)]. \qquad \text{(B.30)}$$

In the case of linear regression,

$$y(t+1) = \boldsymbol{b'x}(t) + \varepsilon(t). \qquad \text{(B.31)}$$

MSE is reduced to the OLS estimate for $\boldsymbol{b}$. For a sample with T observations,

$$b = \sum_{t=1}^{T} \boldsymbol{x}(t)y(t+1) \Big/ \sum_{t=1}^{T} \boldsymbol{x}(t)\boldsymbol{x}'(t). \qquad \text{(B.32)}$$

Another important concept in the time series analysis is the *maximum likelihood estimate* (MLE). Consider the general ARMA model (B.22). The problem is how to estimate the ARMA parameters on the basis of given observations of $y(t)$. The idea of MLE is to find such a vector $\boldsymbol{r'} = (a_1, \ldots, a_p, \ldots, b_1, \ldots, b_q, \sigma^2)$ that maximizes the likelihood function for the given observations $(y_1, y_2, \ldots, y_T)$:

$$f_{1,2,\ldots,T}(y_1, y_2, \ldots, y_T; \boldsymbol{r'}). \qquad \text{(B.33)}$$

The likelihood function (B.33) has the sense of probability of observing the data sample $(y_1, y_2, \ldots, y_T)$. In this approach, the ARMA model and the probability distribution for the white noise should be specified at first. Often, the normal distribution leads to reasonable estimates even if the real distribution is different. Further, the likelihood function must be calculated for the chosen ARMA model. Finally, the components of the vector $\boldsymbol{r'}$ must be estimated. The latter step may require sophisticated numerical optimization technique (Hamilton, 1994).

To avoid possible overfitting of data samples with ARMA(p, q) model, the maximum likelihood-based criteria can be used (see Section 14.1 for details). If unit roots are present in the data sample, ARMA(p, q) should be expanded into the integrated model, ARIMA(p, d, q). Modern statistical software packages offer the means for estimating optimal combinations of the ARIMA parameters p, d, and q.

B.2 Trends and Seasonality

Finding trends is an important part of the time series analysis. The presence of trend implies that time series has no mean reversion. Moreover, mean and variance of a trending process are not constant and depend on the sample. It is said that time series with trend is *nonstationary*. If a process $y(t)$ is *stationary*, its mean, variance, and autocovariance are finite and do not depend on time. In this case, autocovariance (B.24) depends only on the lag parameter k but not on time t. The definition of stationarity given above is named also *covariance-stationarity* or *weak stationarity* because it does not impose any restrictions on the higher moments of the process. S*trict stationarity* implies that higher moments (such as skewness and kurtosis) also do not depend on time. Note that any MA process is covariance-stationary. However, the $AR(p)$ process is covariance-stationary only if the roots of its characteristic polynomial are outside the unit circle.

It is important to discern *deterministic trend* and *stochastic trend* as they both have different nature, yet their graphs may sometimes look very similar. Indeed, let's compare the random walk with drift as an example of stochastic trend

$$y(t) = c + y(t-1) + \varepsilon(t), \tag{B.34}$$

with a simple model of deterministic trend

$$y(t) = at + \varepsilon(t). \tag{B.35}$$

The charts for both processes are very close (see Fig. B.3). However, while the deterministic model has a simple and accurate forecast, the random walk may change its direction any time.

Seasonal effects and various exogenous factors may significantly affect the properties of a time series. Sometimes, there is a need to eliminate these effects in order to focus on the stochastic specifics of the process. Various differencing filters can be used for achieving this goal. In other cases, seasonal effect itself may be the object of interest. The general approach for handling seasonal effects is introducing

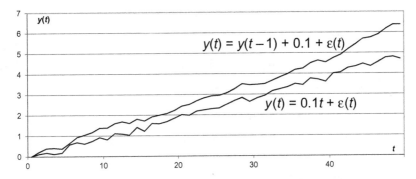

Fig. B.3. An example of deterministic and stochastic trends.

dummy variables $D(n, t)$, where $n = 1, 2, \ldots, N$; N is the number of factors. For example, $N = 12$ for modeling the monthly effects. Then, the parameter $D(n, t)$ equals 1 at a specific month n and equals zero for all other months. Sometimes, the variables that can have only values of 0 or 1 are called *binary variables*. The ARMA(p, q) model with dummy variables has the following form:

$$y(t) = a_1 y(t - 1) + a_2 y(t - 2) + \cdots + a_p y(t - p) + \varepsilon(t)$$

$$+ b_1 \varepsilon(t - 1) + b_2 \varepsilon(t - 2) + \cdots + b_q \varepsilon(t - q) + \sum_{n=1}^{N} d_n D(n, t).$$

$$(B.36)$$

Note that forecasting with the model (B.36) requires estimation of $(p + q + N)$ parameters.

B.3 Multivariate Time Series

Sometimes, the current value of a variable depends not only on its past values but also on past and/or current values of other variables. Then, it is said that the dynamic interdependent variables constitute *multivariate time series*. A multivariate time series $\mathbf{y}(t) = (y_1(t), y_2(t), \ldots, y_n(t))'$ is a vector of n processes that have data available for the same moments of time. Usually, it is assumed that all these processes are either stationary or have the same order of integration. In practice, the multivariate moving average models are rarely used. Therefore, I focus here on the *vector autoregressive model* (VAR).

As an example, consider a bivariate VAR(1) process

$$y_1(t) = a_{10} + a_{11}y_1(t-1) + a_{12}y_2(t-1) + \varepsilon_1(t), \quad \text{(B.37)}$$

$$y_2(t) = a_{20} + a_{21}y_1(t-1) + a_{22}y_2(t-1) + \varepsilon_2(t), \quad \text{(B.38)}$$

that can be presented in the matrix form

$$\boldsymbol{y}(t) = \boldsymbol{a}_0 + \mathbf{A}\boldsymbol{y}(t-1) + \varepsilon(t). \quad \text{(B.39)}$$

In (B.39), $\boldsymbol{y}(t) = (y_1(t), y_2(t))'$, $\boldsymbol{a}_0 = (a_{10}, a_{20})'$, $\varepsilon(t) = (\varepsilon_1(t), \varepsilon_2(t))'$, and $\mathbf{A} = \begin{pmatrix} a_{11} & a_{12} \\ a_{21} & a_{22} \end{pmatrix}$.

The right-hand sides in the example (B.39) depend on past values only. However, dependencies on current values can also be included (the so-called *simultaneous dynamic model*). The simultaneous dynamic models can be reduced to the standard VAR. For example, the following simultaneous system:

$$y_1(t) = a_{11}y_1(t-1) + a_{12}y_2(t) + \varepsilon_1(t), \quad \text{(B.40)}$$

$$y_2(t) = a_{21}y_1(t) + a_{22}y_2(t-1) + \varepsilon_2(t), \quad \text{(B.41)}$$

can be represented as

$$\begin{pmatrix} y_1(t) \\ y_2(t) \end{pmatrix} = (1 - a_{12}a_{21})^{-1} \begin{pmatrix} a_{11} & a_{12}a_{22} \\ a_{11}a_{21} & a_{22} \end{pmatrix} \begin{pmatrix} y_1(t-1) \\ y_2(t-1) \end{pmatrix}$$

$$+ (1 - a_{12}a_{21})^{-1} \begin{pmatrix} 1 & a_{12} \\ a_{21} & 1 \end{pmatrix} \begin{pmatrix} \varepsilon_1(t) \\ \varepsilon_2(t) \end{pmatrix}. \quad \text{(B.42)}$$

In the general case of n-variate time series, VAR(p) has the form

$$\boldsymbol{y}(t) = \boldsymbol{a}_0 + \mathbf{A_1}\boldsymbol{y}(t-1) + \cdots + \mathbf{A_p}\boldsymbol{y}(t-p) + \varepsilon(t), \quad \text{(B.43)}$$

where $\boldsymbol{y}(t)$, $\boldsymbol{a}_0$, and $\varepsilon(t)$ are n-dimensional vectors and $\mathbf{A_i}$ ($i = 1, \ldots, p$) are $n \times n$ matrices. Usually, it is assumed that the white noises $\varepsilon_i(t)$ are mutually independent.

In terms of the lag operator

$$\bar{\mathbf{A}}_p(\boldsymbol{L}) = I_n - \mathbf{A_1}L - \cdots - \mathbf{A_p}L^p, \quad \text{(B.44)}$$

where I_n is the n-dimensional unit vector, (B.43) can be presented as

$$\bar{A}_p(\boldsymbol{L})\boldsymbol{y}(t) = \boldsymbol{a}_0 + \varepsilon(t). \quad \text{(B.45)}$$

Two covariance-stationary processes $x(t)$ and $y(t)$ are jointly covariance-stationary if their covariance $\text{cov}(x(t), y(t-s))$ depends on lag s only. The condition for the covariance-stationary VAR(p) is the generalization of (B.11) for AR(p). Namely, all values of z satisfying the equation

$$|I_n - \mathbf{A_1}z - \cdots - \mathbf{A_p}z^p| = 0 \qquad (B.46)$$

must lie outside the unit circle. Equivalently, all solutions of the equation

$$|I_n\lambda^p - \mathbf{A_1}\lambda^{p-1} - \cdots - \mathbf{A_p}| = 0. \qquad (B.47)$$

must satisfy the condition $|\lambda| < 1$.

References

Abrahams, J. (1986). "A survey of recent progress on level-crossing problems for random processes." In *Communications and Networks: A Survey of Recent Advances*, edited by I. F. Blake and H. V. Poor, pp. 6–25. Berlin: Springer-Verlag.

Admati, A. R. and P. Pfleiderer (1988). "A theory of intraday patterns: Volume and price variability." *Review of Financial Studies* 1, 3–40.

Ait-Sahalia, Y., P. A. Mykland, and L. Zhang (2005). *Ultra high frequency volatility estimation with dependent microstructure noise.* NBER Working Papers 11380.

Akerlof, G. A. and R. J. Shiller (2010). *Animal Spirits: How Human Psychology Drives the Economy, and Why it Matters for Global Capitalism.* Princeton: Princeton University Press.

Aldridge, I. (2010). *High-Frequency Trading: A Practical Guide to Algorithmic Strategies and Trading Systems.* Hoboken, NJ: Wiley.

Aldridge, I. and S. Krawciw (2017). *Real-Time Risk: What Investors Should Know About Fintech, High-Frequency Trading and Flash Crashes.* Hoboken, NJ: Wiley.

Alexander, C. (1999). "Optimal hedging using cointegration." *Philosophical Transactions of the Royal Society* A357, 2039–2058.

Alexander, C. (2001). *Market Models: A Guide to Financial Data Analysis.* New York: Wiley.

Alexander, C., I. Giblin, and W. Weddington, III (2001). *Cointegration and Asset Allocation: A New Active Hedge Strategy.* ISMA Discussion Papers in Finance.

Algaba, A., D. Ardia, K. Bluetau, S. Borms, and K. Boudt (2020). "Econometrics meets sentiment: An overview of methodology and applications." *Journal of Economic Surveys* 34, 512–547.

Almgren, R. and N. Chriss (2000). "Optimal execution of portfolio transactions." *Journal of Risk* 3(2), 5–39.

Almgren, R., C. Thum, E. Hauptmann, and H. Li (2005). "Equity market impact." *Risk* 18, 57–62.

Almgren, R. and J. Lorenz (2007). "Adaptive arrival price." Available on the web: http://www.algotradingstrategies.com/Algotrading.pdf.

Amihud Y. (2002). "Illiquidity and stock returns: Cross-section and time-series effects." *Journal of Financial Markets* 5, 31–56.

Amihud, Y. and H. Mendelson (1980). "Dealership markets: Market making with inventory." *Journal of Financial Economics* 8, 31–53.

Andersen, T. G., T. Bollerslev, F. X. Diebold, and P. Labys (2000). "Great realizations." *Risk* 13(3), 105–108.

Andersen, T. G., T. Bollerslev, F. X. Diebold, and C. Vega (2003). "Micro Effects of Macro Announcements: Real-time Price Discovery in Foreign Exchange." *The American Economic Review* 93, 38–62.

Andersen T. G. and T. Bollerslev (1998). "Deutsche mark-dollar volatility: Intraday activity patterns, macroeconomic announcements, and longer run dependencies." *Journal of Finance* 53(2), 219–265.

Ang, A. (2014). *Asset Management: A Systematic Approach to Factor Investing*. New York: Oxford University Press.

Antonacci, G. (2015) *Dual Momentum Investing*. New York: McGraw Hill Education.

Arnott, R., C. R. Harvey, V. Kalesnik, and J. Linnainmaa (2019). "Alice's Adventures in Factorland: Three Blunders That Plague Factor Investing." *The Journal of Portfolio Management* 45(4), 18–36.

Aronson, D. (2006). *Evidence-Based Technical Analysis: Applying the Scientific Method and Statistical Inference to Trading Signals*. Hoboken, NJ: Wiley.

Arthur, B. W. (1994). "Inductive reasoning and bounded rationality." *American Economic Review* 84, 406–411.

Artzner, P., F. Delbaen, J.-M. Eber, and D. Heath (1999). "Coherent measures of risk." *Mathematical Finance* 9, 203–228.

Asness, C., A. Frazzini, R. Israel, and T. Moskowitz (2014). "Fact, fiction, and momentum investing." *Journal of Portfolio Management* 40, 75–92.

Avellaneda, M., and J.-H. Lee (2010). "Statistical arbitrage in U.S. equities market." *Quantitative Finance* 10, 761–782.

Back, K. and S. Baruch (2004). "Information in securities markets: Kyle meets Glosten and Milgrom." *Econometrica* 72, 433–465.

Baker, M. and J. Wurgler (2006). "Investor sentiment and the cross-section of stock returns." *Journal of Finance* 61, 1645–1680.

Balduzzi, P., E. J. Elton, and T. C. Green (2001). "Economic News and Bond Prices: Evidence From the U.S. Treasury Market." *Journal of Financial and Quantitative Analysis* 36, 523–543.

Ball, R. and S. P. Kothari (1991). "Security returns around earnings announcements." *The Accounting Review* 66, 718–738.

Barndorff-Nielsen, O. E. and N. Shephard (2002). "Econometric analysis of realized volatility and its use in estimating stochastic volatility models." *Journal of the Royal Statistical Society B, Part 2* 64, 253–280.

Barndorff-Nielsen, O. E., P. R. Hansen, A. Lunde, and N. Shephard (2008). "Designing realised kernels to measure the ex-post variation of equity prices in the presence of noise." *Econometrica* 76, 1481–1536.

Baron, D. P. (2009). "A Positive Theory of Moral Management, Social Pressure, and Corporate Social Performance." *Journal of Economics & Management Strategy* 18, 7–43.

Baitinger, E., A. Dragosch, and A. Topalova (2017). "Extending the risk parity approach to higher moments: Is there any value added?" *The Journal of Portfolio Management* 43(2), 24–36.

Baltas, N. and Kosowski R. (2013). "Momentum strategies in futures markets and trend-following funds." Available at: http://dx.doi.org/10.21 39/ssrn.1968996.

Barberis, N., A. Shleifer, and R. Vishny (1998). "A model of investor sentiment." *Journal of Financial Economics* 49, 307–343.

Barroso, P. and P. Santa-Clara (2015). "Momentum has its moments." *Journal of Financial Economics* 116, 111–120.

Beaver, W. H. (1968). "The information content of annual earnings announcements." *Journal of Accounting Research* 6, 67–92.

Beja, A. and M. B. Goldman (1980). "On the dynamic behavior of prices in disequilibrium." *Journal of Finance* 35, 235–248.

Behr, P., A. Guettler, and F. Miebs (2013). "On portfolio optimization: Imposing the right constraints." *Journal of Banking & Finance* 37(4), 1232–1242.

Benabou, R. and J. Tirole (2010). "Individual and corporate social responsibility." *Economica* 77, 1–19.

Benichou, R., Y. Lemperiere, E. Sérié, J. Kockelkoren, P. Seager, J.-P. Bouchaud, and M. Potters (2017). "Agnostic risk parity: Taming known and unknown-unknowns." *The Journal of Investment Strategies* 6(3), 1–12.

Berg, F., J. Kölbel, and R. Rigobon (2019). *Aggregate confusion: The divergence of ESG ratings.* MIT Sloan Research Paper No. 5822-19. Available at SSRN: https://ssrn.com/abstract=3438533.

Bertsimas, D. and A. W. Lo (1998). "Optimal control of execution costs." *Journal of Financial Markets* 1, 1–50.

Biais, B., D. Martimort, and J. C. Rochet (1995). "An empirical analysis of the limit order book and the order flow in the Paris bourse." *Journal of Finance* 50, 1655–1689.

Black, F. and R. Litterman (1990). *Asset Allocation: Combining Investor Views with Market Equilibrium.* New York: Goldman Sachs Fixed Income Research.

Blitz, D., M. X. Hanauer, M. Vidojevic, and P. van Vliet (2018). "Five concerns with the five-factor model." *The Journal of Portfolio Management* 44(4), 71–78.

Bloomfield, R., M. O'Hara, and G. Saar (2004). "The make-or-take decision in an electronic market: Evidence on the evolution of liquidity." *Journal of Financial Economics* 75, 165–199.

Bodie, Z. and R. C. Merton (1998). *Finance.* Upper Saddle River, NJ: Prentice-Hall.

Bollen, J., H. Mao, and X. Zeng (2011). "Twitter mood predicts the stock market." *Journal of Computational Science* 2, 1–8.

Bommes, E. C. Y.-H. Chen, and W. K. Härdle (2018). "Textual sentiment and sector specific reaction." Available at: https://ssrn.com/abstract= 3658203.

Bondarenko, O. (2003). "Statistical arbitrage and securities prices." *Review of Financial Studies* 16, 875–919.

Booth, D. and E. Fama (1992) "Diversification returns and asset contributions." *Financial Analysts Journal* 48, 26–32.

Bordino, I., S. Battiston, G. Caldarelli, M. Cristelli, A. Ukkonen, and I. Weber (2012). "Web Search Queries Can Predict Stock Market Volumes." *PLoS One* 7(e40014).

Bouchaud, J.-P., J. Kockelkoren, and M. Potters (2006). "Random walks, liquidity molasses and critical response in financial markets." *Quantitative Finance* 6(2), 115–123.

Bouchaud, J.-P. M. Potters, and J. P. Aguilar (1997). "Missing information and asset allocation." Available at: arXiv:cond-mat/9707042.

Bouchaud, J.-P. and M. Potters (2000). *Theory Of Financial Risks: From Statistical Physics to Risk Management.* Cambridge: Cambridge University Press.

Bouchaud, J.-P., Y. Gefen, M. Potters, and M. Wyart (2004). "Fluctuations and response in financial markets: The subtle nature of 'random' price changes." *Quantitative Finance* 4, 176–190.

Boudoukh, J., R. Feldman, S. Kogan, and M. Richardson (2013). *Which news moves stock prices? A textual analysis.* NBER Working Paper No. 18725.

Boudoukh, J., M. Richardson, and R. F. Whitelaw (1994). "Industry Returns and the Fisher Effect." *Journal of Finance* 49, 1595–1615.

Brock, W. A. and C. H. Hommes (1998). "Heterogenous beliefs and routes to chaos in a simple asset pricing model." *Journal of Economic Dynamics and Control* 22, 1235–1274.

Brock, W. A., J. Lakonishok, and B. LeBaron (1992). "Simple technical trading rules and stochastic properties of stock returns." *Journal of Finance* 47, 1731–1764.

Bryzgalova, S., J. Huang, and C. Julliard (2020). "Bayesian solutions for the factor zoo: We just ran two quadrillion models." Available at SSRN: https://ssrn.com/abstract=3481736.

Bullen P. S., D. S. Mitrinovic, and P. M. Vasic (1988). *Means and Their Inequalities.* D. Reidel Publishing Company.

Cai, H. and A. B. Schmidt (2020a). "What's so special about the time series momentum?" *Journal of Investment Strategies* 9(2), 33–43.

Cai, H. and A. B. Schmidt (2020b). "Comparing mean–variance portfolios and equal-weight portfolios for major US equity indexes." *Journal of Asset Management* 21, 326–332.

Calvet, L. and A. Fisher (2002). "Multi-fractality in asset returns: Theory and evidence." *Review of Economics and Statistics* 84, 381–406.

Campbell, J. Y., A. W. Lo, and A. C. MacKinlay (1997). *The Econometrics of Financial Markets.* Princeton: Princeton University Press.

Carhart, M. (1997). "On Persistence in Mutual Fund Performance." *Journal of Finance* 52, 57–82.

Cenesizoglu, T., Q. Liu, J. J. Reeves, and H. Wu (2016). "Monthly Beta Forecasting with Low-, Medium- and High-Frequency Stock Returns." *Journal of Forecasting* 35, 528–541.

CFTC-SEC (2010). "The market events of May 6, 2010." Available at: https://www.sec.gov/news/studies/2010/marketevents-report.pdf.

Challet, D., A. Chessa, A. Marsili, and Y. C. Chang (2001). "From minority games to real Markets." *Quantitative Finance* 1, 168–176.

Chan, E. P. (2009). *Quantitative Trading: How to Build Your Own Algorithmic Trading Business.* Hoboken, NJ: Wiley.

Chan, L. K., H. L. Chen, and J. Lakonishok (2002). "On mutual fund investment styles." *Review of Financial Studies* 15, 1407–1437.

Chari, V. V., R. Jagannathan, and A. R. Ofer (1988). "Seasonalities in security returns: The case of earnings announcements." *Journal of Financial Economics* 21, 101–121.

Chen, H., P. De, J. Hu, and B.-H. Hwang (2014). "Wisdom of crowds: The value of stock opinions transmitted through social media." *Review of Financial Studies* 27, 1367–1403.

Chen, N.-F., R. Roll, and S. A. Ross (1986). "Economic forces and the stock market." *The Journal of Business* 59(3), 383–403

Chiarella, C., R. Dieci, and X. He (2009). "Heterogeneity, market mechanisms, and asset price dynamics." In *Handbook on Financial Markets: Dynamics and Evolution*, pp. 277–344. Elsevier.

Chiarella, C. and X. He (2001). "Asset pricing and wealth dynamics under heterogeneous expectations." *Quantitative Finance* 1, 509–526.

Choi, H. and H. Varian (2012). "Predicting the Present with Google Trends." *Economic Record* 88(s1), 2–9.

Choueifaty, Y. and Y. Coignard (2008). "Toward maximum diversification." *The Journal of Portfolio Management* 35(1), 40–51.

Chopra, V. K. and W. T. Ziemba (1993). "The effect of errors in means, variances, and covariances on optimal portfolio choice." *The Journal of Portfolio Management* 19(2), 6–11.

Clarke, R., H. de Silva, and S. Thorley (2006). "Minimum-variance portfolios in the U.S. equity market." *The Journal of Portfolio Management* 33(1), 10–24.

Clarke, R., H. de Silva, and S. Thorley (2011). "Minimum variance portfolio composition." *Journal of Portfolio Management* 31(2), 31–45.

Cohen, K. J., S. F. Maier, R. A. Schwartz, and D. K. Whitcomb (1981). "Transaction costs, order placement strategy, and bid-ask spread." *Journal of Political Economy* 89, 287–305.

Cooper, M. J. (1999). "Filter rules based on price and volume in individual security overreaction." *Review of Financial Studies* 12, 901–935.

Cowles, A. and H. E. Jones (1937). "Some a posteriori probabilities in stock market action." *Econometrica* 5, 280–294.

Dacorogna, M. M., R. Gencay, U. Müller, R. B. Olsen, and O. V. Pictet (2001). *An Introduction to High-Frequency Finance*. San Diego: Academic Press.

Daniel, K. and T. J. Moskowitz (2016). "Momentum crashes." *Journal of Financial Economics* 122, 221–247.

Das, S. R. and M. Y. Chen (2007). "Yahoo! for Amazon: Sentiment extraction from small talk on the web." *Management Science* 53, 1375–1388.

Davidson, A. C. and D. V. Hinkley (1997). *Bootstrap Methods and Their Applications*. Cambridge: Cambridge University Press.

De Carvalho, R. L., X. Lu, and P. Moulin (2012). "Demystifying equity risk-based strategies: A simple alpha plus beta description." *The Journal of Portfolio Management* 38(3), 56–70.

Deguest, R., L. Martellini, and A. Meucci (2013). "Risk parity and beyond — From asset allocation to risk allocation decisions." Available at: https://ssrn.com/abstract=2355778.

de Jong, F. and B. Rindi (2009). *The Microstructure of Financial Markets*. Cambridge: Cambridge University Press.

DeLong, J. B, A. Shleifer, L. H. Summers, and R. J. Waldmann (1990). "Positive feedback investment strategies and destabilizing rational speculation." *Journal of Finance* 45, 379–395.

DeMiguel, V., L. Garlappi, and R. Uppal (2009). "Optimal versus Naïve diversification: How inefficient is the 1/N portfolio strategy?" *Review of Financial Studies* 22, 1915–1953.

DeMiguel, V., Y. Plyakha, R. Uppal, and G. Vilkov (2013). "Improving portfolio selection using option-implied volatility and skewness." *Journal of Financial and Quantitative Analysis* 48, 1813–1845.

Denev, A. and S. Amen (2020). *The Book of Alternative Data: A Guide for Investors, Traders and Risk Managers*. Wiley.

Derman, E. (2011). *Models Behaving Badly: Why Confusing Illusion with Reality Can Lead to Disaster, on Wall Street and in Life*. Free Press.

Dimson, E., P. Marsh, and M. Staunton (2020). "Divergent ESG ratings." *The Journal of Portfolio Management* 47(1), 75–87.

Dixon, M. F., I. Halperin, and P. Bilokon (2020). *Machine Learning in Finance: From Theory to Practice*. Springer.

Donefer, B. S (2010). "Algos gone wild: Risk in the world of automated trading strategies." *Journal of Trading* 5(2), 31–34.

Dowd, K. (2002). *An Introduction to Market Risk Measurement*. Hoboken, NJ: Wiley.

Duchin, R. and H. Levy (2009). "Markowitz versus the Talmudic portfolio diversification Strategies." *Journal of Portfolio Management* 35, 71–74.

Dunis, C., J. Laws, and P. Naim (2003). *Applied Quantitative Methods for Trading and Investment*. Hoboken: Wiley.

Easley, D. and M. O'Hara (1987). "Price, trade size, and information in securities markets." *Journal of Financial Economics* 19, 69–90.

Easley, D. and M. O'Hara (1992). "Time and the process of security price adjustment." *Journal of Finance* 47, 576–605.

Edwards, R. D. and J. Magee (2001). *Technical Analysis of Stock Trends*, 8th edition. AMACOM.

Eisler, Z., J. Kertesz, F. Lillo, and R. N. Mantegna (2009). "Diffusive behavior and the modeling of characteristic times in limit order executions." *Quantitative Finance* 5, 547–563.

Elliott, R. J., J. Van der Hoek, and W. P. Malcolm (2005). "Pairs trading." *Quantitative Finance* 5(3), 271–276.

Elton, E. J., M. J. Gruber, S. J. Brown, and W. N. Goetzmann (2009). *Modern Portfolio Theory and Investment Analysis*. Hoboken, NJ: John Wiley & Sons.

Emrich, S. (2009). "Using smarter algorithms vs. smarter use of algorithms." *A Guide to Global Liquidity II. Institutional Investors Journals* 1, 40–51.

Engle, R. F. (1982). "Autoregressive conditional heteroscedasticity with estimates of the conditional variance of United Kingdom inflation." *Econometrica* 50, 987–1007.

Engle, R. F., R. Ferstenberg, and J. Russell (2012). "Measuring and modeling execution cost and risk." *The Journal of Portfolio Management* 38(2), 14–28.

Engle, R. F. and Granger C. W. J. (1987). "Co-integration and error correction: Representation, estimation and testing." *Econometrica* 55(2), 251–276.

Engle, R. F. and A. J. Patton (2004). "Impact of trades in an error-correction model of quote prices." *Journal of Financial Markets* 7, 1–25.

Evans, K. P. (2011). "Intraday jumps and US macroeconomic news announcements." *Journal of Banking and Finance* 35, 2511–2527.

Fabozzi, F. J. and J.C. Francis (1977). "Stability tests for alphas and betas over bull and bear market conditions." *The Journal of Finance* 32, 1093–1099.

Fabozzi, F. J., P. Kolm, D. Pachamanova, and S.M. Focardi (2007). *Robust Portfolio Optimization and Management.* New York: Wiley.

Fama, E. (1970). "Efficient capital markets: A review of theory and empirical work." *Journal of Finance* 25, 383–417.

Fama, F. and K. R. French (1993). "Common risk factors in the returns on stocks and bonds." *Journal of Financial Economics* 33, 3–56.

Fama, E. F. and K. R. French (1996). "Multifactor explanations of asset pricing anomalies." *Journal of Finance* 51, 55–84.

Fama, E. F and K. B. French (2004). "The capital asset pricing model: Theory and evidence." *Journal of Economic Perspectives* 18(3), 25–46.

Fama, E. F. and K. R. French (1997). "Industry costs of equity." *Journal of Financial Economics* 43, 153–193.

Fama, E. F. and K. R. French (2015). "A five-factor asset pricing model." *Journal of Financial Economics* 16, 1–22.

Fama, E. F. and J. D. MacBeth (1973). "Return and equilibrium: Empirical tests." *Journal of Political Economy* 81, 607–636.

Farmer, J. D., A. Gerig, F. Lillo, and S. Mike (2006). "Market efficiency and the long-memory of supply and demand: Is price impact variable and permanent or fixed and temporary?" *Quantitative Finance* 6(2), 107–112.

Farmer, J. D. and S. Joshi (2002). "The price dynamics of common trading strategies." *Journal of Economic Behavior & Organization* 49(2), 149–171.

Farmer, J. D., P. Patelli, and I. I. Zovko (2005). "Predictive power of zero-intelligence in financial markets." *Proceedings of the National Academy of Sciences USA* 102, 2254–2259.

Feller, W. (1968). *Introduction to Probability Theory and Its Applications,* Vol. 1, 3rd Edition. New York: Wiley.

Ferreira, F., C. Silva C. and J-Y. Yen (2014). "Information ratio analysis of momentum strategies." Available at: http://dx.doi.org/10.2139/ssr n.2396099.

Flannery, M. J. and A. A. Protopapadakis (2002). "Macroeconomic factors do influence aggregate stock returns." *Review of Financial Studies* 15, 751–782.

Foucault, T. (1999). "Order flow composition and trading costs in a dynamic limit order book." *Journal of Financial Markets* 2, 99–134.

Foucault T., O. Kadan, and E. Kandel (2005). "Limit order book as a market for liquidity." *The Review of Financial Studies* 18, 1171–1217.

Frazzini, A. and O. Lamont (2007). *The earnings announcement premium and trading volume.* NBER Working Paper 13090.

Friede, G., T. Busch, and A. Bassen (2015). "ESG and financial performance: Aggregated evidence from more than 2000 empirical studies." *Journal of Sustainable Finance & Investment* 5(4), 210–233.

Gabaix, X. (2009). "Power laws in economics and finance." *Annual Review of Economics* 1, 255–293.

Gabaix, X., P. Gopikrishnan, V. Plerou, and H. E. Stanley (2003). "A theory of power-law distributions in financial market fluctuations." *Nature* 423, 267–270.

Gandelman, N. and R. Hernández-Murillo (2014). *Risk aversion at the country level.* Federal Reserve Bank of St. Louis. Working paper 2014-005B.

Garcia, D. (2013) "Sentiment during recessions." *Journal of Finance* 68, 1267–1300.

Garman M. (1976). "Market microstructure." *Journal of Financial Economics* 3, 257–275.

Gatev, E., W. N. Goetzmann, and K. G. Rowenhorst (2006). "Pairs trading: Performance of a relative-value arbitrage." *The Review of Financial Studies* 19, 797–827.

Gatheral, G. (2010). "No-dynamic-arbitrage and market impact." *Quantitative Finance* 10, 749–759.

Gencay, R., F. Selcuk, and B. Whitcher (2001). *An Introduction to Wavelets and Other Filtering Methods in Economics and Finance.* San Diego: Academic Press.

Gerakos, J. and R. Gramacy (2013). *Regression-Based Earnings Forecasts.* Chicago Booth Research Paper No. 12-26.

Gerber, S., H. Markowitz, and P. Pujara (2015). "Enhancing multi-asset portfolio construction under modern portfolio theory with a robust co-movement measure." Available at: http://ssrn.com/abstract=2627803.

Gilbert, T. (2011). "Information aggregation around macroeconomic announcements: Revisions matter." *Journal of Financial Economics* 101, 114–131.

Gilbert, T., C. Scotti, G. Strasser, and C. Vega (2010). *Why do certain macroeconomic news announcements have a big impact on asset prices?* Applied Econometrics and Forecasting in Macroeconomics and Finance Workshop. Federal Reserve Bank of St. Luis.

Glosten, L. R. and L. E. Harris (1988). "Estimating the components of the bid/ask spread." *Journal of Financial Economics* 21, 123–142.

Glosten, L. R, R. Jagannathan, and D. E. Runkle (1993). "On the relation between the expected value and the volatility of the nominal excess return on stocks." *Journal of Finance* 48, 1779–1801.

Glosten, L. and P. Milgrom (1985). "Bid, ask and transaction prices in a specialist market with heterogeneously informed traders." *Journal of Financial Economics* 14, 71–100.

Goettler, R., C. Parlour, and U. Rajan (2005). "Equilibrium in a dynamic limit order market." *Journal of Finance* 60, 2149–2192.

Goeij, P., Hu, J. and Werker, B.J. (2010). *The price of macroeconomic announcement news.* Netspar Discussion Paper No. 02/2009-053. Available at SSRN: http://ssrn.com/abstract=1573642.

Gomber, P., U. Schweickert, and E. Theissen (2015). "Liquidity Dynamics in an Electronic Open Limit Order Book: An Event Study Approach." *European Financial Management* 21, 52–78.

Graham, B., and D. Dodd (2008). *Security analysis.* 6th Edition. McGraw-Hill.

Gray, W. R. and J. R. Vogel (2016). *Quantitative Momentum: A Practitioner's Guide to Building a Momentum-Based Stock Selection System.* Wiley.

Green, R. C. and B. Hollifield (1992). "When will mean–variance efficient portfolios be well diversified?" *Journal of Finance* 47, 1785–1809.

Grinold, R. C. and R. N. Kahn (2000). *Active Portfolio Management.* McGraw-Hill.

Grossman, S. J. and J.E. Stiglitz (1980). "On the Impossibility of Informationally Efficient Markets." *American Economic Review* 70, 393–408.

Grundy, B. D. and S. J. Martin (2001). "Understanding the Nature of Risks and the Sources of Rewards to Momentum Investing." *Review of Financial Studies* 14, 29–78.

Hamilton, J. D. (1994). *Time series analysis.* Princeton University Press.

Hansen, P. R. (2005). "A test for superior predictive ability." *Journal of Business and Economic Statistics* 23, 365–380.

Hansen, P. R., J. Large, and A. Lunde (2008). "Moving average-based estimators of integrated variance." *Econometric Reviews* 27, 79–111.

Harris, L. (2002). *Trading and Exchanges: Market Microstructure for Practitioners.* Oxford University Press.

Hart, O. and L. Zingales (2017). "Companies should maximize shareholder welfare not market value." *Journal of Law, Finance, and Accounting* 2, 247–274.

Hartmann, C. H.-P. Burghof, and M. Mehlhorn (2018). "Identifying noise traders entering the market with Google and Twitter." Available at: https://ssrn.com/abstract=3271789.

Harvey, C., Y. Liu, and H. Zhu (2016). "... and the cross-section of expected returns." *Review of Financial Studies* 29 (1), 5–68.

Hasbrouck, J. (2007). *Empirical Market Microstructure: The Institutions, Economics, and Econometrics of Securities Trading.* Oxford University Press.

Hasbrouck, J. (1991). "Measuring the informational content of stock trades." *Journal of Finance* 46, 179–207.

Hasbrouck, J. and D. J. Seppi (2001). "Common factors in prices, order flows and liquidity." *Journal of Financial Economics* 59, 383–411.

Hashimoto, Y., T. Ito, M. Ohnishi, H. Takayasu, M. Takayasu, and T. Watanabe (2008). *Random walk or a run: Market microstructure analysis of the foreign exchange rate movements based on conditional probability.* NBER Working Paper 14160.

Haugen, R. and N. Baker (1991). "The efficient market inefficiency of capitalization-weighted stock portfolios." *Journal of Portfolio Management* 17(3), 35–40.

Hautsch, N. and Hess, D. (2007). Bayesian learning in financial markets: Testing for the relevance of information precision in price discovery." *Journal of Financial and Quantitative Analysis* 42, 189–208.

Hautsch, N. and R. Huang (2012). "The market impact of a limit order." *Journal of Economic Dynamics and Control* 36, 501–522.

Heitz, A. R., G. Narayanamoorthy, and M. Zekhnini (2019). "The disappearing earnings announcement premium." Available at SSRN: https://ssrn.com/abstract=3296537.

Hendershott, T. and P. C. Moulton (2011). "Automation, speed, and stock market quality: The NYSE's Hybrid." *Journal of Financial Markets* 14, 568–604.

Hendershott, T., C. M. Jones, and A. J. Menkveld (2011). "Does Algorithmic trading improve liquidity?" *Journal of Finance* 66, 1–33.

Heston, S. L., R.A. Korajczyk, and R. Sadka (2010). "Intraday patterns in the cross-section of stock returns." *Journal of Finance* 65, 1369–1407.

Heston, S. L. and N. R. Sinha (2017). "News vs. sentiment: Predicting stock returns from news stories." *Journal of Financial Analysts* 73(3), 67–83.

Hilborn, R. C. (2000). *Chaos and Nonlinear Dynamics: An Introduction for Scientists and Engineers.* Oxford University Press.

Hirschman, A. O. (1964). "The paternity of an index." *The American Economic Review* 54(5), 761.

Ho, J. C. and C.-H. D. Hung (2012). "Predicting Stock Market Returns and Volatility with Investor Sentiment: Evidence from Eight Developed Countries." Available at: https://ssrn.com/abstract=2279339.

Ho, T. and H. R. Stoll (1981). "Optimal dealer pricing under transactions and return uncertainty." *Journal of Financial Economics* 9, 47–73.

Ho, T. and H. R. Stoll (1983). "The dynamics of dealer markets under competition." *Journal of Finance* 38, 1053–1074.

Hommes, C. H. (2006). "Heterogeneous agent models in economics and finance." In *Handbook of Computational Economics, Vol. 2: Agent-Based Computational Economics*, edited by H. Amman, D. Kendrick, and J. Rust, pp. 1109–1186. North-Holland.

Hommes, C. and B. LeBaron (eds.) (2018). *Computational Economics: Heterogeneous Agent Modeling* (Handbooks in Economics). North-Holland.

Hong, H. and M. Kacperczyk (2009). "The price of sin: The effects of social norms on markets." *Journal of Financial Economics* 93(1), 15–36.

Hong, H. G. and J. Wang (2000). "Trading and returns under periodic market closures." *Journal of Finance* 55, 297–354.

Hora, M. (2006). "Tactical liquidity trading and intraday volume." Available at SSRN: http://ssrn.com/abstract=931667.

Hsu, J. C., V. Kalesnik, and E. Kose (2018). "What is quality?" *Financial Analysts Journal* 75(2), 44–61.

Hsu, P.-H. and C.-M. Kuan (2005). "Reexamining the profitability of technical analysis with data snooping checks." *Journal of Financial Econometrics* 3, 606–628.

Hsu, P.-H., Y.-C. Hsu, and C.-M. Kuan (2010). "Testing the predictive ability of technical analysis using a new stepwise test without data snooping bias." *Journal of Empirical Finance* 17(3), 471–484.

Huang, D., F. Jiang, J. Tu, and G. Zhou (2015). "Investor sentiment aligned: A powerful predictor of stock returns." *Review of Financial Studies* 28, 791–837.

Huberman, G. and W. Stahl (2005). "Optimal liquidity trading." *Review of Finance* 9, 165–200.

Huck, N. and K. Afawubo (2015). "Pairs trading and selection methods: Is cointegration superior?" *Applied Economics* 47, 599–613.

Hull, J. C. (2006). *Options, Futures, and Other Derivatives*. 6th Edition. Upper Saddle River, NJ: Prentice Hall.

Jacobs, B. I. and K. N. Levy (2016). *Equity Management: The Art and Science of Modern Quantitative Investing*. 2nd Edition. McGraw-Hill Education.

Jacobs, H., S. Müller, and M. Weber (2013). "How should individual investors diversify? An empirical evaluation of alternative asset allocation policies." *Journal of Financial Markets* 19, 62–85.

James, G., D. Witten, T. Hastie, and R. Tibshirani (2013). *An Introduction to Statistical Learning With Applications in R.* 1st Edition. New York: Springer-Verlag.

Jegadeesh, N. and S. Titman (1993). "Returns to buying winners and selling losers: Implications for stock market efficiency." *Journal of Finance* 48, 65–91.

Jegadeesh, N. and S. Titman (2001). "Profitability of momentum strategies: An evaluation of alternative explanations." *Journal of Finance* 56, 699–720.

Jegadeesh, N. and S. Titman (2011). "Momentum." *Annual Review of Financial Economics* 3, 493–509.

Jagannathan, R. and T. Ma (2003). "Risk reduction in large portfolios: Why imposing the wrong constraints helps." *The Journal of Finance* 58, 1651–1684.

Jarrow, R. A., M. Teo, Y. K. Tse, and M. Warachka (2005). "Statistical arbitrage and market efficiency: Enhanced theory, robust tests and further applications." Available at SSRN: http://ssrn.com/abstract=659941.

Johnson, B. (2010). *Algorithmic Trading and DMA: An Introduction to Direct Access Trading Strategies.* Myeloma Press.

Johnston, J. and J. DiNardo (1997). *Econometric Methods.* New York: McGraw-Hill.

Jorion, P. (1986). "Bayes–Stein estimation for portfolio analysis." *Journal of Financial and Quantitative Analysis* 21, 279–292.

Jorion, P. (2000). *Value at Risk: The New Benchmark for Managing Financial Risk.* New York: McGraw-Hill.

Jurczenko, E., T. Michel, and J. Teiletche (2013). "Generalized risk-based investing." Available at SSRN: https://ssrn.com/abstract=2205979.

Jurek, J. W. and H. Yang (2007). "Dynamic portfolio selection in arbitrage." Available at SSRN: http://ssrn.com/abstract=882536.

Kahneman, D. and A. Tversky (2000). *Choices, Values and Frames.* Cambridge University Press.

Kaufman, P. J. (2005). *New Trading Systems and Methods.* 4th Edition. Wiley.

Kearney, C. and S. Liu (2014). "Textual sentiment in finance: A survey of methods and models." *International Review of Financial Analysis* 33, 171–185.

Kenett, D. Y., M. Tumminello, A. Madi, G. Gur-Gershgoren, R. N. Mantegna, and E. Ben-Jacob (2010). "Dominating clasp of the financial sector revealed by partial correlation analysis of the stock market." *PLoS One* 5, e15032.

Kenett, D. Y., M. Raddant, L. Zatlavi, T. Lux, and E. Ben-Jacob (2012). "Correlations in the global financial village." *International Journal of Modern Physics Conference* 16, 13–28.

Kenett, D.Y., X. Huang, I. Vodenska, S. Havlin, and H.E. Stanley (2015). "Partial correlation analysis: Applications for financial markets." *Quantitative Finance* 15, 569–578.

Kerstner, L. (2003). *Quantitative Trading Strategies: Harnessing The Power of Quantitative Techniques to Create a Winning Trading Program*. New York: McGraw-Hill.

Khandani, A. E. and A. W. Lo (2011). "What happened to the quants in August 2007? Evidence from factors and transactions data." *Journal of Financial Markets* 14(1), 1–46.

Kirilenko, A. A., A. S. Kyle, M. Samadi, and T. Tuzun (2017). "The flash crash: High-frequency trading in an electronic market." *Journal of Finance* 72, 967–998.

Kissell, R. L. (2020). *Algorithmic Trading Methods: Applications Using Advanced Statistics, Optimization, and Machine Learning Techniques.* 2nd Edition. Academic Press.

Kissell, R. and M. Glantz (2003). *Optimal Trading Strategies.* AMACOM.

Kole, E. and D. van Dijk (2017). "How to identify and forecast bull and bear markets?" *Journal of Applied Econometrics* 32, 120–139.

Kolm, P. and G. Ritter (2017). "On the Bayesian interpretation of Black–Litterman." *European Journal of Operational Research* 258, 564–572.

Kolm, P. N., R. Tütüncü, and F. J. Fabozzi (2014). "60 Years of portfolio optimization: Practical challenges and current trends." *European Journal of Operational Research* 234, 356–371.

Kräussl, R. and E. Mirgorodskaya (2017). "Media, sentiment and market performance in the long run." *European Journal of Finance* 23, 1059–1082.

Kritzman, M., S. Page, and D. Turkington (2010). "In defense of optimization: The fallacy of 1/N." *Financial Analysts Journal* 66(2), 31–39.

Kyle, A. (1985). "Continuous auctions and insider trading." *Econometrica* 53, 1315–1335.

Lachanski, M. and S. Pav (2017). "Shy of the character limit: 'Twitter mood predicts the stock market' revisited." *Economics of Journal Watch* 14(3), 302–345.

Landau, L. D. and E. M. Livshitz (1989). *Quantum Mechanics.* Moscow: Nauka.

Latane, H. A. and C. P. Jones (1977). "Standardized unexpected earnings — A progress report." *Journal of Finance* 32, 1457–1465.

LeBaron, B. (1994). "Chaos and nonlinear forecastability in economics and finance." *Philosophical Transactions of the Royal Society of London* 348A, 397–404.

LeBaron, B. (2001). "Stochastic volatility as a simple generator of apparent financial power laws and long memory." *Quantitative Finance* 1, 621–631.

LeBaron, B. (2006). "Agent based computational finance." In *Handbook of Computational Economics, Vol. 2: Agent-Based Computational Economics,* edited by H. Amman, D. Kendrick, and J. Rust, pp. 1187–1234. North Holland.

LeBaron, B., W. B. Arthur, and R. Palmer (1999). "The time series properties of an artificial stock market." *Journal of Economic Dynamics and Control* 23, 1487–1516.

Ledoit, O. and M. Wolf (2003). "Improved estimation of the covariance matrix of stock returns with an application to portfolio selection." *Journal of Empirical Finance* 10, 603–621.

Ledoit, O. and M. Wolf (2004). "Honey, I shrunk the sample covariance matrix." *Journal of Portfolio Management* 30, 110–119.

Ledoit, O. and M. Wolf (2008). "Robust performance hypothesis testing with the Sharpe ratio." *Journal of Empirical Finance* 15, 850–859.

Lee, W. (2011). "Risk-based asset allocation: A new answer to an old question?" *The Journal of Portfolio Management* 37(4), 11–28.

Lesyk, S., P. Gunthorp, and A. Dougan (2020). "Inverting factor strategies: No more 'Monkey Business'." Available at: https://www.ftserussell.com/research/inverting-factor-strategies.

Levy, H. and H. M. Markowitz (1979). "Approximating expected utility by a function of mean and variance." *The American Economic Review* 69(3), 309–317.

Levy, M., H. Levy, and S. Solomon (2000). *The Microscopic Simulation of Financial Markets: From Investor Behavior to Market Phenomena.* San Diego: Academic Press.

Lewis M. (2014). *Flash Boys: A Wall Street Revolt.* W. W. Norton & Company.

Litterman, R. and K. Winkelmann (1998). *Estimating Covariance Matrices. Risk Management Series.* New York: Goldman, Sachs, & Co.

Liu, B. (2020). *Sentiment Analysis (Mining Opinions, Sentiments, and Emotions).* 2nd Edition. Cambridge: Cambridge University Press.

Liu, J., and F. A. Longstaff (2004). "Losing money on arbitrages: Optimal dynamic portfolio choice in markets with arbitrage opportunities." *Review of Financial Studies* 17, 611–641.

Liu, J., and A. G. Timmermann (2009). "Risky arbitrage strategies: Optimal portfolio choice and economic implications." Available at SSRN: http://ssrn.com/abstract=1356397.

Livnat, J. and R. R. Mendenhall (2006). "Comparing the postearnings announcement drift for surprises calculated from analyst and time series forecasts." *Journal of Accounting Research* 44, 177– 205.

Lo, A. W. (2004). "Adaptive market hypothesis: Market efficiency from evolutionary perspective." *Journal of Portfolio Management* 30, 15–29.

Lo, A. W. and A. C. MacKinlay (1990). "Data-snooping biases in tests of asset pricing models." *Review of Financial Studies* 3, 431–467.

Lo, A. W. and A. C. MacKinlay (1999). *A Non-Random Walk Down Wall Street*. Princeton, NJ: Princeton University Press.

Lo, A. W., C. MacKinlay, and J. Zhang (2002). "Econometric models of limit order execution." *Journal of Financial Economics* 65, 31–71.

Lo, A. W., H. Mamaysky, and J. Wang (2000). "Foundations of technical analysis: Computational algorithms, statistical inference, and empirical implementation." *Journal of Finance* 55, 1705–1770.

Lopez de Prado, M. (2018a). *Advances in Financial Machine Learning*. Wiley.

Lopez de Prado, M. (2018b). "The 10 reasons most machine learning funds fail." *The Journal of Portfolio Management* 44(6), 120–133.

Loughran, T. and B. McDonald (2011). "When is a liability not a liability? Textual analysis, dictionaries, and 10-Ks." *The Journal of Finance* 66(1), 35–65.

Lowenstein, R. (2000). *When Genius Failed: The Rise and Fall of Long-Term Capital Management*. New York: Random House.

Luenberger, D. G. (1998). *Investment Science*. Oxford University Press.

Lunde, A. and A. Timmermann (2004). "Duration dependence in stock prices: An analysis of bull and bear markets." *Journal of Business & Economic Statistics* 22, 253–273.

Lux, T. (1998). "The socio-economic dynamics of speculative markets: Interacting agents, chaos, and the fat tails of return distributions." *Journal of Economic Behavior and Organization* 33, 143–165.

Lux, T. (2001a). "Power laws and long memory." *Quantitative Finance* 1, 560–562.

Lux, T. (2001b). "Turbulence in financial markets: The surprising explanatory power of simple cascade models." *Quantitative Finance* 1, 632–640.

Lux, T. and M. Marchesi (2000). "Volatility clustering in financial markets: A micro-simulation of interacting agents." *International Journal of Theoretical and Applied Finance* 3, 675–702.

Magdon-Ismail, M. and A. F. Atiya (2004). "Maximum drawdown." *Risk* 17(10), 99–102.

Maillard, S., T. Roncalli, and J. Teiletche (2010). "On the properties of equally weighted risk contribution portfolios." *The Journal of Portfolio Management* 36 (4), 60–70.

Malinova, K., and A. Park (2009). *Intraday trading patterns: The role of timing.* Working paper 335. University of Toronto, Canada.

Malkiel, B. G. (2003). *A Random Walk Down Wall Street.* New York: Norton & Company.

Mandelbrot, B. B. (1997). *Fractals and Scaling in Finance.* Berlin: Springer-Verlag.

Mantegna, R. N. and H. E. Stanley. (2000). *An Introduction in Econophysics: Correlations and Complexity in Finance.* Cambridge University Press.

Markowitz, H. (1952). "Portfolio Selection." *The Journal of Finance* 7 (1), 77–91.

Marshall, B. R., R. H. Cahan, and J. M. Cahan (2008). "Does intraday technical analysis in the U.S. equity market have value?" *Journal of Empirical Finance* 15(2), 199–210.

Marshall, B. R., N. H. Nguyen, and N. Visaltanachoti (2017). "Time series momentum and moving average trading rules." *Quantitative Finance* 17(3), 405–421.

Menkhoff, L. and M. P. Taylor (2007). "The obstinate passion of foreign exchange professionals: Technical analysis." *Journal of Economic Literature* 45, 936–972.

Merton, R.C. (1990). *Continuous Time Finance.* Blackwell.

Meucci, A. (2009) "Managing diversification." *Risk* 22(5), 74–79.

Miller, M. and F. Modigliani (1961). "Dividend policy, growth, and the valuation of shares." *Journal of Business* 34, 411–433.

Mizrach, B. (2008). "The next tick on NASDAQ." *Quantitative Finance* 8, 19–40.

Moran, M. T. and B. Liu (2020). *The VIX Index and Volatility-Based Global Indexes and Trading Instruments.* New York: CFA Institute Foundation.

Moskowitz, T., Y. H. Ooi, and L. H. Pedersen (2012). "Time series momentum." *Journal of Financial Economics* 104(2), 228–250.

Nadler, D. and A. B. Schmidt (2014a). "Portfolio theory in terms of partial covariance." Available at SSRN: http://ssrn.com/abstract=2436478.

Nadler, D. and A. B. Schmidt (2014b). "Market impact of macroeconomic announcements: Do surprises matter?" Available at SSRN: http://ssrn.com/abstract=2449796.

Nadler, D. and A.B. Schmidt (2015). "Impact of macroeconomic announcements on the etf trading volumes." *Journal of Trading* 10(3), 31–35.

Nadler, D. and A.B. Schmidt (2016a). "Persistent interest portfolios: Marrying web search data with mean variance theory." *The Journal of Investing* 25(3), 135–141.

Nadler, D. and A.B. Schmidt (2016b). "Impact of macroeconomic announcements on us equity prices: 2009–2013." *Journal of Forecasting* 25(3), 135–141.

Nadler, D. and A. B. Schmidt (2019a). "Momentum strategies for the ETF-based portfolios." Available at SSRN: https://ssrn.com/abstract=326 9475.

Nadler, D. and A.B. Schmidt (2019b). "Beta hedging: Performance measures, momentum weighting, and rebalancing effects." *Journal of Investment Strategies* 8, 1–9.

Nagy, Z., A. Kassam and L. E. Lee (2016). "Can ESG add alpha? An analysis of ESG tilt and momentum strategies." *The Journal of Investing* 25(2), 113–124.

Neely, C., D. E. Rapach, J. Tu, and G. Zhou (2010). *Out-of-sample equity premium prediction: Economic fundamentals vs. moving-average rules.* Federal Reserve Bank of St. Louis. Working Paper No. 2010–008A.

Neely, C. J., P. A. Weller, and J. M. Ulrich (2009). "The adaptive markets hypothesis: Evidence from the foreign exchange market." *Journal of Financial and Quantitative Analysis* 44, 467–488.

Novy-Marx, R. (2013). "The other side of value: The gross profitability premium." *Journal of Financial Economics* 108, 1–28.

Novy-Marx, R. (2014). "Predicting anomaly performance with politics, the weather, global warming, sunspots, and the stars." *Journal of Financial Economics* 112, 131–146.

Novy-Marx, R. (2015). *Backtesting strategies based on multiple signals.* NBER Working Paper #21329.

Obizhaeva, A. A. and J. Wang (2013). "Optimal trading strategy and supply/demand dynamics." *Journal of Financial Markets* 16, 1–32.

Oehmke, M. and M. M. Opp (2020). "A theory of socially responsible investment." Swedish House of Finance Research Paper No. 20-2. Available at SSRN: https://ssrn.com/abstract=3467644.

Oliveira, N., P. Cortez, and N. Areal (2017). "The impact of microblogging data for stock market prediction: Using Twitter to predict returns, volatility, trading volume and survey sentiment indices." *Expert Systems with Applications* 73, 125–144.

Omrane, W. B., and H. Van Oppens (2004). *The predictive success and profitability of chart patterns in the euro/dollar foreign exchange market.* IAG Working Paper No. 95-03. Available at SSRN: http://ssrn.co m/abstract=484384.

O'Hara, M. (1995). *Market Microstructure Theory.* New York: Wiley.

Pagan, A. R. and K. A. Sossounov (2003). "A simple framework for analysing bull and bear markets." *Journal of Applied Econometrics* 18, 23–46.

Pak, A. and P. Paroubek, P. (2010). "Twitter as a corpus for sentiment analysis and opinion mining." Available at: https://www.researchgate.net/publication/220746311_Twitter_as_a_Corpus_for_Sentiment_Analysis_and_Opinion_Mining.

Park, C.-H. and S. H. Irwin (2007). "What do we know about profitability of technical analysis?" *Journal of Economic Surveys* 21, 786–826.

Parlour, C. A. (1998). "Price dynamics in limit order markets." *Journal of Financial Studies* 11, 789–816.

Parlour, C. A. and D. J. Seppi (2008). "Limit order markets: A survey." In *Handbook of Financial Intermediation and Banking*, edited by A. W. A. Boot and A. V. Thakor, pp. 61–96. Elsevier.

Pastor, L., R. F. Stambaugh, and L. A. Taylor (2020). "Sustainable investing in equilibrium." Available at: https://ssrn.com/abstract=3498354.

Pedersen, L. H. (2015). *Efficiently Inefficient: How Smart Money Invests and Market Prices Are Determined*. Princeton: Princeton University Press.

Pedersen, L. H., S. Fitzgibbons, and L. Pomorski (2020). "Responsible investing: The ESG-efficient frontier." Available at SSRN: https://ssrn.com/abstract=3466417.

Perold, A. F. (1988). "The implementation shortfall: Paper versus reality." *Journal of Portfolio Management* 24, 4–9.

Peters, E. (1996). *Chaos and Order in Capital Markets*. New York: John Wiley & Sons.

Peters, E. (2000). *Chaos and Order in Capital Markets*. New York: Wiley.

Petersen, M. A. (2005). *Estimating standard errors in finance panel data sets: Comparing approaches*. NBER Working Paper 11280.

Politis, D. N. and J. P. Romano (1994). "The stationary bootstrap." *Journal of American Statistical Association* 89, 1303–1313.

Poon, S.-H. and C. W. J. Granger (2003). "Forecasting volatility in financial markets." *Journal of Economic Literature* 41, 478–539.

Poundstone, W. (2006). *Fortune's Formula*. New York: Hill and Wang.

Preis, T., H. S. Moat, and H. E. Stanley (2013). "Quantifying trading behavior in financial markets using google trends." *Scientific Reports* 3(1684).

Reigneron, P.-A., V. Nguyen, S. Ciliberti, P. Seager, and J.-P. Bouchaud (2019). "The case for long-only agnostic allocation portfolios." Available at: https://ssrn.com/abstract=3403154.

Reiss, P.C. and F.A. Wolak (2007). "Structural econometric modeling: Rationals and examples from industrial organization." In *Handbook of Econometrics*, edited by J.J. Heckman and E.E. Leamer, 6A-64, pp. 4280–4415. Elsevier.

Roll, R. (1977). "A critique of the asset pricing theory's tests." *Journal of Financial Economics* 4(2), 129–176.

Roll, R. (1984). "A simple implicit measure of the effective bid-ask spread in an efficient market." *Journal of Finance* 39, 1127–1139.

Romano, J. P. and M. Wolf (2005). "Stepwise multiple testing as formalized data snooping." *Econometrica* 73, 1237–1282.

Ross, S. A. (1976). "The arbitrage theory of capital pricing." *Journal of Economic Theory* 13, 341–360.

Ross, S. M. (2007). *Introduction to Probability Models*. 9th Edition. San Diego: Academic Press.

Rosu, I. (2009). "A dynamic model of the limit order book." *Review of Financial Studies* 22, 4601–4641.

Satchell, S. and A. Scowcroft (2000). "A demystification of the Black-Litterman model: Managing quantitative and traditional portfolio construction." *Journal of Asset Management* 1,138–150.

Savor, P. G. and M. I. Wilson (2013). "How much do investors care about macroeconomic risk? Evidence from scheduled economic announcements." *Journal of Financial and Quantitative Analysis* 48, 343–375.

Savor, P. G. and M. I. Wilson (2016). "Earnings announcements and systematic risk." *The Journal of Finance* 71(1), 83–138.

Sawilowsky, S. S. (2005). "Misconceptions leading to choosing the t test over the Wilcoxon Mann-Whitney U test for shift in location parameter." *Journal of Modern Applied Statistical Methods* 4(2), 598–600.

Scotti, C. (2013). "Surprise and uncertainty indexes: Real-time aggregation of real-activity macro surprises." *Board of Governors of the Federal Reserve System International Finance Discussion Papers*, No. 1093.

Scott, S. L. and H. R. Varian (2013). "Predicting the Present with Bayesian Structural Time Series." SSRN Working Paper #2304426, http://ssrn.com/abstract=2304426.

Schied, A. and T. Schöneborn (2008). "Risk aversion and the dynamics of optimal liquidation strategies in illiquid markets." *Finance and Stochastics* 13(2), 181–204.

Schiereck, D. and C. Voigt (2008). "Intraday pattern of principal and agent account trading: An empirical investigation." Available at SSRN: http://ssrn.com/abstract=1123649.

Schmidt, A. B. (1999). "Modeling the demand — Price relations in a high-frequency foreign exchange market." *Physica* A271, 507–514.

Schmidt, A. B. (2000). "Modeling the birth of a liquid market." *Physica* A283, 479–485.

Schmidt, A. B. (2002). "Why technical trading may be successful: A lesson from the agent-based modeling." *Physica* A303, 185–188.

Schmidt, A. B. (2003). "Non-ideal effects in highly asymmetric ionic mixtures at moderate coupling." *Physica* A319, 115–124.

Schmidt, A. B. (2004). *Quantitative Finance for Physicists: An Introduction.* Burlington, MA: Elsevier.

Schmidt, A. B. (2009a). "Simulation of execution costs in the global institutional spot FX market." *Journal of Trading* 4(4), 62–68.

Schmidt, A. B. (2009b). "Detrending the realized volatility in the global FX market." *Physica* 388, 1887–1892.

Schmidt, A. B. (2010a). "Optimal execution in the global FX market." *Journal of Trading* 5(3) 68–77.

Schmidt, A. B. (2010b). "Microstructure and execution strategies in the global spot FX market." In *Econophysics Approaches to Large-Scale Business Data and Financial Crisis,* pp. 49–63. Berlin: Springer-Verlag.

Schmidt, A. B. (2011). *Financial Markets and Trading: Introduction to Market Microstructure and Trading Strategies.* Hoboken, NJ: Wiley.

Schmidt, A. B. (2013). *Everything That Can Happen to You Happens Today: Autofictional Notes.* CreateSpace.

Schmidt, A. B. (2015). "Impact of trading in the multi-dealer spot foreign exchange." *Journal of Trading* 10(2), 72–78.

Schmidt, A. B. (2016). "Effects of high-frequency trading in the multi-dealer spot foreign exchange." *Journal of Trading* 11(1), 68–75.

Schmidt, A. B. (2018). "Managing portfolio diversity within the mean variance theory." *Annals of Operations Research* 282, 315–329.

Schmidt, A. B. (2020a). "Corrections in the US equity indexes and sector ETFs." *Journal of Index Investing* 10(4), 59–75.

Schmidt, A. B. (2020b). "Optimal ESG portfolios: An example for the Dow Jones Index." *Journal of Sustainable Finance and Investment.* Available at: https://doi.org/10.1080/20430795.2020.1783180.

Schmidt, A. B. (2020c). "Impact of earnings announcements for Dow Jones Index Stocks." Available at: https://papers.ssrn.com/sol3/papers.cfm?abstract_id=3537660.

Schwab Center for Financial Research (2018). "Market Correction: What Does It Mean?" Available at: https://www.schwab.com/resource-center/insights/content/market-correction-what-does-it-mean.

Sharpe, W. F. (1963). "A simplified model for portfolio analysis." *Management Science* 9, 277–293.

Shephard, N. (2005). *Stochastic Volatility.* Selected readings. Oxford University Press.

Silvapulle, P. and C. W. J. Granger (2001). "Large returns, conditional correlation and portfolio diversification: A-value-at-risk approach." *Quantitative Finance* 1, 542–551.

Sinha, N. R. (2016). "Underreaction to news in the US stock market." *Quarterly Journal of Finance* 6(2), 1–46.

Stoll, H. R. (1978). "The supply of dealer services in securities market." *Journal of Finance* 33, 1133–1151.

Stambaugh, R. F., J. Yu, and Y. Yuan (2012). "The short of it: Investor sentiment and anomalies." *Journal of Financial Economics* 104, 288–302.

Statman, M. (2019). *Behavioral Finance. The Second Generation.* CFA Institute Research Foundation.

Stefanini, F. (2006). *Investment Strategies of Hedge Funds.* Wiley.

Subrahmanyam, A. (1991). "Risk aversion, market liquidity, and price efficiency." *Review of Financial Studies* 4, 417–442.

Sullivan, R., A. Timmermann, and H. White (1999). "Data-snooping, technical trading rule performance, and the bootstrap." *Journal of Finance* 54, 1647–1691.

Tafti, A., R. Zotti, and W. Jank (2016). "Real-time diffusion of information on twitter and the financial markets." *PLoS ONE* 11(8), e0159226.

Taylor, S. J. (2005). *Asset Price Dynamics, Volatility, and Prediction.* Princeton: Princeton University Press.

Tetlock, P. C. (2007). "Giving content to investor sentiment: The role of media in the stock market." *Journal of Finance* 62, 1139–1168.

Tetlock, P. C., M. Saar-Tsechansky, and S. Macskassy (2008). "More than words: Quantifying language to measure firms' fundamentals." *Journal of Finance* 63(3), 1437–1467.

Thorp, E. O. (2006). "The Kelly criterion in blackjack sports betting and the stock market." In *Handbook of Asset and Liability Management, Volume 1: Theory and Methodology*, edited by S. A. Zenios and W. T. Ziemba, pp. 385–428. North Holland.

Timmermann, A. (2006). "Forecast combinations." In *Handbook of Economic Forecasting*, edited by G. Elliott, A. G. W. Granger, and A. Timmermann, pp. 135–196. Elsevier.

Tsay, R. S. (2005). *Analysis of Financial Time Series.* Hoboken, NJ: Wiley.

Tu, J. and G. Zhou (2009). "Markowitz meets Talmud: A combination of sophisticated and naïve diversification strategies." *Journal of Financial Economics* 99, 204–215.

Tumminello, M., F. Lillo, and R. Mantegna (2010). "Correlation, hierarchies, and networks in financial markets." *Journal of Economic Behavior & Organization* 75, 40–58.

Vidyamurthy, G. (2004). *Pair Trading: Quantitative Methods and Analysis.* Hoboken, NJ: Wiley.

Vincent, A. and M. Armstrong (2010). "Predicting Break-Points in Trading Strategies with Twitter." Available at: https://ssrn.com/abstract=16 85150.

Weber, P. and B. Rosenow (2005). "Order book approach to price impact." *Quantitative Finance* 5, 357–364.

White, H. (2000). "A reality check for data snooping." *Econometrica* 68, 1097–1126.

Whittaker, J. (1990). *Graphical Models in Applied Multivariate Statistics.* Wiley.

Willenbrock, S. (2011). "Diversification return, portfolio rebalancing, and the commodity return puzzle." *Financial Analysts Journal* 67(4), 42–49.

Williams, C. D. (2015). "Asymmetric responses to earnings news: A case for ambiguity." *The Accounting Review* 90, 785–817.

Yardeni, E., J. Abbott, and M. Quintana (2020). "Market briefing: S&P 500 bull & bear markets & corrections." Yardeni Research. Available at: https://www.yardeni.com/pub/sp500corrbear.pdf.

Yin, C., R. Perchet, and F. Soupé (2021). "A practical guide to robust portfolio optimization." *Quantitative Finance* 21(1), 1–18.

Zhang, L., P. A. Mykland, and Y. Ait-Sahalia (2005). "A tale of two time scales: Determining integrated volatility with noisy high-frequency data." *Journal of the American Statistical Association* 100, 1394–1411.

Index

A

adaptive market hypothesis, 70–71
ADR arbitrage, 199
adverse selection, 11, 20, 34, 40–41, 51, 54–55
Akaike information criterion, 228, 238
algorithmic trading, ix, 62, 253
all-or-none orders, 9
alternative data, ix, xxviii, 217–218
alternative trading systems, 17, 19
Amihud–Mendelson model, 29
APT, xxix, 169–170, 201, 204
arbitrage, 199
arbitrage pricing theory, xxvii, 165, 168
arbitrage risks, 199, 209
arbitrage strategies, xxix, 197, 199, 215
arbitrageurs, 4, 209
ARMA, 86, 191, 205, 220, 228, 238, 244, 285–286, 289
ARMA-GARCH, 78
ARMA model, 225, 281, 284, 287
arrival price, 254
auction, 12, 17–18, 24, 35, 37
autocorrelations, 62
autoregressive conditional heteroscedasticity, 90
autoregressive model, 281
autoregressive moving-average, 68
autoregressive process, 281

B

back-testing, 181, 215, 237, 240, 247, 252
bar, 181
Bayes' rule, 39, 42
Bayesian information criterion, 238
BB, 264, 267–269
bear market, 76–79, 96, 123, 132, 135, 143, 167, 176, 207–209, 228
benchmark-driven algorithms, 254–255
Bertrand competition model, 37
beta hedging, 198, 206
bid/ask spread, 6, 8, 10–11, 14, 25, 28–29, 32–34, 40–41, 43–45, 48, 50–52, 54, 60–62, 73, 215, 240, 247, 264, 269
binomial distribution, 275–276
Black–Litterman model, 151
Black–Scholes theory, 89
block bootstrap, 244
BO, 264
book value, 176
bootstrap, 239, 243
bootstrapped, 245
bounded rationality, 105

broker, 3, 5–6, 12, 15, 17–20, 22, 129, 212
brokerage, ix, 253
Brownian bridge, 213–214
Brownian motion, 33, 37, 41–42, 44, 62, 71, 93, 205, 216, 245, 252, 266
buy-side, 6, 23, 44, 256
B&H, 188, 190–191, 229–230, 241–242
B&H strategy, 229

C

call auctions, 15–16
Calmar ratio, 243
cancel-and-replace limit orders, 8
Capital Asset Pricing Model (CAPM), xxviii–xxix, 96, 131, 148, 151–152, 159–160, 163, 165–168, 173–176, 198, 206, 220
capital market line, 165
CARA, 32, 104
Cauchy distribution, 74, 278–280
causality, 201
CCAPM, 167
chartists, 62, 105, 107–109
Chicago Board Options Exchange's (CBOE), 232
co-location, 20
coherent risk measures, 98
cointegrated, 202–204
cointegration, 201
Commodity Futures Trading Commission, 12
constant absolute risk aversion (CARA), 31–32, 104
constant correlation model, 150
constant relative aversion function (CRRA), 31, 104, 123, 214–215
convertible arbitrage, 200
cost-driven algorithms, 254, 257
covariance, 124, 127–129, 143, 148–151, 166, 206, 236
covariance-stationary, 89, 275, 288
covariance-stationary processes, 291
cross-sectional momentum (CSM), 208–209

crossing networks, 12–13, 19–20
cumulative impulse response (CIR), 56–57

D

dark pools, 12–13, 19–20
data snooping, 181, 238–239, 245, 248–251
dealer, 4, 6, 17, 25, 27–29, 33, 35–36, 38–39, 41, 57
dealer markets, xxviii, 43, 102
dealers, 5, 11–10, 12–13, 16–19, 21–23, 26, 32, 34, 37, 41–42
deterministic arbitrage, 197
deterministic trend, 288
distribution, 271, 276
diversity booster (DB), xxix, 121, 130, 139, 142
diversity strength, 142–143
DMVP, 142–143
DMVPT, 158
dummy variables, 171, 228, 289

E

ECNs, 19
efficient market hypothesis (EMH), 55, 69–71, 102, 176
electronic communication network, 18
equal risk balance portfolio (ERBP), 162
equal risk contributions portfolio (ERCP), 161–162
equity hedge, 199
ergodicity, 67, 86, 275
error correction model, 203
ESG, 143–145, 148
ETL, 99
event arbitrage, 20
event-driven arbitrage, 201, 212
EWP, 129, 134–135, 138–139, 142, 148, 157–159, 162, 206
exchanges, 12–13, 17, 19, 22–24, 61, 254
expected tail loss (ETL), 87, 98

exponential moving average (EMA), 88–89, 184, 186–187, 191
exponentially weighed moving average (EWMA), 89, 92

F

fair game, 72
Fama–French, 175, 196, 208
Fama–French models, 173
fill ratio, 13
fill-or-kill orders, 9
filter rules, 182–183
Financial Industry Regulatory Authority (FINRA), 18, 23
first passage time, 44, 205, 266
fixed-income arbitrage, 200
flash crash, 21, 23
flash orders, 22
Foucault model, 46, 48
FPT, 267, 269
fractals, 67, 84
fractional Browning motion, 85–86
front running, 17, 22
fundamentalists, 105, 107–109

G

gambler's ruin problem, 27, 42
GARCH, 86, 90–92, 220, 222, 225, 228, 244
Garman, 32
Garman's model, 26–29
Gaussian, 74–76, 109, 238, 271, 276
Glosten–Harris, 55
Glosten–Harris model, 51, 54
Glosten–Milgrom, 41, 252
Glosten–Milgrom model, 38–40, 155
Granger causality, 202–203
Grossman & Stiglitz, 70

H

head-and-shoulder pattern (HaSP), 194, 196
hidden limit orders, 8

high-frequency trading (HFT), 19–22, 88, 93, 181, 248, 252
historical volatility, 87–88, 96
Hurst exponent, 85
hybrid market, 16–18

I

ICAPM, 167
illiquidity, 11, 36
implementation shortfall (IS), 187, 254
implied volatility, 131, 232
index arbitrage, 199
informed, 40
informed investors, 4, 34, 37, 41, 55
initial public offering (IPO), 12
insiders, 4, 38, 40–41
integrated, 91, 282, 287
integrated process, 215
integrated volatility, 87, 93
instantaneous volatility, 71
investors, 31, 40, 102, 114
IPOs, 232

K

kurtosis, 99
Kyle's, 11, 34
Kyle's model, 35–39, 41, 54

L

lag operator, 281, 283–284, 290
Levy flights, 74
limit-order, 6–8, 13–14, 19, 43–49, 50, 56, 60, 63, 264, 266–267
limit order book (LOB), 7–8, 11, 13–14, 17–19, 23, 45–47, 49–51, 58–59, 63–64, 268–269
limit-order market, xxviii, 11, 43, 46, 48, 51, 56, 58
liquidity, 4–5, 9, 17, 19–23, 25, 35, 41, 43, 45–46, 48–49, 58, 63, 73, 94–95, 103, 187, 215, 240, 247, 253–254, 261, 264
liquidity aggregators, 254

liquidity traders, 4–5, 32, 34–39, 41, 61, 264
lognormal distribution, 277–278
look-ahead bias, 181, 230
Lorentzian, 278

M

market, 12, 17, 47
market impact, 7, 11, 50, 55, 57–59, 62–64, 114, 148, 187, 218, 224, 230, 253, 256–259, 261–264
market makers, 4–5, 10–11, 16, 23, 25, 34–35, 57, 62–63, 255
market order, 6–8, 14, 16, 18, 43, 45, 47–51, 56, 60, 63, 255
market risk, 165
market sentiment indicator, 218, 232
market-on-close, 9
market-on-open, 9
marketable limit order, 8, 18
market value (MV), 176
market-neutral strategy, 198–201
Markov chain Monte Carlo (MCMC), 239, 246–247
martingale, 55, 72–73, 88
maximum diversification portfolio, 161
maximum drawdown (MDD), 76–77, 86, 157, 243
maximum likelihood estimate (MLE), 287
merger arbitrage, 200
mean–variance portfolio theory (MVPT), xxviii–xxix, 25, 31, 121, 124, 127, 129, 131, 139, 153, 159
minimum-variance portfolio (MinVP), 125, 159
model, 11, 34, 48
momentum, 105, 130–131, 175–176, 182, 187, 191, 193, 196, 198, 207–208, 220
momentum arbitrage, 187, 208
mortgage-backed securities (MBS) arbitrage, 200

moving average convergence/ divergence (MACD), 191–192
moving average, 284
multicollinearity, 172
MVP, 124, 127, 129–132, 135, 138–139, 143, 148–149, 153, 157, 159–162, 206

N

NASDAQ, 12–13, 17–19, 23–24, 76–77, 174, 221
national best bid and offer (NBBO), 23
non-diversifiable risk, 165
normal, 74, 96, 98, 149, 153, 241, 266, 271
normal (Gaussian) distribution, 32, 35–36, 71, 73, 75, 97, 153–154, 204, 273, 276–277, 279–280, 287
normally, 104, 152
normally distributed, 171
nowcast, 225, 236
NYSE, 12–13, 17–19, 23–24, 55, 174, 196, 222, 232

O

OLS, 139, 142, 172, 244, 287
opinion mining, 218, 233
opportunity cost, 43, 254–256
oral auctions, 15
order, 13–15, 17, 19–21
order flow, 10, 16, 22, 62
order-driven market, 12–15, 19, 25
oscillator strategies, 182
oscillators, 192–194
OTC markets, 12–13
out-of-sample testing, 237
over-the-counter (OTC), 12

P

pair trading, 198, 201, 203, 205
PaMVPs, 131–132, 134–135, 138, 143, 148
Pareto distributions, 280
Parlour model, 45–46, 48

partial correlation, xxix, 121, 130–132, 143, 274
partial covariances, 131
participation weighted price, 257
Pearson's correlations, 121, 130–132, 143, 274
pegged order, 9, 247, 267, 269
PeMVPs, 131–132, 134–135, 138–139, 148
percent of volume, 256
persistent processes, 85
Poisson distribution, 276
Poisson process, 26, 33, 41–42, 44, 49
POV, 257
price discovery, 12, 15–16, 19–20, 55, 102, 113
primary markets, 12–13, 17, 19, 24
process, 91
proprietary traders, 3

Q

quote-driven, 17
quote-driven markets, 12, 16

R

random entry protocol, 239, 247–248
random walk, xxvii, 44, 47, 55, 62, 64, 67, 69–73, 78, 88–89, 91, 102, 215, 242–244, 258–259, 266–267, 282, 288
rational, 31, 102
rational investors, xxvii, 4, 69, 166
relative strength index (RSI), 193–194
realized volatility, 87, 89, 93–94
relative-value arbitrage, 200, 212
resampling, xxix, 172, 239, 243, 246–248, 250, 269
rescaled range (R/S) analysis, 85
return on equity (ROE), 170, 176
risk arbitrage, 200
risk aversion, 25, 29–34, 41, 63, 86, 104, 122–123, 127–128, 142, 144, 148, 166–167, 215, 225, 260–261, 265

risk parity portfolio, 161
risk premium, 105, 169, 225
risk-averse investors, 62, 185, 214–215, 241
Roll's model, 51–55

S

scale-free processes, 75
scheduling, 254
Securities and Exchanges Commission (SEC), 12, 18, 22–23
secondary market, 12
self-affinity, 84
self-similarity, 84
sell-side, 6
sentiment analysis, 218, 231, 233
sequential trading, 247, 252
Sharpe ratio, 96, 122, 129, 135, 145, 148, 157, 160–161, 188, 190, 206–207, 230, 236, 240–243, 251
short-squeeze, 234
shrinkage estimator, 149–151
simple moving average (SMA), 88–89, 183–184, 186, 188, 191, 194
skewness, 99
smart betas, xxviii, 165, 175
smart routing, 254
Sortino ratio, 242
stable distributions, 74, 278–280
standard Brownian motion, 71
standardized unexpected earnings (SUE), 220–221, 224
stationarity, 67, 86
stationary, 91
stationary bootstrap, 244
statistical arbitrage, 20, 197, 199, 217
stochastic oscillators, 193
stochastic trend, 288
Stoll's, 34
Stoll's model, 32–33
stop orders, 9
strict stationarity, 288
structural model, 51, 55, 59, 64, 117
systematic risk, 165

T

taker, 5, 8, 10, 25–26, 43, 62–63, 103, 166, 255, 264, 269
Technical analysis-based strategies (TABSs), 179–182, 187, 192, 194–196, 217
technical traders, 4, 112–114
time series momentum (TSM), 187–188, 190–191, 208
time-weighted average price (TWAP), 255
tracking error, 129, 202, 216, 242, 251
trend strategies, 180, 182
tweets, 217–218, 233–234

U

unit root, 91, 99, 202, 283, 287
utility function, 31–32, 34, 47, 49, 104, 110, 123, 214, 260, 263–264, 267, 269

V

value at risk (VaR), 87
value investors, 4
vector autoregressive model (VAR), 56–57, 64, 96–99, 289–291
volatility signature, 94
VAR2, 58
VAR4, 59
volatility index (VIX), 232
volume-weighted average price, 255
VWAP, 256–257, 262

W

weak stationarity, 288
well-diversified portfolio, 169
Wiener process, 71
winsorization, 172

Y

yield curve arbitrage, 200